Special Praise for
When the Servant Becomes the Master
(Second Edition)

"*When the Servant Becomes the Master* has become my 'go-to' resource countless times. It is part of almost every conversation I have with anyone who courageously reaches out for help for a loved one or themselves. This comprehensive review of addiction provides the reader with knowledge to better understand addiction and an entry point to embarking on a healing journey. Written with the perfect balance of data, research, humor, and love, this book fosters hope and arms the reader with practical solutions, suggestions, and facts. *When the Servant Becomes the Master* has been incorporated into our family program and our new-hire orientation process."

Julie K. DeNofa

President, Sobriety Matters

"Dr. Powers has the unique ability to articulate seemingly complex concepts in a way that is accessible, memorable, and enjoyable to read. This updated, second edition of *When the Servant Becomes the Master* remains a reliable resource for me in assisting those interested in deepening their understanding of the disease of addiction and strengthening their ability to be a part of the solution. Whether for a family member, a professional, or someone battling active addiction, this book is a worthy and impactful read!"

Ilana Zivkovich, LCSW, LCDC, CDWF

Chief Clinical Officer, Northbound Treatment Services

"*When the Servant Becomes the Master* takes the complexities and misconceptions about addiction and sets the record straight with thoughtful insights and credible research. If you work in the field of addiction treatment, this is a must-have for your professional library. If you or someone you love suffers from addiction and you want to better understand the addictive process as well as the process of recovery, then I strongly encourage you to read this book."

Robert Hilliker, LCSW-S, LCDC
Managing Partner of the Lovett Center
Clinical Director of the Center for Integrative Healing

"For everyone from addicts and their families to professionals with a desire to know more about this baffling disease, *When the Servant Becomes the Master* is a must-read. Despite my years in the practice of addiction medicine, I experienced many 'aha moments' as I read. I am glad this book is now available to explain the suffering and the science of addiction in such a way as to be easily understood by the reader. Dr. Powers brings to light and illustrates that addiction is a disease and not just an affliction of the weak or immoral. He explains and underscores the effectiveness of treatment and draws parallels of success and failure with other chronic diseases such as diabetes and hypertension. I would like to make this book required reading for all my patients and their families. If you are challenged by the notion of addiction as a disease, read this book and decide for yourself."

Mike Leath, MD, RPh
Medical Director of Outpatient Services
Memorial Hermann Prevention and Recovery Center,
Houston, Texas

Special Praise for
When the Servant Becomes the Master
(First Edition)

"*When the Servant Becomes the Master* should be required reading for those entering the field of addiction! Jason Powers combines intelligence and humor and makes a very difficult topic clear, precise, and easy to understand."

Rhonda S. McBride, PhD, LCDC, author of
Peace, Power, and a Sound Mind **and**
Inspirations for the Awakening Soul

"Whenever someone in recovery writes a book about addiction, I usually expect a personal story about that person's trials, tribulations, and miraculous revival into a new person. This book is different. It is well researched, complete, and balanced. Jason Powers, MD gets it. He understands what addiction is, not because he has it himself, but because he has taken so much time to learn about the disease from different angles, and without bias. He clearly and carefully attacks myths and misinformation, and brings the reader up to date with the latest popular and scientific literature on addiction. I wish this could be required reading for every health professional."

Carlton K. Erickson, PhD
Distinguished Professor of Pharmacology/Toxicology
Associate Dean for Research and Graduate Studies
Director, Addiction Science Research & Education Center
The University of Texas at Austin

"*When the Servant Becomes the Master* gives any addict who may suffer from the misconception of 'being broken' that hope can and will come from healing. Where else can you find amazing storytelling, current vital statistics, autobiographical data, scientific theory, and true clinical education, all presented in a unique, entertaining format on a topic such as addiction?"

Keith H. Liles, BA, LCDC, ADC III, ICADC

CEO and Chief Clinical Officer, Extended Aftercare, Inc.

National Addiction Professional of the Year

2011 Texas Addiction Counselors' Hall of Fame Inductee

"*When the Servant Becomes the Master* presents an authentic and practical understanding of addiction and recovery from a personal and heartfelt perspective. Using both science-supported and relevant anecdotal information, Dr. Powers offers the reader a meaningful glimpse into the nature of addiction and the behaviors associated with it. More importantly, he offers ample facts, sound guidance, and helpful solutions to assist those on the path of inquiry for themselves or a loved one."

Matt Feehery, CEO

Memorial Hermann Prevention & Recovery Center

"Dr. Powers has been able to combine his vast clinical experience with his thorough review of related literature into a passionate and persuasive guide for patients, loved ones, and clinicians. He helps guide us not just through the extensive material but also to a more humane yet 'medically driven' view of what we in the field have come to know as the true meaning of the disease of addiction."

Ed Fallick, DO

Medical Director, Young Adult Program

Memorial Hermann Prevention & Recovery Center

When the Servant Becomes the Master
Second Edition

When the Servant Becomes the Master

A Comprehensive Addiction Guide for Those Who Suffer from the Disease, the Loved Ones Affected by It, and the Professionals Who Assist Them

Second Edition

Jason Z W Powers

CENTRAL RECOVERY PRESS

Las Vegas

CENTRAL RECOVERY PRESS

Central Recovery Press (CRP) is committed to publishing exceptional materials addressing addiction treatment, recovery, and behavioral healthcare topics.

For more information, visit **www.centralrecoverypress.com**

©2012, 2017 by Jason Z W Powers
All rights reserved. First edition 2012. Second edition 2017.
Printed in the United States of America.

Publisher: Central Recovery Press
             3321 N. Buffalo Drive
             Las Vegas, NV 89129

22 21 20 19 18 17   1 2 3 4 5

Library of Congress Cataloging-in-Publication Data
Name: Powers, Jason Z. W., author.
Title: When the servant becomes the master : a comprehensive addiction guide for those who suffer from the disease, the loved ones affected by it, and the professionals who assist them / Jason Z. W. Powers.
Description: Second edition. | Las Vegas, NV : Central Recovery Press, 2017.
Identifiers: LCCN 2017020652 (print) | LCCN 2017030634 (ebook) | ISBN 9781942094555 (ebook) | ISBN 9781942094548 (paperback)
Subjects: LCSH: Substance abuse. | Substance abuse—Treatment. | Compulsive behavior. | Addicts—Rehabilitation. | BISAC: SELF-HELP / Substance Abuse & Addictions / General. | PSYCHOLOGY / Psychopathology / Addiction. MEDICAL / Reference.
Classification: LCC RC564 (ebook) | LCC RC564 .P69 2017 (print) | DDC 616.86—dc23 LC record available at https://lccn.loc.gov/2017020652

Jason Powers photo by Sarah Powers.

Publisher's Note: This book contains general information about addiction and addiction treatment and recovery. It is not an alternative to medical advice from your doctor or other professional healthcare provider.

CRP books represent the experiences and opinions of their authors only. Every effort has been made to ensure that events, institutions, and statistics presented in our books as facts are accurate and up-to-date. To protect their privacy, some of the names of people and institutions in this book have been changed.

Cover and interior design by David Leicester Hardy.

Table of Contents

Foreword to the Second Edition

The more things change, the more they remain the same.

Over the last two decades our understanding of addiction has expanded exponentially. We have identified the specific brain structures that are activated by drugs of abuse. We have delineated the sequence of brain changes that occur as an individual moves from casual user to habitual user. We know how to block the medically dangerous complications of withdrawal. We have conclusively demonstrated the genetic contribution to becoming addicted, as well some of the candidate genes involved. Yet at the same time, we find ourselves in the worse opiate epidemic in more than a century, with death and disability sapping the hopes and lives of a generation. And, as we find ourselves asking how this could be, it is easy to forget that the war on cancer did not produce great dividends in its first decades, either.

For the person who raises a glass of wine at a friend's wedding or enjoys a cigar after a successful round of golf, it is hard to imagine how anyone would drink enough to wreck his or her heart or liver or drag on a cigarette through a tracheotomy. Yet it happens all too frequently. The brain's reward pathways, so easily fooled and manipulated by alcohol and other drugs, are old and strong and critical to survival. Remembering where to go for the pleasure of quenching one's thirst or hunger is a powerful advantage. But once these circuits are deflected by drugs, they are difficult to redirect.

Few things challenge our belief in free will more than addiction. If we don't choose our genes and if using alcohol and other drugs reshapes our neural pathways, what is left to choose? The field of addiction treatment is dedicated to helping people find the motivation to change, and to unspooling the harms of drugs on the brain and restoring people whose addiction has shredded their moral compass to the human family.

Dr. Powers, in his revised and updated work, has provided a compassionate and medically rigorous interpretation of what we know now about addiction. For the person with only passing familiarity, it will answer many questions raised by a cultural rather than scientific understanding of addiction. For those like me who have spent years in the field, his insights allow us to see past our own mental clutter to what really works and how to use it.

David Sack, MD
Chief Medical Officer, Elements Behavioral Inc.

Foreword to the First Edition

Addiction—to alcohol and other drugs, tobacco, gambling, sex, or food—is the nation's number-one public health problem. Drug use, abuse, and dependence have been the easiest to model in the laboratory, like here at the University of Florida's McKnight Brain Institute. Gambling, sex, Internet, and other process addictions have been more difficult to model. Food addiction has been the focus of recent studies and, as with classical drugs of abuse, has been modeled in rats using glucose or fructose self-administration.[1] There are even labs studying rats that became obese after a rapid shift from lab chow to fat-filled fast foods.[2]

Basic science studies have proved that drugs of abuse hijack and ultimately change the brain. I have worked in this area since the 1970s. First, we demonstrated that opiate drugs caused liking and self-administration, which, if prolonged and continued, produced tolerance and dependence. Discontinuation is associated with abstinence signs and symptoms. Our work in the 1970s led to the identification of the noradrenergic pontine locus coeruleus as the neuroanatomical site for the majority of abstinence symptoms. Reversing opiate withdrawal with opiates like morphine or methadone was understood. Clonidine, an alpha-2 adrenergic agonist, had opiate-like effects, reversed withdrawal, and challenged the notion that opiate withdrawal reversal was synonymous with an opiate.[3] Clonidine became a widely used treatment for acute opiate withdrawal, an adjunct for rapid opiate detoxification and Naltrexone induction, and an analgesic potentiator.

Perhaps the most important findings were largely ignored or overlooked. First, most of the first patients who successfully detoxified using clonidine relapsed quickly, and all relapsed within twelve months. This was not unlike the experience with methadone; detoxification was not and is not a treatment for addiction. Second, animals who had their locus coeruleus lesioned did not have significant opiate withdrawal when opiates were discontinued, but also had no change in drug liking or taking.[4] Withdrawal may make drug use more addicting, but drug use is much more about the acquired drive for the drug than anything else.

Dr. Jason Powers, a recovering addict himself, describes substance use, dependence, treatment, and recovery from a scientific viewpoint, as well as a viewpoint from someone in long-term recovery. The analysis is compelling because of the approach: using information, science, and practical discussion of what works and what does not work. Addiction research has established that addiction has a neuroanatomy and neurochemistry.[5] All drugs of abuse self-administered by lab animals cause craving and wanting, and all cause dopamine release in the nucleus accumbens and long-term changes in the brain's dopamine and other systems.[6] Addiction treatment and recovery have been best studied in patients like Jason Powers, MD. Five-year treatment outcome studies have been reported for Florida and for thirty-five of our fifty states, with strikingly similar results. Regardless of the type of substance abuse, recovery at five years is the rule rather than the exception.[7]

What works? Long-term, supervised, abstinence-based treatments. Drug abuse treatment data, with five years as a standard and urine testing as an impartial barometer, clearly show that more than 80 percent of patients are back at work, drug- and alcohol-free, at five years. Evidence-based treatments should work whether coerced or voluntary. This is the case for impaired professionals. Evidence-based treatments should also work whether or not the patient is cooperative or believes in the treatment. This is the case for the treatment of strep throat, but not for addiction. Treatment outcomes always depend on adherence and compliance, and for addiction, as with hypertension, this is the case. Treatment works, but often successfully treated patients are anonymous and silent about their addiction and recovery.

Jason Powers, in sharing his experience with the disease and lessons learned, provides hope in addiction science and treatment. He reviews all drugs and treatment options comprehensively, but without unnecessary verbiage or jargon. Intervention, treatment, and recovery sometimes come late. Signs of the disease are subtle, often disguised by the patient and covered up by loved ones. Drug, dose, route, duration, genes, and other host (user) factors play a role in how much brain cell compromise or loss occurs. Everyone has struggled trying to help someone who appears to have been burnt out by drug use. The person has problems thinking and remembering, loses attachments, and has mood problems. Basic research suggests that drugs influence and change gene expression and the making of signals and proteins in the brain and elsewhere, and also that the brain is not the least-forgiving organ. The brain changes caused by drugs or alcohol can be permanent and irreversible. Still, abstinence and recovery can change the person and stop the downward spiral. Stabilization, hope, and help, mixed with the tincture of time, do wonders, if not miracles. Jason Powers is living proof of this!

Drug use early in life changes the brain and makes further use more likely. Drug dependence cannot be treated by detoxification alone, though that is often the first step. Once dependence is reversed, mood changes, depression, sexual dysfunction and compulsivity, overeating, and obesity may result. All contribute to slips and relapses. Treatment is more than detox, more than going to meetings; it is walking the walk—eating and exercising, helping others, and all sorts of things that the recent Betty Ford panel described in "What Is Recovery?"[8] It is a daunting task, but with a sponsor, program, and guides, it happens every day.

Mark S. Gold, MD
Distinguished Professor and Chair of Psychiatry
University of Florida College of Medicine
Member of the McKnight Brain Institute

Preface to the Second Edition

So much has happened in the short time since *When the Servant Becomes the Master* was first published in 2012. New medical treatments and enhanced talk therapies, creative use of technology, and the formal recognition of the American Board of Addiction Medicine by the American College of Medical Examiners are but a few atop the list of developments that have taken place in addiction treatment.

In 2016, the US surgeon general released a comprehensive report on addiction—marking the first time a surgeon general has ever been so bold. Medical and clinical thought leaders have been actively examining fundamental assumptions about addiction and its treatment. Questions about the nature of addiction, the disturbing rate of relapse, the prescription opioid and new-generation heroin epidemics, and how best to treat addiction are some of the critical issues assuming center stage. These questions are being debated everywhere from professional and trade conferences to blogs, and at times I've seen discussions become quite heated behind closed doors. Naturally, you may wonder if we have arrived at any answers to these questions.

I wish we had arrived at THE answers to these and other essential questions, but unfortunately consensus continues to elude us. At the end of the day, we are still awash in opinions. But all is not lost. There are reasons to be hopeful. When the *Diagnostic and Statistical Manual of Mental Disorders, Fifth Edition (DSM-5)*, was published in May of 2013, the earlier categories of substance abuse and dependence were replaced with the single classification of substance use disorder. Moreover, for the first time in the history of the DSM (dating to 1952), addiction is described as a disease.

Addiction is now more widely accepted as a disease based on objective brain changes observed via brain scans in addicts. Although these observed brain changes aren't new findings (as presented in the first edition of *When the Servant Becomes the Master)*, their use in increasing our understanding of addiction as a complex disease with myriad expressions is an important advancement.

In another more recent shift, the American Society of Addiction Medicine (ASAM) and major addiction journals have begun advocating the use of nonstigmatizing "person-first" language in communicating about addiction,[9] as has the subspecialty of addiction medicine (established in 2015 by the American Board of Medical Specialties). The words we use matter, and person-first language can reduce stigma by distinguishing between the individual and the conditions with which they are afflicted. Thus, rather than referring to an "addict," we refer to a "person with addiction."

If you have read the first edition of *When the Servant Becomes the Master*, you are aware that I strongly support all efforts to destigmatize addiction. That being said, like many other experienced addiction treatment professionals, I continue to be comfortable using some of the more traditional terminology, including that of "addict." I disagree that this term is inherently negative. In fact, for many of us in the treatment community, "addict" is used with kindness and compassion. Also, for the purposes of a substantial book such as this, referring to "a person with addiction" can create unnecessarily awkward syntax, so you won't see it used here with regularity.

Addiction treatment has been moving toward more cost-effective and person-centered levels of care. Increasingly, patients are receiving outpatient rather than inpatient treatment. The value of community- and peer-based approaches as crucial adjuncts to professional addiction treatment has become clear. These approaches include peer-provided support, recovery coaching, aftercare urine drug-screen monitoring, and relationship-building skills training, to name just a few. Since addiction requires long-term (as in lifetime) management, resources that are available in the recovering person's community at lower cost are appropriately being viewed as essential assets.

There is progress in the emphasis on evidence-based practices in addiction treatment as well. Although many treatment centers continue to rely on traditional rather than evidence-based practices, evidence-based practices will soon be expected to be the norm. These include the use of (1) medications proven to improve myriad treatment outcomes, (2) innovative technology, and (3) promising balanced-treatment approaches such as Positive Recovery, which incorporates positive psychology with effective existing modalities to promote recovery.

There has been a proliferation of new technologies that support recovery from addiction. These include technologically based applications, such as mobile apps that help provide recovery support via computers and smart phones, other smart phone technologies, and GPS devices used to keep track of and alert key people in the addict's life (partners, physicians, licensing boards, and so forth), should he or she venture into high-risk places like bars or specific neighborhoods where drugs are procured. These alerts are essentially layers of accountability and can help prevent relapse.

Unfortunately, there are also significantly troubling trends in addiction since the initial publication of *When the Servant Becomes the Master*. Designer drugs (synthetic psychoactive substances) created in clandestine labs the world over have become much more prevalent. I had been hopeful that legislation that casts a wide criminal net over any substance with a similar chemical makeup instead of focusing on specific chemical compounds would make these nasty drugs a passing fad. However, resourceful chemists motivated by money continue to churn out more and different designer drugs with names and appearances that mimic harmless household products, such as bath salts and potpourri. These designer drugs are capable of causing violent behavior, psychosis, elevated heart rate, and even death.[10]

Furthermore, as has been well publicized, the prescription opioid epidemic has only gotten worse over the last several years—decimating the lives of more individuals and families in more parts of the country, and precipitating a dramatic increase in heroin use, addiction, and overdose.

On a more positive and personal note, I graduated from the University of Pennsylvania's Positive Psychology Masters Program; I'm privileged and honored to be part of the Methodist Houston Medical Center Hospital Liver Transplant Review Board; and I developed and have been busy applying the Positive Recovery model in my work. Positive Recovery is a novel approach to treating addictive disorders, as well as an effective vehicle for staff training and personal and professional development. I have been most interested in improving outcomes and in helping addiction treatment staff thrive.

Relapse rates are just too high, both during and soon after treatment; addiction treatment staff have high turnover and burnout rates; and addiction medicine has the largest gap in all of healthcare between the existence of evidence-based treatment modalities and their actual application. My mission is to help addicts recover and help addiction professionals (present company included) be more informed, be more effective, and flourish at work, in life, and in their recovery. The second edition of *When the Servant Becomes the Master* continues this mission.

Acknowledgments

Where to begin? I want to start by thanking my family, without whom I would be lost. Amy, Sarah, Danyel, Mia, Sugar, Dandy, and Waffles: you have given me more joy and meaning than I deserve. Thank you, Amy, again, for all your love and support, and the remote. Sarah, thank you for making me laugh so much. You are a blessing, a creative force, and a ham on rye. Danyel, aka Mini-me, thank you for your prudent guidance at times and the unlimited hours upon hours of being called upon to play basketball, Ping-Pong, and football. Mia, your cuteness hasn't diminished over the years. Thank you for the tea parties, the howling, and the nighttime drawing stories. Thank you again, Allison Lack, for your skillful graphics.

A debt of gratitude goes out to a dear friend, George Joseph, whose friendship, support, and guidance have been cherished and who took a chance on me way back when. Thank you to the Force Forum for your support, especially after the second flood! Also, I am honored and fortunate to have such an amazing group of talented individuals to work with at The Right Steps and Promises Austin. Together we save and transform lives!

Thanks to Chris Davis: your wisdom and love of the trade lift me up and motivate me to be the best version of a healer that I can be. Terry Rusten and David Sack, thanks for your mentorship and rescue from more than one existential crisis. Julie DeNofa, thank you for all your wisdom and guidance, support, friendship, help, and insight. Thank you to Ilana Zivkovich for being a marble-jar friend, a co-external processesor, and an amusing teacher.

Thanks to those who helped me with the writing process: Leanna Gadbois-Sills, Kevin Cochrane, Ted Powers, Casey Green, and others at The Right Steps. For helping keep my daily routine and much of my professional life together, thank you, Ashley Sickler. Thanks to Mark Gold, MD, for writing the Foreword to the original edition of *When the Servant Becomes the Master*. Finally, many, many thanks to my gifted editor, Dan "As You Wish" Mager, and the wonderful team at Central Recovery Press.

Introduction

This is a book about the disease of addiction. Although I am a physician, I knew nothing about addiction until I was a patient in rehab. Well, I had a head full of ideas about addiction, to be honest, but few were accurate. My judgment was that I ended up in rehab because I was broken, a moral failure, a wretch. In rehab, I was offered shocking data. The professionals there informed me that my addiction was a disease. Initially I was skeptical—addiction classified as a disease conflicted with my preconceived notions. But if I was so smart, why was I the patient? So I listened and learned. The more I learned, the more I realized how much there was to learn. In my search to answer some fundamental and important questions, I explored as much information as I could and read everything I could get my hands on about addiction.

I also wanted to discover why some people continue to drink, drug, and engage in other dysfunctional behaviors despite seriously harmful consequences and despite the desire to stop using or acting out. Honestly, I was initially only concerned about why *I* could not quit despite a desire to do so, and the ever-increasing mountain of wreckage my behavior continued to create. My concern for others was secondary, but grew substantially over time. This book is the fruit of that labor. It is the result of my journey to make sense of the question, "What is addiction?" What I discovered was that something was wrong with me. However, that something was not to be found in my character, but in the ancient and subconscious recesses of my brain. Like me, if you are looking for a simple explanation, be prepared to be disappointed.

A word about the title is due here. Addiction comes from the Latin *addicere*, which can be translated as "relinquishing one's power to do something." What happens in addiction is that the tools people use to manage their lives begin to manage them. This is when the servant becomes the master.

In the addiction treatment community, what has been observed for an extended period of time has only recently become substantiated by science. That is, professionals working closely with addicts have known for decades that addiction is a disease process, not a moral failing or character flaw. Objective proof defining addiction as a disease can be found in the recent advancements in scientific imaging, brain research, and other medical breakthroughs. As a result, over the last several years, general public perception about addiction has significantly, though slowly, changed. Even within the dogmatic scientific community there has been a major, albeit slow, shift in awareness, and acceptance. Whereas before it was difficult to contend that addiction is a disease, it is slowly becoming a standard and accepted truth. Yet, despite the recent surge of objective knowledge, old ways of viewing addicts persist. Unfortunately, despite all the scientific data that reveal addiction to be as authentic a disease as any other, the outdated view that stigmatizes addicts as people of weak character who choose to indulge themselves too much continues to persist.

Even with all of the progress in research over the last few decades, we are still in the relatively early stages of our scientific understanding of addiction. Every discovery yields ten new questions. As a result, misunderstanding, judgment, and lack of consensus will likely continue. Addiction prolongs isolation of the sick person from his or her loved ones and communities. Since support from family and community is an effective element of successful treatment and relapse prevention, reducing the stigma of addiction is essential to health and healing. Alienation perpetuates this disease.

Thanks to the brilliant minds in research and clinical practice, we continue to make enormous strides. Applications of medications that at one time had nothing to do with addiction are now proving promising in curtailing the use of alcohol and certain other drugs. Behavioral disorders once thought to be merely obsessions and compulsions are now known to stimulate brain chemistry changes remarkably similar to substance addiction. It is exciting to be practicing in the field of addiction medicine during this time of expansive growth in our knowledge base. I continue to be amazed by our recent breakthroughs and eagerly look forward to those that lie ahead.

This book is intended to provide the most comprehensive and thorough resource for all things related to addiction. My hope is that you will find some of the information I have gathered over the years as useful and interesting as I have. My goal is to explain addiction's scientific and nonscientific elements in an easy-to-read format for a wide audience. Hopefully, anyone—from addicts, families, and friends to professionals and others who are interested in learning about the current understanding of addiction—will find this book helpful. Many times after I've lectured in the community, there have been repeated requests for this body of work, so after a while I decided to get busy. This has been a long but enjoyable process because I love everything about the study of addiction, including its rich history, the disease, the drugs (nowadays for educational purposes only), medications to combat the disease, treatment approaches, interventions, and relapse-prevention strategies.

Initially, I had trouble understanding addiction as a disease. I once thought that classifying addiction as a disease was a cop-out—addicts were too self-indulgent and refused to stop their behavior. If you are also challenged by the notion of addiction as a disease, read on and decide for yourself. When I finally ended up in rehab, I was sure it was due to the well-established "fact" that I was always going to be broken.

Because we do not teach enough about addiction in the United States, I learned very little about addiction to alcohol and other drugs in medical school. However, even with more education, I doubt I would be as convinced of the disease model as I am today had I not been through what I experienced myself. There was an internal conflict over whether I was a defective person or not. I had a lot of evidence mounting that I was endowed with defects! After rehab, I pored over every article, book, and piece of research I could get my hands on out of a need to know if addiction was really a disease. The results of that journey led to this book.

It is important to note that in speaking about the disease of addiction today, we have moved past describing the *concept* of addiction as a disease. That would be akin to calling diabetes or cancer disease concepts. This is not a concept anymore; this *is* a disease. And the disease is not simple.

For the content of this book, I owe much to the pioneers, leaders, and researchers whose work and discoveries help us both understand and treat patients effectively. Gratitude is owed to my predecessors in addiction medicine: Erickson, Gold, Volkow, Koob, Johnson, Begleiter, O'Malley, Jellinek, Li, Smith, Cloninger, Amen, and countless others. Over the last several years I have compiled a wide array of biologic, psychiatric, psychological, genetic, pharmacologic, and integrative medical research from literature, conferences, and leaders in the field of addiction treatment. This book also contains the wisdom that can only be found among those directly in the know: recovering addicts.

It has been my pleasure and honor to meet and work with thousands of amazing people (and their loved ones) in recovery from alcohol and other drugs, as well as from food, sex, love, gambling, and gaming. I treat people from all walks of life: high-profile athletes and celebrities, engineers, writers, teachers, wives, husbands, sons, daughters, friends, doctors, lawyers, salespeople, plumbers, policemen and policewomen, and so on. The disease of addiction does not discriminate as far as race, creed, sex, or socioeconomic status is concerned. Addiction can potentially affect anyone. No one is immune. No matter who is affected, successful treatment fosters a truly magical transformation in everyone willing to apply him- or herself to the solutions. On a daily basis I bear witness to health and healing. Treatment works and recovery is possible.

The success of recovering people is amazing because, in their own way, each one is a hero rather than a victim. Their struggles speak to the best human beings can be. In recovery, addicts are asked to make some momentous changes. It is nothing short of incredible what some addicts will do to get better. Most human beings with other diseases make few, if any, significant lifestyle changes. Change is hard. Changing almost everything is nearly impossible, when you think about it. Some addicts make changes that are akin to climbing Mount Everest blind and without a rope.

A daily victory over a chronic, relapsing, and powerful disease exemplifies excellence, service, spirit, accountability, honor, honesty, courage, willingness, humility, and many other virtues that reflect the best human beings have to offer. I believe every human being is perfectly imperfect in his or her own ways. Addicts happen to make an art form of their imperfection during their active addiction. As a result, their lives and the lives of those around them suffer. But if they can maximize the opportunities for learning and change, immeasurable growth is the awe-inspiring by-product of the recovery process. Addiction will take any person to horrible places and cause incredible suffering, regardless of who he or she is. It is said that religion is for people who don't want to go to hell, and recovery is for people who have been to hell and don't want to go back.

"No pleasure is in itself evil, but the things which produce certain pleasures entail annoyances many times greater than the pleasures themselves."—**Epicurus**

Chapter 1: The Disease of Addiction

A lcohol and other drugs are good. At first glance, this may appear to be an outrageous, even blasphemous statement. Research has demonstrated that people take drugs (alcohol is a drug) in order to feel good or to change the way they feel. In fact, drugs are a fast, effective, and easy way to accomplish a change in feelings. They are powerful, often having the ability to change the chemistry in the brain with much more strength than what happens naturally. Drugs are effective—albeit in the short term, with long-term consequences—often causing change rapidly and predictably. Drugs are also easy because it often takes little effort to obtain and use them. The fact is that people use drugs because they are believed to be good. They exert their effects in the *pleasure pathways* of the brain. Pleasure is good, right?

Drugs are many other things, too. Drugs are tools, drugs reward, drugs motivate, drugs numb, drugs can give meaning to life, and drugs have social significance. One of the oldest known recorded recipes in the history of humanity is for brewing alcohol. Alcohol especially is a drug with a long-standing social value. People use drugs in health and healing, recreation, and spiritual ceremonies.

Drugs are bad. Drugs are responsible for so many ills; an entire volume of books can be written on the negative consequences they have caused throughout history. While most major causes of preventable death are declining, alcohol and other drugs are a glaring exception—the death toll from them doubled in the preceding decade. In contrast, traffic accidents have been decreasing for decades because of important investments in auto safety. In 2009, more deaths in the United States were caused by drugs than by motor vehicles for the first time since the government started tracking drug-related deaths in 1979.[11] Opioids—prescription painkillers and heroin—have been the main driver of drug overdose deaths. Opioids were involved in 33,091 deaths in 2015, and opioid overdoses have quadrupled since 1999.[12]

Are drugs good or bad, then? The truth is, drugs are both, and neither. When someone can have a beer once a week and never run into trouble, is that beer bad? When someone has a beer that leads to more beers and that leads to incarceration, is that good? When cocaine is used therapeutically in eye surgery, is it bad? When cocaine is used at a party one night and leads to a two-week binge that leads to psychosis, is it good? The nature of any drug is not intrinsic to the substance itself; the circumstances and context of its use must also be considered.

In any case, we have an enormous "drug" problem. The US Department of Health and Human Services (HHS) Substance Abuse and Mental Health Services Administration (SAMHSA) conducts the National Survey on Drug Use and Health annually. In 2014 (the most recent year for which results are available), an estimated twenty-seven million people aged twelve or older—10.2 percent of the US population—were current illicit drug users. In other words, one in ten individuals aged twelve or older in the United States used illicit drugs in the past month. In the US, 9.4 percent of all adolescents (aged twelve to seventeen), or slightly more than 2.3 million adolescents, were current users of illicit drugs in 2014.[13]

As many as 10 percent of those who use alcohol and other drugs will develop addiction.[14] Alcohol and other drug misuse costs our society over $600 billion every year.[15] Sadly, the disease of addiction has never received adequate public education, appropriate funding, or comprehensive and consistent prevention and treatment strategies in relationship to its costs. As a result, most people who develop addiction will never receive treatment. Many end up dead or in jail. The majority of our prisons are filled with those who are guilty of drug-related crimes.

A 2008 study by the Justice Policy Institute reported that every dollar spent on drug treatment returns an estimated eighteen dollars in benefits to the community.[16] Unfortunately, we usually punish those with the disease of addiction rather than treat them. Allowing any disease to be managed by police and district attorneys is as misguided as allowing physicians to represent plaintiffs in courts of law. The US "war on drugs" has served no purpose but to fill prison beds and keep them filled. It is estimated that 70 percent of individuals in state prisons and local jails have abused drugs regularly, compared with approximately 9 percent of the general population. Studies show that treatment cuts drug abuse in half, reduces criminal activity up to 80 percent, and reduces arrests up to 64 percent. However, fewer than one-fifth of these offenders receive treatment. Treatment not only lowers recidivism rates, it is also cost-effective. It is estimated that for every dollar spent on addiction treatment programs, there is a four to seven dollar reduction in the cost of drug-related crimes. With some outpatient programs, total savings can exceed costs by a ratio of twelve to one.[17]

This is primarily a book about addiction to alcohol and other drugs. There are other forms of addiction known as process addiction. These forms of addiction—to gambling, food, and sex—will be covered in Chapter Twelve.

The Three Blind Men and the Elephant

Early on in my search to discover the definition and nature of addiction, I found the more I learned, the more it became clear how complicated addiction is. A pervasive misconception is that it is merely due to using too much of a substance for too long. While use of mind-altering substances is a necessary component for addiction to activate, it is not nearly enough. We cannot make the diagnosis of addiction based solely on patterns of use. For one thing, most people who use drugs are not addicts, and many addicts are not daily users. Moreover, addiction is not defined by any particular substance or behavior(s), but rather is characterized by a pathological relationship between the individual and substances and/or behaviors that include obsessive thinking and compulsive acting.

A useful analogy I frequently use to explain the multifaceted and complex nature of addiction is the ancient Asian fable of "The Three Blind Men and the Elephant."

> One day, three blind men who were acquainted with one another got together and talked for a long time about many things. At one point, one of them exclaimed, "I've heard that an elephant is an amazing animal. It's too bad that we can't see one because we're blind."
>
> "It's indeed unfortunate that we're unable to glimpse this unusual animal," said another.
>
> The third, quite annoyed, joined in and said, "We don't need to see it with our eyes. Like with other things, if we can only touch an elephant, we can know what it looks like."
>
> It so happened that a merchant with a herd of elephants was passing by and happened to overhear their conversation. "If you gentlemen really want to feel an elephant, follow me; I will show you," he said.
>
> Happily surprised, the three men took each other by the hand and followed while the merchant led the way. Each one began to contemplate how he would feel the elephant and thought about how he would form an image of the animal.
>
> After they reached the herd, the merchant asked them to sit on the ground to wait. In a few minutes he led the first blind man to feel the elephant. With outstretched hand, he touched first the left front leg and then the right. He felt the two legs from the top to the bottom, and with a beaming face, reported, "So, an elephant is just like that." Then he slowly returned to the group.

The second blind man was led to the rear of the elephant where he touched the tail, which wagged a few times, and he exclaimed with satisfaction, "Ha! That is truly a strange animal! Now I know."

When the third blind man's turn came, he touched the elephant's trunk, which moved back and forth, turning and twisting, and he thought, That's it! I've learned what I wanted to know.

The three blind men thanked the merchant and went on their way. Each of them was excited about this experience and had a lot to say, yet as they walked they did not discuss it.

Finally, one said, "Let's sit down and have a discussion about this extraordinary beast." The other two readily agreed.

The second began, "The elephant is like our straw fans swinging back and forth to give us a breeze. However, it's not so big or well made. The main portion is rather wispy."

"No, no!" the first blind man stated with certainty. "The elephant resembles two big trees without any branches."

"You're both completely wrong," the third man said. "The elephant is like a snake; it's long and round, and very strong."

They argued for hours, each one insisting that his perception alone was correct. Of course, none of them was correct, for none of them had examined the entire elephant. After all, how can anyone describe the whole until he has learned the total of the parts?

Attempts to define addiction are often similarly limited. When we focus on only one element, we miss the entire picture. Each of the blind men was correct in his assessment of what he experienced, but none of them discovered the true nature of the beast. So, if we concentrate only on which drug is used or for how long, we miss the mark. If we examine only behavior, we describe only part of the puzzle. If we talk only about genetics and family patterns, we fall short. If we accept that addiction only occurs with trauma, poor self-esteem, peer pressure, or other behavioral and mental illnesses, we miss out as well. Addiction involves pleasure at first. However, it is maintained not by that initial bliss, but by avoiding the pain and angst associated with not using. Addiction involves many elements, and only by considering all of them are we able to grasp its true nature.

Each of the blind men was correct in his assessment of the elephant, but without the others would never achieve a full understanding of the whole. When I set out to discover the nature of addiction, I had to release many preconceived notions I once had about human behavior, choice, and the definition of diseases. Many times, our preconceptions leave little room for new information. A full cup has no space.

This lesson is not wasted on many of my patients, because they often come into treatment with a preconceived notion of what their treatment will be, armed with their own treatment plans. When they first hear our treatment plan for them, they often display resistance, since it is usually not as *convenient* as the one they have in mind. I use the fable above to challenge their reluctance to accept suggestions. Often they are so attached to their own ideas and preferences that they are unaware of just how unaware they are as to what is in their best interests. Over time, many of these patients allow other views in and their understanding and openness expands. This sort of humility is important and healthy, not only for addicts in recovery, but for all of us. We have only one set of eyes, one set of experiences, and one mind. The world is full of wisdom. All we have to do is let it in.

Alcoholism Is Addiction

Alcoholism and drug addiction have often been thought of as two distinct and different entities, while they are, in fact, so similar that both can be considered as variants of the same disease. Alcohol is a mood-and mind-altering drug of abuse like any other. Therefore, it makes little sense to separate *alcoholism* from *addiction* and *alcoholics* from *addicts*.

In some circles, alcohol may be considered different because it is legal and used in a wide variety of social and business circumstances. However, increasingly, the medicinal and even recreational use of marijuana is becoming legal in states across the US. The line between legal and illegal substances is artificial and arbitrary. Every year, thousands of people abuse, become addicted to, and overdose on legally prescribed opioids. Based on the harm it causes, excellent arguments can be made that alcohol should also be illegal, but we attempted that as a society during Prohibition and the rest is history.

Ethanol, the active ingredient in alcohol, works in the same part of the brain, the mesolimbic dopamine system (MDS), as every other drug of abuse, including cocaine, heroin, and crystal meth. All mood- and mind-altering substances converge in action and dysfunction in the MDS with no distinction between legal and illegal, between liquid or solid or gaseous, or any other variable. When ethanol, opioids, cocaine, marijuana, or amphetamines are ingested and exert their effects in the MDS, they are all potential agents of addiction.

If someone is taking twenty Valium a day prescribed by a physician, the MDS does not say, "This is a prescription substance called diazepam that is manufactured by Roche and is legally prescribed three times daily, so I won't be activated." If someone drinks a fifth of scotch most nights of the week because he or she needs to entertain guests, the MDS does not say, "This is only because I am working and does not really count because there are others around and alcohol is legal." No, the MDS cannot differentiate based on the context in which substances are used, and when ethanol or other drugs of abuse are ingested, predictable changes occur.

Alcohol is used to change the way we feel; it is used as a coping mechanism, and its abuse causes all the same kinds of problems as the abuse of other drugs. When we look at the progression of alcohol use in spite the presence of increasingly serious negative consequences—in terms of family, legal, social, spiritual, physical, and emotional problems—it mirrors the progression of use in spite the presence of increasingly serious negative consequences of virtually any other substance of abuse.

Alcoholics are addicts, and addiction to alcohol is the same as addiction to any other addictive substance. If your drug of choice is cocaine, do you have cocaineism? If your drug of choice is marijuana, do you have marijuanaism? The answer is no. Appropriately, we also don't separate *heroinism* and *cocaineism* and *Vicodinism*. So I ask: why is it that we make a distinction at all? In my opinion and that of many others, it's all the same disease—the disease of addiction. Even the Big Book of Alcoholics Anonymous states that the act of drinking alcohol is only a symptom of the larger disease. The point is, no matter what the substance of abuse may be, we are talking about the disease of addiction, and I will refer to those who suffer from it as addicts.

A Word on Language

Words matter, and research shows that even for seasoned clinicians the term *abuser* or *addict* can increase the stereotypical stigma associated with addiction. I use the term *addict* as I would use the term *diabetic*. I use it descriptively for any individual who has the disease of addiction. To many thought leaders, including some of my trusted mentors, the term *addict* has a negative or misleading connotation due to stigma and the historical misunderstanding of addiction. While I fully support all efforts to destigmatize addiction, as an addict in recovery myself, I do not have a problem with the term *addict,* and do not find it inherently stigmatizing. Again, to me, it is merely descriptive. It is the same as saying *asthmatic.*

That being said, it's important to be thoughtful about words we use in the field of addiction medicine and treatment. Many frequently use terms that are rife with judgment and shame. For example, a positive urine drug screen is commonly referred to as "dirty." Why would a positive test be called dirty? Dirty implies that there is something gross or wrong. A urinalysis looking for an infection is not called dirty; it is called positive. A blood sugar test for diabetes that turns out high is called "high" or "positive." Addicts are subject to an undercurrent of judgment not found elsewhere in medicine. Wherever possible, prejudicial and inappropriate terminology should be identified and eliminated.

With these points in mind, and after careful deliberation, I decided to continue to use the term *addict* in this work with ownership and neutrality, and within the context of efficient communication and nonjudgmental description. In fact, for myself and others in the field like my friend Michael Baron, MD and chair of the Controlled Substance Monitoring Database Committee of the Department of Health for the state of Tennessee, the word *addict* is endearing.

Addiction Defined

The million-dollar question to which people want a clean and simple answer is, "What is addiction?" As I noted earlier, the answer is far from straightforward: a complex disease, an unhealthy habit, a process, and more. I define addiction as *a brain disease and habit-forming process that is continued despite negative behavioral, psychological, biological, social, emotional, and spiritual consequences.*

But perhaps an easy way to think about the dysfunction or disorder known as addiction is to briefly explore overall well-being (aka "happiness"). People just want to be happy, whether that means avoiding pain or moving toward the positive. Aristotle said happiness is the only end people pursue for itself; everything else people do is in order to achieve some aspect of well-being. This is close to my heart, as I believe that *addiction can develop when happiness is pursued in the wrong way.* Recovery, then, is more likely when happiness is pursued effectively.

There is no specific mention of alcohol or other drugs in the definition above. Notice how this definition applies to addiction to substances like alcohol and other drugs, or processes like gambling, eating, sex, and shopping. The American Society of Addiction Medicine (ASAM), the foremost authority on addiction in the world, defines addiction as follows:

> *Addiction is a primary, chronic disease of brain reward, motivation, memory, and related circuitry. Dysfunction in these circuits leads to characteristic biological, psychological, social, and spiritual manifestations. This is reflected in an individual pathologically pursuing reward and/or relief by substance use and other behaviors. Addiction is characterized by inability to consistently abstain, impairment in behavioral control, craving, diminished recognition of significant problems with one's behaviors and interpersonal relationships, and a dysfunctional emotional response. Like other chronic diseases, addiction often involves cycles of relapse and remission. Without treatment or engagement in recovery activities, addiction is progressive and can result in disability or premature death.*[18]

Here too, there is no mention of particular substances or behaviors.

Later I will explore how the interactions among environment, drug, and person can lead to addiction. I will also review the progression of the disease. In Chapter Five, the elements of preoccupation, obsession, compulsion, and impaired thinking are described within a model known as the addiction cycle.

The medical and behavioral health communities use standard language when defining mental/psychiatric disorders, including addiction. We use a guidebook to define, diagnose, and help us communicate about mental illnesses: the *Diagnostic and Statistical Manual of Mental Disorders,* Fifth Edition (*DSM-5*). As I mentioned earlier, one of the changes in *DSM-5* is that the diagnostic categories of *substance abuse* and *substance dependence* were eliminated in favor of the single category of *substance use disorders,* which can be further assessed as *mild, moderate,* or *severe* based on the level of severity. The level of severity is determined by the number of different diagnostic criteria met by an individual.

Substance use disorders are diagnosed when the recurrent use of alcohol and/or other drugs causes clinically and functionally significant impairment, such as health problems, disability, and failure to meet major responsibilities at work, school, or home. According to the *DSM-5,* a diagnosis of substance use disorder involves evidence of impaired control, social impairment, risky use, and pharmacological criteria.[19]

In part because of the complexity of the process and what's at stake, whenever the *DSM* is revised, as it was in 2013, there is controversy and disagreement. This was certainly the case with regard to the changes related to alcohol and other drug use problems. Physicians, therapists, counselors, and other clinicians are required to use the *DSM,* and insurance reimbursement and other forms of payment are often dependent upon a *DSM* diagnosis. Its language can be highly technical and tedious, and with respect to addiction, it ignores the ASAM definition.

Jerome C. Wakefield, DSW, PhD, professor in the Silver School of Social Work at New York University, eloquently articulated some of the greatest concerns related to these changes in the current version of the *DSM*: "*DSM-5* has not only conceptually muddled the notion of an addictive disorder in its revised diagnostic criteria for substance use disorder but also irresponsibly made it more difficult to diagnose opioid addiction in the midst of a deadly iatrogenically generated opioid addiction epidemic; it is left to the rest of us to try to move forward in clarifying the notion of addiction. However, the rest of us are mired in a highly polarized cross-disciplinary debate about the fundamental nature of addiction."[20]

Every edition of the *DSM*, from the first in 1952 to *DSM-5,* is presented as a work of science, but they are really more representative of the prevailing sociocultural and political environment (with all of the relevant financial implications) than they are of actual science. The *DSM* attempts to define illness rather than uncover its cause or help improve treatment outcomes. All this notwithstanding, as imperfect as *DSM-5* is, it's the best diagnostic resource we have currently, and provides a *good enough* reference for anyone interested in medicine's *official* taxonomy of psychiatric disorders.

Recognizing Addiction

Defining addiction is one thing; recognizing it when there is doubt is another. Identifying addiction is obvious when the specified diagnostic criteria are clearly present. In other words, where addiction is evident, finding evidence of *continued use despite harmful negative consequences, loss of control,* and other indications is not a challenge. But addiction is a process that takes time. Most of the time, it can be tricky to spot. Until cases are obvious, shrewd detective work and a high index of suspicion are the best tools we have. Addiction's essential behavioral components mean that objective medical tests such as a brain scan or blood test cannot make the diagnosis. There is no "easy button" here.

The exact point at which addiction commandeers the brain, that is, when addiction is activated, is impossible to ascertain. Before addiction is present, there is often problematic use. Problematic use can precede addiction or simply indicate that someone has progressed beyond social or experimental use. It is impossible to predict which problematic users will progress to full-blown addiction because many behaviors in problematic use look exactly like addiction-mediated behaviors. On the surface, a DUI is not enough to make a diagnosis. Anyone is capable of making poor decisions and could have bad luck. The trouble is that both addicts and nonaddicts are just as likely to deny a problem exists when confronted with the negative consequences of their use. Denial is an inherent aspect of addiction, making those with the disease earnest refuters. Beyond denial, addicts often take heroic steps to conceal their problem.

Most people who drink are not addicts. Most people who use other drugs are not addicts. Addiction is a process activated only after the right combination of host, drug, and environment comes into play. Problematic and risky use of alcohol and other drug-taking behaviors alone do not fulfill the diagnostic criteria for addiction. For all these reasons, often addiction is not identified until it has been present for far too long.

Not surprisingly, I am frequently asked to explain how to recognize when addiction is present. Major behavioral changes are important red flags, provided that we acknowledge that these red flags could also signify any number of other underlying disorders. The bottom line here is this: as the number of biopsychosocial problems rises, so does the likelihood that addiction is present.

Common Symptoms of an Addictive Disorder

- Tolerance leads to more use, so higher and higher quantities of the substance (or behavior) are required to achieve the desired effect. More and more time and effort are required to keep up with the progressive habit.

- Tardiness becomes the norm. Active addiction is like a demanding full-time job. Elaborate and incredible excuses are used to "explain" why the person is frequently late or absent.

- Withdrawal symptoms such as shaking, sweating, insomnia, fatigue, irritability, anxiety, and so forth begin to materialize and disappear contingent on where the person is in his or her cycle of using, and whether he or she has limited or no access to the object of addiction.

- Responsibilities are ignored. School, work, or home obligations increasingly go unfulfilled.

- Relationships are strained. Conflicts arise with friends, family, and work-related peers or employers.

- Relationships change. Existing friendships change. New and completely different relationships start.

- Jobs are changed or lost, sometimes frequently.

- Hobbies and other leisure activities are abandoned—socializing and soccer games interfere with drug use.

- Promises are broken and commitments go unfulfilled.

- Isolation begins or increases. Addiction causes withdrawal from intimate friends and the community.

- Concealing of using and related behaviors arises. Nonproblematic users have nothing to hide.

- Dishonesty starts, continues, and escalates.

- Suspicious and secretive behaviors are present.

- Unexplained mood swings or mood changes start or become more obvious.

- Legal troubles arise.

- Risky and impulsive behaviors start or escalate.

- Defensiveness is evident whenever the issue of a possible alcohol or other drug problem arises. Addicts will often blame others, minimize significant problems, turn the tables and attack those who are expressing concern, or say things such as "I can quit any time I want."

- Physical changes arise that may indicate drug use, such as bloodshot eyes, weight loss, or deterioration of hygiene and appearance.

- Health issues arise. Addiction causes chronic conditions like high blood pressure and short-term medical issues like falling, bruising, cuts, and so forth. Also, frequent infections and/or other unexplained illnesses are possible signs.
- Memory and concentration become impaired.
- Financial problems arise and become more frequent.

Again, any of these red flags is possible with other conditions—any list of possible warning signs is at best an imperfect tool. However, these indicators correlate with the presence of addiction. When you have concerns about another person's alcohol or other drug use, the best initial approach is to let him know that you are worried. It's generally never a mistake to express your own feelings and concerns with dignity and respect. Letting that person know your concerns and the reasons behind them is an opportunity to give caring and compassion, as well as to strengthen the bonds you share with him.

Consider the more common scenario in which someone you care about has a large piece of spinach (or other food) stuck in her teeth, unbeknownst to her. Taking the step of letting her know of your observation may be somewhat uncomfortable for both you, but it provides her with important information she can use to take action (if she so chooses) and is evidence of your concern and the close connection the two of you share. It is that level of intimacy and caring that binds us and motivates us into action.

In a disease process, there are predictable patterns of signs and symptoms. Addiction in any form creates the same patterns of behavior and harmful consequences in the individuals afflicted by it. Note that a plethora of red flags from the list above can just as easily indicate a sex addiction or gambling addiction. In Chapter Twelve, we address the similarities between substance and process forms of addiction like gambling and sex. For now, suffice it to say that any problematic addictive process has the same recognizable symptoms.

Is Addiction Really a Disease?

Many still argue that addiction is not a disease. Although there are decades of good scientific data, there is by no means a general consensus about how best to understand addiction. In the historical record there is ample evidence of cultures that appreciated the true nature of addiction. The ancient Greeks and Egyptians expressed their understanding of addiction as a disease in some of their recovered writings. Benjamin Rush, MD, who signed the Declaration of Independence, was a physician in colonial times who wrote *Inquiry into the Effects of Ardent Spirits on the Human Mind and Body*, a book about alcoholism as a disease. He, and later the Washingtonians, Oxford Groups, Alcoholics Anonymous, and others, understood that addiction is an entity larger than morality, habit, faith, volitional decision-making, character, and willpower.

In the twenty-first century we have the science to both validate and elucidate the recognition of addiction as a disease. Certain consistent disease-specific elements have been recognized about addiction through the years, including toxic effects of drugs, predisposing factors, tolerance, craving, withdrawal symptoms, progression of the disease, loss of control, inability to quit on one's own, and other psychological, physical, and emotional effects.

I have heard addicts referred to as people who make poor choices or are lazy, stupid, or sinful; are products of poor parenting; have no willpower; have no faith; and worse. I appreciate the concern that labeling addiction as a disease may appear to absolve the addict of responsibility for his or her behavior. Obviously, many addicts behave in untoward ways that often create significant problems for others, as well as for themselves. Millions upon millions of people have been adversely affected in some form or fashion by an addict's behavior. It can be difficult to find someone who has not been so affected. Despite the science, any disease that causes people to behave poorly will usually stir some resentment and incur judgment, and in many cases, a degree of condemnation.

As a result, addicts have historically been treated as moral or character failures, treated as outcasts, and subjected to outrageous, sometimes inhumane treatments. For example, some addicts were sterilized at the turn of the twentieth century in an attempt to reduce, or even cure, addiction in society. Others had the frontal lobe of their brain removed. Some addicts were even subjected to having hot metal poured down their throats in an attempt to stop drunkenness. Misunderstanding of addictive disease was the source of these and other grossly inappropriate "treatments."

Throughout US history, the majority of the population has believed that addiction is an issue of morality, character, and willpower. That began to change in 1956 when the American Medical Association, the foremost medical organization in the United States, declared alcoholism to be a treatable illness.[21] That was over sixty years ago. Based on that declaration and the 2016 report on addiction by the US surgeon general stating that addiction results from changes in the brain that occur with the repeated use of alcohol and other drugs,[22] one could assume that we have made some progress.

However, unfortunately, as recently as 1988 the United States Supreme Court found drinking to be willful misconduct in one of their cases.[23] That wording—*willful* misconduct—is a powerful reinforcer of the stigma linked to addiction. Too many people continue to believe that addicts can get better through good, old-fashioned Puritan self-discipline. But the evidence that addiction is a disease is overwhelming.

When I started lecturing on addiction to groups, I was often approached afterward with requests to explain what I had just presented to some of the attendees' other family members or friends in the community. What is interesting is that I do not perform original bench research; I relay research conducted by others. I may have some intuition and experience mixed in, but most of the information I present has been around for years. I find it truly amazing that we have come so far on one hand, yet have made little progress in the public understanding and psyche on the other. There continues to be an enormous amount of prejudice and bias against addicts.

As long as addiction continues to be steeped in stigma, our efforts to effectively treat and prevent this disease will be undermined. Many individuals with addiction will remain underground for fear of ridicule. Society will support punishment rather than treatment, and professionals will continue to provide less-than-optimal treatment services.

Is It a Choice?

In understanding addiction and in breaking down a common misconception, it is important to first address the key issue of free will, or choice. Many people believe that addiction cannot be a disease specifically because it involves an element of choice. I hear that cancer happens to people who are unfortunate, but addiction happens to those who make poor choices. The majority of people who drink and use other drugs do not develop the disease of addiction. The simple act of using a drug does not addiction make. Choosing to use a drug is not enough to cause addiction. Choice alone cannot create any disease, for that matter. You may choose to eat cheeseburgers, but you do not choose to have a heart attack. You may choose not to exercise, but you do not choose diabetes. You may choose to not eat enough fiber, but you do not choose colon cancer. No one chooses addiction, either.

Interestingly, choice is actually an element in many diseases. Yet there is more compassion for other diseases that contain elements of choice than there is for addiction. Addicts are quickly judged, even when the facts do not support such a judgment. I, for one, do not assign blame to those with addiction for having a disease any more than I blame water for being wet. I do not assign blame for any disease.

Intrinsic to choice is free will, personal accountability, and the ability to stop "bad" behaviors. Choice responds to deterrence and punishment. On the other hand, in the case of disease, there is less free will and therefore less personal accountability. There are symptoms, and disease usually responds to treatment. Smoking and eating a poor diet are strong risk factors that can lead to colon cancer, among other diseases. Eating a poor diet and leading a sedentary lifestyle may also lead to diabetes, liver disease, heart disease, high blood pressure, heart attacks, and strokes. There is also an association between one alcoholic drink daily and an increased risk of breast cancer in women. Now, if someone who develops any of those diseases attempts to get treatment, do they encounter negative judgment and resistance, and stigma in their families, society, or the medical system? Do they get punished for having a disease that involves an element of choice? Of course not. Nor should they. Nor should anyone.

Did their behavior favor the development of the disease? Good question. The crux lies in the fact that free will can be present in many diseases that are thought to "befall the innocent." Not everyone who uses alcohol or other drugs becomes addicted, and not all addicts are daily users. Not everyone who smokes or eats poorly develops cancer, high blood pressure, heart disease, or diabetes, and not everyone who develops cancer, high blood pressure, heart disease, or diabetes smokes or eats poorly, either. The main point here is that choice is a possible contributing factor in many major diseases and does not always lead to the worst possible outcomes.

I appreciate that it takes acts of will for the disease of addiction to develop. That's why addiction is also akin to a bad habit. However, bad habits aren't caused by the degree of brain dysfunction that perpetuates addiction. With repetitive use, symptoms develop, some of which (based on the ASAM definition) include the inability to consistently abstain, impairment in behavioral control, and diminished recognition of significant problems with one's behaviors and interpersonal relationships. Consistent with these symptoms, at a certain point the element of choice has been eliminated.

There are places where the line between no addiction and addiction can be fuzzy, but the same is true of the lines that separate child from adolescent and adolescent from adult, as well as day from night. In effect, there is an element of free will or choice until there isn't any longer, even though the exact moment this occurs is diffuse and may be difficult to identify. In addiction there is a line beyond which choice has been removed. At that point, there is no longer a choice to use as much as there is a need.

Samuel Taylor Coleridge, a late-eighteenth/early-nineteenth–century British poet and philosopher who started the Romantic movement and influenced American Transcendentalism, was also an opiate addict who adeptly described his loss of choice as his addiction progressed: "My case is a species of madness, only that it is a derangement of the Volition, and not of the intellectual faculties."[24] Coleridge explains that addiction is not merely a pesky habit that can be rejected by reason. Addiction is all-encompassing: a disease of the body, mind, soul, and will.

In the evolution of alcohol and other drug use from social use to regular use to problematic use to addiction, there is an ethereal line on the other side of which addiction lies. On one side of this line the person retains the ability to stop, and the other side of the line is where choice is eliminated. Addiction is therefore considered to be a state where the brain is effectively hijacked—addiction overpowers the brain's reward, motivation, and impulse-control pathways. And once that threshold is crossed, the ability to choose and control alcohol and other drug use is gone forever. In other words, once the disease is activated, there is no going back. Consistent with a saying in AA, once a cucumber has been turned into a pickle, it can never return to being a cucumber again.

Another curious and cynically humorous observation on addiction that one hears in the twelve-step recovery community is that addiction is the only disease that tells you that you don't have it. It often seems as though the addict is the last to know he or she has addiction. Just as it is obvious to objective observers when there is a pickle mixed in with cucumbers at the grocery store, it is obvious when there is an active addict is in your midst. When the addict is asked to get some treatment or, as in this example, to move from the fresh produce section to the pickle aisle, the disease tells him or her, "No, you are a cucumber; don't listen to anyone else!" Denial is an inherent aspect of addiction.

Still, the biggest misconception about addicts and addiction continues to involve the issue of free will and willpower. Addicts can decide to do many things, but addiction is one disease that cannot be managed merely by "trying harder." The problem is that addicts actually can have *too much* willpower. That is right: addicts have too much willpower. This may seem an incredible statement on the surface, but it is one that can be explained by defining willpower.

Willpower is the combination of discipline and diligence. It is the trait of resolutely controlling your own behavior. Addiction is characterized by the continuing use of alcohol and other drugs despite negative consequences. For the addict and his or her loved ones, some of these consequences can be terribly painful, extremely expensive, or even catastrophic. They show up as signs: health begins to fail, family and friends repeatedly beg the addict to stop, the legal system may "express concern," and employment is affected. When the signs are obvious that the addict should stop, what character trait, above all others, must be summoned to continue using? That's correct—willpower.

Discipline and diligence are needed to continue pushing on in the face of such roadblocks. While the social, spiritual, financial, and legal consequences would deter most people from continuing down this path, addicts seem to be able to persist against insurmountable odds because they are able to wield their willpower so successfully. It takes discipline and diligence to formulate better plans for obtaining, using, and recovering from drugs. Devising better hiding places for the booze or other drugs and circulating among different liquor stores or doctors and pharmacies takes careful planning and cunning. Covering one's tracks, lying, and evading trouble likewise require considerable effort. Without willpower, problematic substance use would be less likely to develop into addiction.

Too much willpower shows up in another way. Addicts often need to "run the show." Addiction is the only disease where the patient comes into treatment with his or her own treatment plan. When we assess a new patient and make our recommendation, we are frequently met with resistance not found elsewhere in the field of medicine. Imagine you were diagnosed with a cancerous tumor, and the physician recommended a course of treatment that would grant you the greatest chance of success. Now, factor in that such treatment would not be convenient and might require you to make some sacrifices. How would you respond? My guess is that most folks would accept the sacrifices and move forward. No one tells the cancer doctor what to do, but in my field patients often tell me exactly how to treat them.

Treatment is geared toward getting the addict out of his or her current so-called comfort zone. In that sense, treatment should be inconvenient and difficult. There are various *good* reasons why someone who is in the middle of a life-threatening crisis cannot enter treatment immediately: the dog needs food, the cleaning needs to be done, or the person needs to have an elective appendix transplant. Addicts are using their willpower when they determine their own treatment plans. Addicts are not encouraged to develop more willpower. Actually, they are encouraged to let go of their willpower long enough to start the healing process.

Recovery requires more than "swearing off of it." People who are not addicts can choose whether or not to use alcohol and other drugs, even excessively (though of course, continued use may lead to addiction). Addicts, on the other hand, continue the use of mind-altering substances despite themselves. That is, even when the intention is to do otherwise, addicts will continue to use and to do so despite a desire to quit and despite the negative physical, emotional, psychological, and spiritual consequences that follow.

Willpower is not an effective treatment for addiction, or for any disease, for that matter. When I hear others say, "Why don't they just quit?" it reflects how little these folks appreciate that addiction is a disease like other chronic diseases. No one tells the diabetic to *just quit that sugar stuff!* Willpower is not considered a treatment for other diseases, so why would anyone assume it is the treatment for addiction? Try using willpower next time you have diarrhea and see how successful you are. If willpower could treat diseases, then effective treatment would mostly consist of cheerleading. Why not tell patients with all diseases to try harder?

It is vital to emphasize that lack of choice and lack of willpower do not absolve the addict from personal responsibility. I am the first one in line to hold addicts personally accountable for their actions. Treatment gives addicts a chance to modify their behavior because it focuses on the underlying issue (addiction) rather than the symptoms (behavior).

Genetic Factors in Addiction

Genetic factors contribute significantly to someone's vulnerability in developing addiction. Researchers can demonstrate that a disease is inherited by looking at studies of biological twins, environmental conditions, and chemical markers. We have discovered that addiction is not found on a single gene, but rather is the result of various genes that, in combination with each other and environmental factors, increase the likelihood of its development. There is no one cause; there are many contributing factors. Family history and genetic transmission are only one piece of the puzzle.

Long ago it was noticed that alcoholism, one form of addiction, ran in families. The ancient Greeks understood this. Plutarch, a Greek historian (AD

46–120), commented on how alcoholism was more frequent among offspring of alcoholics.[25] Many diseases run in families and have known genetic factors. Not surprisingly, addiction is among them. Genetic factors help explain, in part, the lack of choice people have in whether or not they get a specific disease. When genetic studies demonstrated that alcoholism had a real genetic component, a major milestone was reached in the debate on whether alcoholism was a true disease or was due to character flaws and poor choices. Genetic factors lend credence to discussions about diseases in ways not otherwise possible.

In my estimation, we may look and look but we will never find a single "addiction gene." Even if I am wrong and we do isolate a magic biologic marker, environmental and psychosocial factors must also be considered. While a genetic predisposition indicates a higher probability that a disease may activate under the right circumstances, addiction can develop without biological predisposition and often does not develop even with such predisposition. With respect to substance addiction, genetic factors alone will never "turn on" addiction without the actual use of mind-altering substances. Addiction may not be a purely genetic disease, but it does have significant genetic components.

Again, many opponents of the "disease of addiction" concept contend that labeling it as a disease releases the addict from responsibility. The behaviors of addicts can be disheartening, and there are many who have been hurt by those with addiction. Rather than minimizing an addict's responsibility for his or her behavior, recognizing the fact addiction is influenced by biology can assist in improving outcomes. No disease grants anyone a free pass to behave inappropriately. The untreated diabetic and the untreated addict should be held equally accountable to make lifestyle changes.

The first few decades of studies on addiction focused on alcoholics. Alcohol has been the most widely studied drug merely because it has been around the longest, and, as a legal drug, is readily available and so has had the most widespread use. Times are changing, though. Increasingly, marijuana is becoming legal for medical and recreational purposes. Its popularity and use are increasing commensurately. Even with ever greater public awareness of the opioid epidemic, prescription drugs continue to be used and abused at alarming rates. All addicts appear to have roughly equivalent familial patterns of use, but what we know about the genetics of addiction comes from studies of mostly just one drug: alcohol. However, studies with other drugs like cocaine and opioids demonstrate very similar genetic elements to those of alcohol. It is not too much of a stretch, then, when addiction professionals extrapolate results from studies specific to alcohol to other drugs. That being said, only actual empirical research can confirm clinical suspicion.

The early studies on alcoholism demonstrated around a 50 percent increased risk of developing the disease for those who have alcoholic parents compared with the general population. Later, more than a dozen twin studies confirmed that genetic predispositions exist because identical twins are twice as likely as fraternal twins to both have alcoholism. Overall, we know today that the genetic contribution for alcoholism is somewhere between 40 and 60 percent.[26]

Interestingly, type 2 diabetes also has a 40 to 60 percent genetic component. Examining diabetes can help clarify what a genetic predisposition is, as well as help explain how addiction shares other properties with chronic diseases, thus providing further evidence that addiction is a disease and not merely a set of poor choices or character flaws.

What happens to the human body with poor diet and lack of exercise is predictable and reproducible, with or without any genetic predisposition. With years of fat accumulation and excess food intake (especially high-calorie food) combined with minimal exercise, the body's ability to utilize sugar weakens and diabetes develops. We know that family members of persons with type 2 diabetes will develop that disease earlier in life than those without strong genetic influences *if* this predisposition is combined with the same degree of poor diet and lack of exercise.

Those predisposed to diabetes may actually be drawn to eating a heavily fat- and sugar-laden diet, leading to early onset of the disease. Many compulsive overeaters who crave sugar-rich foods have genetic dysfunctions in their dopamine receptors that may cause them to self-medicate feelings of inadequacy with foods that cause weight gain and speed up the development of diabetes. So in this case, as in the case of addiction, the predisposed may not initially have as much choice as some think. Once they have the disease, it must be managed. Diet and exercise, and often medication management, must be part of the overall scheme to prevent diabetes from destroying their health and wreaking havoc on their home life and their happiness, as well as that of their loved ones or caretakers.

Adoption studies, which are especially helpful in exposing genetic versus environmental factors, consistently demonstrate a strong familial component to alcoholism. In adoption studies, it has been shown that having a parent with alcoholism more than doubles the risk of a child developing alcoholism (addiction). Over the years we have attempted to find true biologic markers that definitively identify the disease. Although we have not been successful in discovering the "one" addiction gene, in the search for a different type of biologic marker, Dr. Henri Begleiter, distinguished professor of psychiatry and neuroscience at the SUNY Downstate Medical Center at Brooklyn, conducted a study that demonstrated that certain changes were seen on electroencephalograms (EEG), or brain scans, of alcoholics and their nondrinking preadolescent sons. He discovered evidence of a biologic marker.[27] This discovery was later confirmed by other scientists who observed a reduced brain wave.[28] The existence of these and other biologic markers helps to solidify the rightful place of addiction as a disease. If addiction were due to poor choices and lack of willpower, how could there be biologic markers and genetic predispositions?

Another national thought leader, maverick, and one of my most trusted mentors, Dr. Howard Wetsman, MD, also emphasizes the genetic aspect of addiction. He has made excellent progress in treatment outcomes using a metabolite of folic acid to help those with addiction and a genetic variant that prevents adequate metabolism of folate and consequent production of feel-good neurotransmitters. Wetsman adds, "While about 30 percent of the general population have genetic polymorphisms leading to poor folic acid metabolism, almost 80 percent of the patients arriving for treatment at his facility had such mutations."[29]

The inherited predisposing factor is important, but so is the impact of one's environment. It is the combination of genes with the influence of environment, including such elements as stress and peer group, that give those who are predisposed that 40 to 60 percent chance of developing addiction. On the other hand, there is only a 10 percent risk of developing alcoholism in those with no genetic predisposition, no family history of the disease. The risk of developing alcoholism increases to 25 percent if you have a nonidentical twin sibling with alcoholism; it increases to 40 percent if you have a parent with the disease; and the risk is over 50 percent if you have an identical twin with alcoholism. Forty percent of biological children of alcoholics who are adopted at birth and raised in nonalcoholic homes develop alcoholism. In contrast, only 10 percent of birth children of nonalcoholics who are adopted at birth develop the disease. It did not matter if the adopted children were exposed to drinking in the home or not—biological parental alcoholism was the primary determinant of risk.

Diseases that have genetic components are often studied in animal models. There was an interesting study conducted on rats that yielded profound insight on the subject of inheritability. Rat populations are, for a variety of reasons, easier to study in a lab than humans are. For one thing, humans are highly resistant to laboratory confinement. Rats will also breed with the partners we choose for them. Human beings, on the other hand, are very reluctant to do that.

So, scientists used rats and exposed them to alcohol. When two bowls of water, one with pure water and the other spiked with alcohol, were placed in a cage full of randomly selected rats, 10 percent of the rat population began to congregate around the "vodka water." Most of the rats that tasted the vodka water decided it was not for them, and they drank only the pure water. However, 10 percent or so of the rat population began drinking from the vodka water. Those rats were then selected out to breed with other alcohol-preferring rats. After a few generations, the study revealed, a strain of alcohol-preferring rats was created. That is, there was something that was passed down from generation to generation that actually produced the disease of alcoholism in a lab. The disease was activated in a controlled laboratory setting. Dr. Ting-Kai Li and his colleagues at the Indiana University School of Medicine essentially proved that the development of addiction was not due to learned behavior, nor was it due to the poor moral fiber of the rats.[30]

Animal models such as this one prove that one or more genetic factors that are contributors to the formation of a disease can be passed down through successive generations. "Alcoholic rats" can exhibit a compulsion to ingest alcohol, ingest it to achieve intoxication, and attempt to remain intoxicated as much of the time as possible. These behaviors cannot be explained by poor character, bad parenting, lack of social skills, stupidity, lack of faith, or any other similar reason. Moreover, the alcoholic rats also exhibited other "addict-like" behaviors. They would actually binge drink. They would drink excessive amounts for discrete periods of time and then pass out. They also fought more with one another. Some of them stopped showing up for work, and the researchers had to call Rodent Child Protective Services on quite a few others (just a little science research joke).

A preeminent psychiatrist and genetic researcher in the field, Marc Schuckit, MD, discovered some remarkable associations between family-related markers and risks for alcoholism. His body of work includes identified genetic characteristics that elevate the risk of alcoholism. He examined physiologic differences in response to alcohol between young men with and without family histories of alcoholism. He found that young men with family histories that were positive for alcoholism reported fewer subjective adverse effects from drinking than young men who were family history–negative; those with positive family histories reported feeling less drunk from equivalent amounts of alcohol.

In essence, the close relatives of alcoholics were able to hold their liquor better. This self-rating was confirmed by testing their physical and cognitive responses to alcohol. When measured, the family history–negative young men had more body movement (called body sway) than their counterparts with positive family histories had after drinking equal amounts. The test of body sway was not as vigorous as a field sobriety test, but it did examine how much their posture deviated from the midline when standing. The family history–negative group also scored more poorly on cognitive tests.[31]

Other studies have demonstrated that family history–positive groups exhibit more rewarding effects from alcohol than family history–negative groups. The positive groups had more naturally occurring, pleasurable, rewarding endorphin release and greater enhancement of calming, low-frequency EEG activity.[32] It is almost as though those of us who are biologically predisposed may be "built" to enjoy more of the positive benefits of the drug while experiencing fewer of the negative side effects. More positive reinforcement and less negative reinforcement automatically increase motivation for use. This demonstrates a real difference in responses to drugs (in this specific case, the drug alcohol) that helps explain why some people are more drawn to use drugs than others.

Dr. Schuckit also made another interesting, though unfortunate, discovery. He found that compared to the men with no family history of alcoholism who consumed the same amount of alcohol, those with positive family histories had significantly more alcohol and other drug and psychiatric problems. Even when they drank the same amount, the family history–positive men appeared to have some factor that contributed to more suffering across different areas of their lives.[33] Other studies have reinforced this predisposing factor by demonstrating that a family history of alcoholism makes some of us more reactive to stimuli and stress.

Peter Finn, PhD, and his colleagues showed that while positive and negative family history groups had equal nervous system activity at rest, when exposed to stressful stimuli, the family history–positive group had higher levels of reactivity as measured by perspiration, heart rate, and vein constriction. They also took longer to return to feeling normal than the family history–negative group.[34] In essence, the groups that were genetically predisposed to addiction became more stressed, and stayed that way for longer. Moreover, they didn't choose their reactions; their biological wiring chose their reactions for them. Not surprisingly, the positive family group also experienced notably more stress-reducing effects from alcohol than the negative family group. Increased stress coupled with higher pleasure and more stress-reducing effects of drugs helps explain not only why some are predisposed to use, but also why they use excessively.

In terms of biologic markers, Dr. Schuckit uncovered one more valuable piece of information ten years after his initial study when he conducted follow-up interviews with the original research subjects. What he found was that regardless of whether or not there was a family history of alcoholism, those young men who demonstrated a reduced sensitivity to the intoxicating effects of alcohol had a greater risk of developing addiction later in life.

Researchers such as Dr. Christina Gianoulakis, a professor in the departments of psychiatry and physiology at McGill University, have focused their search for clear genetic predispositions on our natural opioid system. This system is the source of the endorphins, the brain's natural feel-good neurotransmitters and painkillers. It makes us feel euphoric and decreases anxiety. One mechanism through which alcohol produces its rewarding effects is through the activation of this reward system, particularly among those with risk factors for addiction. Dr. Gianoulakis found lowered natural opioid levels in nonalcoholic subjects with strong family histories of alcoholism compared to those with no family history of alcoholism.[35] She also found that the β-endorphin response to a moderate dose of alcohol was increased in the high-risk subjects but not in the low-risk subjects.[36]

The fact that there is a measurable difference in the amount of endorphins that are released in high-risk individuals should make it easier to appreciate the absence of choice and the presence of disease. The increased endorphin response occurs in some people because there is something physiologic that causes an extra amount of feel-good chemicals to be released. It is not due to choice. This and other studies helped to formulate a clear picture that certain high-risk subjects have an inherited deficiency in the endogenous opioid system, which in turn explains why some people feel generally worse than others while at rest, yet feel much better after they use.[37] They are therefore more motivated to keep using. People do not and cannot tell their bodies to respond this way or that way to drugs by releasing a predetermined amount of certain chemicals in their brains. It just happens.

As I described above, alcohol is not de facto "bad." Many people enjoy drinking alcohol, and most do so responsibly. Alcohol is a social lubricant that causes a release of pleasurable chemicals in the brain, reduces stress, and has significant social meaning. After alcohol consumption, endorphins are naturally released. Even the low-risk crowd can get a kick out of drinking. But their rise in endorphins is not as great as it is for high-risk individuals.[38] They just don't derive as much pleasure from drinking.

Another way I explain this is to use the analogy of a broccoli-and-cheese casserole. Before you turn up your nose, keep reading. What I have in mind is a fantastic broccoli-and-cheese casserole made with the freshest and tastiest ingredients. In low-risk individuals, alcohol causes pleasurable brain chemicals to rise about as much as they would if those folks were to eat this excellent broccoli-and-cheese casserole. In contrast, high-risk individuals experience more release of pleasurable brain chemicals.

To many high-risk folks, the experience of using drugs is no casserole. It is more like ambrosia. Because there are different physical responses to drugs, it is easy for me to understand why some people look at addicts and think, "Why can't they just stop?!" In their minds, I can imagine they are saying, "Why don't you just put down the broccoli?!" It is then easy for me to understand why they follow that up with "They must be weak, lazy, or stupid." Many people can easily put down alcohol and other drugs because the reinforcing effects are not that powerful for them. In general, it is difficult to grasp that the same experience can be so different in others. Quite frankly, if I were to see someone facedown in a gutter, having lost their dignity and everything they loved over broccoli, I would be hard-pressed not to judge them too.

Addiction is a challenging puzzle, especially for those who have been directly affected by it. With tongue in cheek, we say that addicts "go big or go home" and that "if something is worth doing, it's worth overdoing." As strange as addicts are to many people, nonaddicts sometimes appear the same way to us. My wife is not an addict, so when we go out, sometimes she will order a glass of wine. She'll take four small sips over two hours and leave the glass half full, and I think she is the insane one! I say to her, "Don't you know what you can do? Geez, if I weren't an addict, I would drink all the time." In making light of our mistakes, the dark humor that we often use in recovery helps to highlight the insanity of the effects of the disease of addiction and is also paradoxically supportive. Recovery fellowships are the only place where raucous laughter follows admissions of failed suicide attempts. Contrary to being a mean-spirited dismissal of one's pain and misery, it's part of how we cope, connect, and support one another. There is a deep mutual understanding among those who have been through active addiction and are now in recovery. Poking fun at our painful experiences helps us make sense of them. As Mark Twain put it, "Humor is tragedy plus time."

What makes a disease a disease, anyway? There are several defining aspects, but specifically, there is a sick organ system and a progression. Most diseases are not *cured;* most diseases are *managed*. What all diseases share in common is several factors: a clear biologic basis, identifiable signs and symptoms, predictable course and outcome, and the inability to control the cause of the disease. Addiction has all of these elements. It has a biologic basis and genetic component, is defined by a set of disease-specific behaviors, follows a progressive course in all those who are afflicted, is chronic, and is fatal if left untreated.

All Diseases Have a Progression

Again, I'll use diabetes as a model of a chronic disease in order to demonstrate the similarities between addiction and other diseases. If the diabetes is not controlled, it progresses in ways that are reproducible and predictable in the human body. When left untreated, every disease follows a specific course.

Untreated diabetes causes fatty changes in the liver; arteriosclerotic plaque and blockage builds up in the arteries, circulatory and mechanical problems arise in the heart, the kidneys start to deteriorate, the nerves become damaged, the eyes fail, and the immune system weakens. Poor souls with untreated diabetes may lose their eyesight, their ability to urinate, and their limbs, and eventually their lives end prematurely. The suffering can be horrible for both the diabetic patient and his or her loved ones. Those who take care of the diabetic may also have a high degree of pain and suffering, as caring for sick relatives can top the list of stressful things we do.

Every untreated disease has a natural, reproducible, and predictable progression of negative consequences, not only for the afflicted individual, but for his or her support system as well. And, no matter who it is who has diabetes, the effects are the same—regardless of whom they may know or how much money they have, untreated diabetics will have fatty livers, kidney failure, nerve damage, loss of vision, and heart disease.

The Progression of Addiction

Once present, like other diseases, untreated addiction follows a predictable and reproducible course in any human being. The patterns caused by untreated addiction are the same no matter who has the disease. Cancer, diabetes, high blood pressure, and other diseases cannot distinguish whether you are good, rich, or successful. If addiction only affected the "bad" people, it would actually be easier to spot. It is a disease that does not discriminate any more than other diseases. Street addicts die of overdoses and medical complications just as do the wealthy and famous, such as Prince, Philip Seymour Hoffman, Jim Morrison, Marilyn Monroe, Elvis Presley, River Phoenix, Judy Garland, Anna Nicole Smith, John Belushi, Heath Ledger, Michael Jackson, and Amy Winehouse.

What happens to that poor soul with untreated addiction? Negative emotional, relationship, psychological, spiritual, and physical consequences begin to surface, recur, and escalate. His or her loved ones also suffer. The use of substances becomes the focal point of life, to the exclusion of other goals. When addiction is left untreated, eventually many addicts end up institutionalized, in jail, or dead.

Bad Behavior

"Everything that gives pleasure has its reason. To scorn the mobs of those who go astray is not the means to bring them around." —Charles Baudelaire

No one who develops addiction chooses to. Active addiction is a horrifically painful existence. While it may appear to be a choice, no one would elect to subject him- or herself to the drama and trauma of addiction. As I have indicated, as with other diseases, addiction has genetic factors, a progression and natural course, and an element of choice that ends early in the course of its progression.

So, why is addiction not uniformly accepted as a disease? As previously noted, one reason is that the behavior of people with addiction is bothersome. People with active addiction break promises and lie and steal and cheat and cause pain. They are not models of social grace, compassion, and virtue. "Bad behavior, bad person" is the easy explanation. Although diabetes can have a huge behavioral component, untreated diabetes does not usually cause someone to steal, repeatedly break promises, or wake up in jail. Diabetes has probably never caused anyone to rob a Krispy Kreme. No, it is fairly easy to call a disease "a disease" when "bad behavior" isn't a normal result of the condition. But diseases like addiction and schizophrenia that have "bad behavior" as a component are immediately and negatively judged until proven otherwise— and the proving otherwise can be difficult to do. As Friedrich Nietzsche put it in *Human, All Too Human: A Book for Free Spirits,* first published in 1878: "Convictions are more dangerous enemies of truth than lies. Lies can be exposed for what they are; while convictions are usually not amenable to logical discussions, data, rational debate."

Schizophrenia is a disease that, when untreated, often results in bothersome behavior. Untreated schizophrenics may not bathe or shave, may talk to themselves or imaginary people, may invade others' personal space, and may sometimes (though not usually) become violent. This behavior can be disturbing. In line with the tendency to negatively judge diseases with bothersome behavior, for a time schizophrenia was attributed to bad parenting. Mothers were originally judged to be at fault. The thinking was that the mothers of schizophrenics were either too smothering or too abandoning. Today, we know this concept is foolish. Schizophrenia is a disease, with chemical and functional disorders of the brain. Although there is still considerable stigma associated with schizophrenia, it is now recognized and understood as a disease—just as we are learning to do today with addiction.

In the past, many mental disorders with bothersome behaviors were linked to brutal treatment approaches. Sterilization, frontal lobotomies, isolation, and water therapy were once common treatments for depression, schizophrenia, and addiction. Exploring the history of mental illness uncovers a sordid past of medical treatments that resemble medieval torture practices. When one concentrates only on the behavioral manifestations of addiction, the emphasis on a "war on drugs" as opposed to offering treatment becomes more understandable. If the behavior is bothersome, "let's punish!" is often an automatic response—one that fails to meet the real needs of the circumstance because the behavior is caused by an underlying disease process.

Even today, in the twenty-first century, the dogma of the drug war and punishment is so entrenched that it is inconceivable in the minds of many to offer treatment to addicts who have been involved in criminal activity. Even now, many politicians are afraid of appearing soft on crime, and so continue to promise to throw the hammer down in the war on drugs. Our criminal justice system is overrun with nonviolent drug offenses. There are 2.3 million people in our prisons—and one in every five of these is incarcerated for a nonviolent drug offense.[39]

We incarcerate more people than any other country and have the highest per capita rate of imprisonment in the world. This is a great moral injustice, especially in light of the fact that private prisons in which one can purchase stock have become a booming industry. As a result, the war on drugs has become big business. The amount of resources we continue to pour into this broken punitive system is astronomical. It is a travesty that we haven't explored alternatives on a large scale. We need to put more resources into addiction education, prevention, and treatment instead of punishing those who are suffering with it. After all, there are more Americans with addiction than with all types of cancer combined (14.5 million in 2014[40]).

Progress . . . to a Point

A comprehensive 2016 report, *Facing Addiction in America: The Surgeon General's Report on Alcohol, Drugs, and Health*, marks the first time a US surgeon general has dedicated a report to substance misuse and related disorders. The report addresses alcohol, illicit drugs, and prescription drug misuse, including the opioid epidemic of which we have been well aware for more than ten years. US Surgeon General Vivek Murthy, MD, reflected on how damaging addiction is on "individuals, families, and communities," highlighting that only 10 percent of people who need treatment receive it.[41]

The report revealed the large discrepancy addiction medicine faces when compared with the rest of medical care. Addiction treatment in the United States remains largely separate from the rest of healthcare and serves only a fraction of those in need of treatment. In other words, there is a massive gap. The Paul Wellstone and Pete Domenici Mental Health Parity and Addiction Equity Act of 2008, and later the Health Care and Education Reconciliation Act of 2010, were intended to eliminate the gap by making addiction treatment more mainstream, thus increasing access. Sadly, the gap remains. The stigma of being labeled an addict, the cultural shame associated with it, denial, and financial impediments continue to keep people hidden in the shadows, away from effective treatment.

In *Facing Addiction in America*, Dr. Murthy emphasized that addiction is not a "moral failing" but a "chronic illness that must be treated with skill, urgency, and compassion." Before my time on this rock is over, I would love to see addiction treated like every other medical disorder. Fortunately, evidence-based addiction treatment efforts have begun to reveal early success. For instance, the Obama administration invested in the research, development, and evaluation of programs to both prevent and treat substance misuse and substance use disorders, as well as to support recovery. Initiatives focused on improving opioid-prescribing practices, expanding access to medication-assisted treatment for opioid use disorders, and increasing the use of naloxone to reverse opioid overdoses are permeating both the public and private healthcare sectors.

And yet there is so much more to do. When addiction is fully recognized as a disease, we peel away some of its stigma. Many people suffering with addiction avoid asking for help from families, friends, employers, and even those in the healthcare industry because there is so much stigma associated with the disease. Often there is an unspoken code in families where addiction is present to not speak about it, with the effect of keeping it secret. This is, in large part, to protect a semblance of normalcy. The fear is that if the addiction were to be made public, it would be some sort of "mark" against the family. However, keeping addiction hidden only leads to more dysfunction and distress for both the individual and the family.

Further, when addiction is accepted as a disease, health insurance companies will be forced to pay adequately for *proper* treatment. Until then, managed care companies can continue to pad their bottom lines with dollars saved by withholding sufficient care from those suffering with addiction. Insurance companies do not authorize surgeons to remove only half a tumor or provide for only three weeks of diabetes treatments, yet they continue to get away with paying for inadequate treatment for addiction.

And yet, research demonstrates that substance-abuse treatment can be expected to both save money and produce new income. In California, various drug treatments were estimated to have saved between $245 million and $1.2

billion after subtracting the cost of treatment from cost savings and income generated in a single year in the early 1990s. Substance-abuse researchers have found profound reductions in a number of costly events after treatment, including the following decreases:

- Patient arrests for driving while intoxicated or driving under the influence decreased from 18 percent (pre-treatment) to 3 percent (post-treatment).

- Patients involved in accidents decreased from 14 percent to 1 percent.

- Patients' family members who sought counseling decreased from 31 percent to 5 percent.

- Patients' children who missed school decreased from 5 percent to 1 percent.

- Patients' spouses who missed work decreased from 10 percent to 1 percent.[42]

According to several more recent estimates, every dollar invested in addiction treatment programs yields a return of between four dollars and seven dollars in reduced drug-related crime, criminal justice costs, and theft. When savings related to healthcare are included, total savings can exceed costs by a ratio of twelve to one.[43]

Identifying a Sick Organ System

In examining the past, we can shed light on how our current medical understanding has evolved. In colonial times in the New World, if I were a trusted physician who was at the top of my game and someone came to me with burning on urination, I would have known that they suffered from evil humors, and I would have induced vomiting or diarrhea; or I would have reached for my trusted leeches that were the best in the land, and I would have started bleeding out the person with vigor. Those were the tools of properly trained physicians of the times. The best I would have had to offer as a trusted servant of health and science was dangerous.

In fact, George Washington died due to complications from this type of treatment for strep throat. He survived two major wars, smallpox, and other serious diseases, but ended up succumbing to strep throat because his physician caused too much blood loss. Unfortunate as it was, the point is that I would have had a very wrong understanding of the disease process of a urinary tract infection in this case, or any other disease process, for that matter. Due to the framework of understanding disease processes back then, I would have missed the mark completely in assessment and treatment.

Today, we take it for granted that bacteria get into the urinary system and create an infection in the genitourinary organ system. The reason we have been able to understand disease processes better is that we have a much better and more accurate understanding of the human body through science. We are now identifying disease processes based on an in-depth and objective understanding of specific diseased organs, cells, and genes. The talk of evil humors, poor character, bad parenting, and God's wrath has increasingly fallen by the wayside as science has replaced conjecture and superstition.

So what does all that have to do with the disease of addiction? In the past, without good science, addiction was seen as a series of bad choices at best or a moral failure at worst. Instead of leeches, though, the medical community and society at large treated addicts with disdain and judgment, and utilized wacky procedures such as frontal lobotomies, castration, sterilization, and excommunication, to name just a few. Based on sound science and current research, we know that the diseased organ system in addiction is in the brain. More specifically, it primarily involves a part of the brain known as the mesolimbic system.

Admittedly, it is overly simplistic to claim that brain changes prove addiction is a disease. The brain also changes through learning, behavior, experience, and directed attention. However, substances and addictive behaviors cause physical changes in the brain's receptors and cause significant impairment in the person's social, emotional, relationship, and/or spiritual life. Addiction generates precise pathological physical adaptations in several regions of the brain at the neuronal level, constituting a brain dysfunction. It's important to note that these changes are pathological even if they result from normal learning mechanisms in response to a substance and its use. Most aspects of any pathological process are normal. For example, even if immune cells are acting in an entirely normal manner in terms of their many disease-fighting mechanisms, if the target is one's own cells and organs, then one has an autoimmune disease. It is a dysfunction of the brain to be so sensitized to opioids or alcohol that it is unable to function as biologically designed due to a need for substance intake, even if this dysfunction occurs via a normal learning system.

Most of the dysfunction occurs in the limbic system, a horseshoe-shaped collection of structures and neural pathways located deep within the brain. Involved with survival, emotion, and reward, the limbic system has many roles. With respect to addiction, one of its crucial roles relates to its connection to the reward pathway and pleasure-producing dopamine. The limbic system contains a common site of action for all addictive substances. Today, we know that this is the sick organ system in addiction.

Historically, it is interesting to note that diabetes, thyroid disorders, leprosy, and cancer were once stigmatized because these diseases were also misunderstood. People were once afraid of contracting diabetes by exposure to other diabetics. Can you imagine being afraid of contagious diabetes? Given our current state of knowledge, contagious diabetes is a silly thought. But at a time when the general understanding was that diseases were contagious, it made sense. One particularly disturbing example occurred in Hawaii, starting in 1866. Back then, people with leprosy living in Hawaii were physically removed to the "desert island" of Molokai. They were simply loaded on boats and dropped off, without social services or help. Why? There was an unusual and misunderstood presentation of that disease process. Since we didn't understand it, we ostracized it.

If this sounds familiar, it is because addiction is not unique as far as how long it is taking us to fully understand it. For a long time, a prevailing state-of-the-art understanding and accepted scientific "truth" was that peptic ulcer disease was caused by a certain personality type, called type A. Specifically, high stress, intensity, and rigidity (hallmarks of type-A personalities) were believed to cause peptic ulcer disease. Treatment usually involved invasive major surgery. Then, in 1982, Barry Marshall and Robin Warren discovered that peptic ulcer disease is actually caused by bacteria. I can imagine what they were up against in challenging the consensus of highly skilled and intelligent physicians of that time. Legend has it that while Marshall and Warren were presenting their findings for the first time at a professional gathering, the audience actually got up and left. What Marshall and Warren were proposing was a direct challenge to the scientific community's consensus, and what they encountered was a common human reaction when prevailing belief systems are challenged.

History teaches that it is no easy task to challenge the accepted dogmatic thinking of the day. I frequently encounter those in healthcare and society at large who cannot imagine that addiction is anything like a disease. I can understand the resistance. What other disease causes us to behave in such unsavory ways? What other disease *appears* to have such strong elements of choice and willpower?

Even though Marshall and Warren initially faced cynicism and scorn, in 2005 they won the Nobel Prize for their paradigm-shattering discovery. The perspective of addiction as a disease similarly challenges the current paradigm, and we have science on our side as well (so, if you are not convinced yet, continue reading). Personality does not cause peptic ulcer disease, and personality does not cause addiction. Specifically, addiction is not due to self-centeredness or an *addictive personality*. It is not caused by poor parenting or character defects. It has a genetic component, biologic components, and behavioral components, and develops as a result of the interactions among the variables of the host (the individual), the agent (the substance), and the environment.

Does It Really Matter What Addiction Is?

Let's face it: addiction is a profoundly complex entity. It's both a bad habit and the result of biologically programmed brain survival instinct gone awry. It's the result of a series of choices, but it ultimately robs the host of volition. And it's the result of both environmental (nurture) and genetic (nature) influences.

As I have pointed out, the debate over the exact nature of addiction lingers on. While many people are busy arguing over semantics, I feel the more important issue may be how each individual explains the problem one has with alcohol, opioids, gambling, or sex, and so on, to him- or herself. Why? The explanation itself is what has the power to either damage or endow. For those interested in preventing unnecessary suffering, it is paramount to adopt realistic and healthy perspectives in life. How we can apply this with regard to addiction?

Martin Seligman, PhD, addresses the factors that facilitate change in his book *What You Can Change and What You Can't: The Complete Guide to Successful Self-Improvement*. As Dr. Seligman suggests, what's more important than whether or not addiction is a disease is how we describe it to ourselves. When someone finds herself with an active addiction, and it finally dawns on her that her life, family, career, and everything else she values are in jeopardy, how should she explain this to herself? She can explain it either as a disease or a vice, as a result of bad choices and bad character, or as sin.

In comparing disease to vice, disease is more temporary, and often curable, whereas vice is more permanent, and stems from "bad" character, and character is resistant to change. A disease is more specific, coming from biology and environment, whereas vice is global, coming from being a "bad" person. Disease is impersonal, whereas vice is a choice. The upshot is that a disease is a more optimistic explanation than vice, and optimism is about changeability. Pessimistic labels lead to greater passivity, whereas optimistic ones often lead to attempts to change. If you believe that addiction is not a disease but rather a character flaw, then the problem is internal and the hope for overcoming it very small.

If I believe that my problem is internal, then *if it's not a disease, then I must be a degenerate, and why bother trying to do anything about the bad things in life? It's who I am.* With this perspective, there is no point in trying to get better. Again, contrast that with the external-disease explanation wherein addiction can be managed and recovery is possible. Here, there is hope, and *I will summon more energy to overcome this; I am a sick person trying to get well rather than a bad person trying to become good.* It follows that addicts who label themselves as "ill" will be less depressed, be less helpless, have higher self-esteem, and, most importantly, make greater efforts to change than addicts who label themselves as "bad" people. Another benefit of the disease label is that it is a ticket into the medical care system.

I agree with my friend and teacher, Marty. I couldn't care less that the data doesn't unequivocally prove addiction is a disease. If explaining it to oneself in this realistic and useful way helps improve the likelihood of a better and happier life, then how is that not beneficial?

Issues about definitions of addiction, terminology, medication in addiction treatment, abstinence-oriented versus abstinence-mandated approaches, dealing with relapse, and so forth elicit strong convictions on both sides of the choice-versus-disease debate and are likely to remain unresolved for the foreseeable future. I truly believe that it is best to keep an open mind and seek the most helpful path.

Chapter 2:

Miseducation, Misinformation, Misunderstanding

Addiction Is Misunderstood by Healthcare Professionals

A nother roadblock in proper prevention and treatment is the lack of training and education our healthcare providers receive. Since less than 1 percent of medical school curriculum teaches future doctors about addiction, as physicians we have little or no understanding about the disease. There was an anonymous survey sent out to many physicians in the United States, the results of which revealed that too many regard addiction as a moral problem, and they believe that treatments are ineffective.

Many doctors neither screen for addiction nor make any effort to intervene with their patients, despite indications of problematic substance use or addiction. A common assumption and misconception is that physicians know the warning signs of addiction and understand how to recognize whether addiction is present. We US-trained physicians learn virtually nothing about addiction. In effect, many well-intentioned physicians practicing medicine routinely fail to identify the presenting signs of addiction. We are not adequately trained to detect addiction. Every other disease, bar none, is mostly recognized and referred for treatment in primary care and emergency room settings. Addiction requires friends and family, employers, and judges to refer individuals with addiction to proper treatment.

As I noted earlier, I knew nothing about addiction until I was a patient in rehab myself. When I was in medical school and residency, respected, smart, excellent, and caring physicians taught that addicts make poor choices and do not get better. In fact, there was a rather bleak colloquialism about alcoholics having a "Librium deficiency." Librium is a sedative medication very similar to alcohol that was once commonly used to treat alcoholics who were in withdrawal. I would literally hear "Alcoholics have a Librium deficiency" repeated throughout my training at various times, as if it were a fact. The sarcastic and cynical nature of that expression reflects a fundamental misunderstanding about addiction and the effectiveness of treatment. Believing that anyone addicted to alcohol would choose that wretched way of life and get admitted to emergency rooms in order to get mind-altering benzodiazepines so they can go back to sitting on their bar stools is the epitome of lack of empathy and education on the subject of addiction.

First Use Is Not to Blame

I often hear that addicts are to blame for their problem because they chose to use in the first place. Choice alone is not responsible for addiction. Most people can use drugs and never develop the disease of addiction. For example, many people drink excessively in their twenties, suffer some negative consequences, and then stop or greatly curtail their use. The majority of these folks will not become alcoholics. Millions of people will experiment with drugs, and some may use them excessively. Most will recognize that the risks and consequences outweigh the benefits, and will stop or greatly curtail their drug use. So the initial decision to use is not the culprit. As described above, addiction is not that simple: most drinkers are not alcoholics, and most problem drinkers are not daily drinkers. In *The Science of Addiction,* Dr. Carlton Erickson demonstrates that most users of mind-altering substances do not progress to addiction. Merely using a drug does not necessarily cause addiction to develop.[44]

The vast majority of people who use drugs do so while maintaining control over their actions and lives. Remember, you may decide to have a cheeseburger, but you do not decide on the heart attack. Those who develop addiction do so due to many more factors beyond early decisions to use.

Are Addicts Less Compliant?

Most diseases have behavioral components, and most diseases are more effectively managed when patients make significant behavioral changes.

Patients with high blood pressure and diabetes are instructed to carefully watch their diets, exercise, quit smoking, and modify other lifestyle factors. Patients with asthma are often encouraged to stop smoking and remove Fluffy, the allergenic cat, from their homes. Patients with addiction are asked to, well, change everything. It is true that addiction is often a relapsing disease. Like cancer, relapse is possible and occurs far too often for anyone's taste, but relapse is not inevitable in addiction. Nonetheless, the frequency of relapse is a compelling reason why many people think addicts do not want to get better and/or that treatment is ineffective. Addiction and recovery have very large behavioral components, and if more people with addiction failed to follow their treatment plans than patients with high blood pressure, asthma, or diabetes, it could be argued that addicts are behaviorally more resistant to treatment.

Interestingly, research comparing addiction to asthma, diabetes, and high blood pressure demonstrated that the opposite was mostly true. There were in fact fewer patients with high blood pressure, asthma, and diabetes who were compliant with their medications and lifestyle changes than addicts who were compliant with their treatment plans. The success rate of treating all four of these chronic diseases is also roughly equal.[45] Surprisingly to some, more patients with the disease of addiction are compliant with the behavioral changes asked of them than are patients with these other "real" and less stigmatizing diseases.

When patients with diabetes, asthma, or high blood pressure have imperfect control of their chronic diseases as a result of not changing their lifestyles or not taking their medications as prescribed, are they judged as being failures? Are they ridiculed and blamed for not having their chronic diseases under control? No, and neither should patients with the chronic disease of addiction. When diabetics eat too much sugar over time and, as a result, they need additional medications and doctor visits to help maintain their health and quality of life, do we stop treatment? When patients with high blood pressure fail to lose weight or stop using salt, do we kick them out of our office? Of course not. We continue treatment, and look for and offer new and better ways to help control the disease, because every effort helps us gain a foothold in the attempt to maximize health and healing. Isn't it time we applied this approach to all diseases?

Treatment Effectiveness

Another misconception about addiction is that treatment is ineffective. Several decades' worth of research demonstrates that treatment is effective in managing, as opposed to curing, addiction. Behavioral and medical treatment engages addicts in recovery, enhances and expands their coping skills, changes their attitudes and behaviors, improves quality of life, decreases crime and transmission of infectious disease, decreases traumatic injury, increases work productivity and tax revenue, and increases the chances of long-term recovery. None of these changes necessarily happen at once, to everyone, or at all . . . as is the case in the practice of medicine.

As I've described, addiction is not an acute illness. An acute illness is a disease process that begins suddenly and is short-lived. Having an appendix that bursts—an acute case of appendicitis—is a good example. Treating acute appendicitis involves recognition of the condition and surgical removal of the diseased tissue. The patient who has had his or her appendix removed does not need to ever worry about that condition recurring. Treating appendicitis for a brief time is appropriate for that acute disease. But addiction is a chronic disease, not a short-lived illness. Addiction does not get cured, nor does it ever spontaneously disappear. So if we treat addiction as if it were an acute disease like appendicitis, we will not achieve any long-lasting results. It would be as inappropriate for me to treat addiction for only a few days as it would be to treat appendicitis for years.

When talking about the effectiveness of treatment and looking at treatment outcomes, we must factor in the chronic nature of addiction. Short-term treatment for any chronic disease is inappropriate and will be ineffective. If I treat high blood pressure with medicine and behavioral modalities only to stop the treatment after three days or three months, I will not be appropriately or effectively treating that chronic disease. The high blood pressure will return soon after treatment is stopped. Relapse rates for substance addiction are similar to those for other well-established chronic illnesses like high blood pressure, diabetes, and asthma. Relapse is very common for all these diseases. The reason is simple: we do not cure most diseases; we manage them, and nearly never are we perfect at it.

Like other chronic diseases, addiction has behavioral and biological aspects. Successful treatment requires that we address both. Furthermore, recovery from addiction is a long-term process that may require repeated attempts at treatment, just as with other chronic conditions. Rarely does a diabetic or high-blood-pressure patient achieve and maintain perfect control of his or her blood sugar or blood pressure, respectively. Long-term management of chronic disease involves trial and error, adaptation, and repeated attempts to achieve the desired outcome.

Changes throughout the course of treatment and multiple attempts at consistent management are the norm, not the exception, in managing chronic diseases. Relapses, or deviations from perfect management, can occur during the course of treatment for any chronic illness, and are used to guide treatment plan modifications. One crucial fact remains: despite the chronic and potentially relapsing nature of addiction, relapse is *not* mandatory. In fact, contrary to popular perception, it is not uncommon to find addicts in stable long-term recovery who have never relapsed.

Extended abstinence is highly predictive of long-term recovery. The chances of remaining in recovery rise if patients are abstinent from mood-altering substances for five years.[46] What can be done to maximize an addict's chance of maintaining recovery? Experience and research make it clear that they ought to remain in treatment for an extended period of time and participate in appropriate professional and mutual-aid aftercare programming. When we look at some studies of outcome measures, there does appear to be a minimum length of treatment that increases effectiveness in maintaining abstinence, and that is ninety days. According to the National Institute on Drug Abuse, ninety days of continuous inpatient treatment increases the likelihood of long-term recovery.[47]

If we can get a patient past the three-year mark, his or her chances of remaining in recovery are higher still, so there is great value in engaging patients in maximized continuous treatment. I often stress here that ninety days, three years, and five years is not the ultimate objective—lifelong recovery is the goal. However, it is difficult to convince addicts, as well as insurance and managed care companies, to agree to ninety days of continuous inpatient treatment. Therefore, we need to be creative and try to combine modalities in order to engage patients in as much continuous treatment as we can so as to maximize the effectiveness of treatment. If we can keep somebody engaged for at least ninety days of combined inpatient and outpatient treatment, we can make much more of a difference than if we were to treat for a few days, a couple of weeks, or thirty days and bid them best of luck.

Science shows that there are other payoffs to longer lengths of stay for patients in treatment. Following appropriate treatment, alcohol- and drug-related medical visits decrease by 53 percent for those who received treatment versus untreated addicts with the same factors.[48] Blood sugar increases in diabetics and blood pressure rises in hypertensives during the course of their treatments do not mean they are moral failures or that we should stop treating them. Imperfect control of chronic diseases is common. When relapses occur, they are no more evidence of character flaws in the patient or that addiction treatment is ineffective than is the case for diabetics who have a relapse of their symptoms. Treatment for addiction is effective and must be applied, and reapplied when necessary, over the long term, as it is with other chronic diseases.[49]

Dispelling Other Myths

"Truth does not become more true by virtue of the fact the entire world agrees with it, nor less so even if the whole world disagrees with it." —Maimonides

We have learned that addiction is a disease, a long-term one, and is not simply the result of poor choices or moral failing. If only these were the only myths we needed to debunk, we could stop now. But there are still those who think that people become addicts because they lack intelligence. Is addiction merely a disease of dumbness? Well, addicts do some awfully stupid things, right? So naturally, the "dumb issue" is raised in relationship to judgment. But often the opposite is true. Personally, I find that I am treating some of the smartest people I have ever met. In my opinion, addiction appears to select out for intelligence, not the other way around. It takes a smart brain to be exposed to mind-altering, brain-damaging substances while maintaining spheres of normalcy in life. By no means am I arguing it is a smart choice to embark on a path that leads to self-destruction, but addiction is hardly an affliction of the dim-witted.

According to a study by Satoshi Kanazawa, data confirm that more-intelligent children in the United States and the United Kingdom grow up to drink more alcohol, more often, than do less-intelligent children. Kanazawa did not come to the same conclusion that I did about why smarter people tend to use mind-altering substances more often. His hypothesis was that intelligence is an evolutionarily new phenomenon, as is alcohol, so the novelty of it explains why smarter folks tend to be heavier drinkers.[50] In any case, whatever conclusions can be drawn from this study and experience, addiction is *not* due to a lack of intelligence.

Then, there are those who believe that people become addicts because they lack faith. Is addiction caused by lack of religious beliefs? The answer is no. Lack of faith does not cause diabetes, high blood pressure, asthma, cancer, or addiction. I treat people who have faith and are "good with God," yet still have the disease of addiction. Furthermore, the management of addiction does not necessarily include a belief in religion, God, or prayer. Agnostics and atheists have addiction and can recover without changing their belief systems. Addiction was once viewed as a vice, and addicts as heathens. Such claims are archaic and judgmental, and contradict vast anecdotal evidence, as well as scientific facts.

That being said, while lack of faith does not cause addiction, it is generally accepted that addiction does have a spiritual component. Alcohol and other drugs occupy a central and vital role in addicts' lives that has some degree of spiritual significance. In fact, spirituality can be such an effective element in the healing process for addiction that it has become a mainstay in the largest recovery community group in the world, Alcoholics Anonymous (AA). Perhaps the impetus for this comes from the "father of analytic psychology," Swiss psychiatrist Carl Jung. Jung shared his thoughts with an alcoholic patient in 1930 that in his experience, only those alcoholics who had a spiritual awakening could overcome the disease of addiction. Jung called this *spiritus contra spiritum*, which roughly translates from the Latin as a spiritual remedy being necessary for addiction, a spiritual malady.

Subsequently, Dr. Jung's patient passed this information on to an associate of Bill Wilson, who then passed it on to AA's future cofounder in 1934. As is well known, a profound spiritual awakening was part of Bill W's process of achieving sobriety, and when he and Dr. Bob Smith formulated the Twelve Steps and started AA in 1935, they emphasized the critical importance of spirituality.

Most addicts may not have a "burning bush" or a "room filled with white light" spiritual experience, yet they still achieve and maintain recovery in large numbers. I heard an addict share, "I was looking for a burning bush experience, but then I learned that a plant in the Middle East emits aromatic hydrocarbons when the temperature gets hot enough and can spontaneously burst into flames. And I thought, I will just stick with my agnostic views, then." Recovery is personal and individualized. It may include spirituality in any form, or it may not. Either way, recovery is possible.

Scientifically, we can explain the physiologic effects of spiritual practices. Prayer and meditation increase serotonin and dopamine in the brain that elevate mood and a sense of well-being. Alcohol and other drugs increase those neurotransmitters in the brain as well, and serve to elevate mood and satisfy and reward the user. Thus, even on a molecular level, we can appreciate the connection between drug use and spiritual practices. One of the reasons people have used mind- and mood-changing substances for thousands of years is to attain altered and "higher" states of consciousness—to connect with that which is greater than oneself, consistent with the seeking of spirituality. Addiction is not caused by a lack of faith.

Some contend that at the heart of any addict is unresolved trauma. Do people become addicts because they have experienced trauma? It is true that trauma can create an incredible amount of pain and anxiety, and a sense of hopelessness. These feelings can cause someone to self-medicate the feelings away by drinking or using other drugs. Many trauma victims develop the disease of addiction in this way. Of course, not all trauma victims self-medicate. Likewise, there are many addicts who have not experienced previous trauma. But many have, and it is vital that any unresolved trauma be addressed—therapy to address the grief and help with the processing of traumatic experiences are essential. However, even though trauma and addiction frequently co-occur, the bottom line is that trauma does not cause addiction. Addiction, once present, is its own disease and must be independently addressed.

Addiction is its own primary illness. Even when there is an underlying issue like trauma that leads to initial use, once addiction has been activated, it is its own "motor." That is, once activated, addiction is a diseased state of the brain that perpetuates itself. It does not need an "issue" to keep going. In relation to this issue, a treatment professional I know often rhetorically asks his patients or the families who seek his counsel, "Why do alcoholics drink?" The answers: *because they are alcoholic*. There are often good reasons that addicts find to explain their use, but in the absence of a good reason, any reason will do. In the end, an addict has his or her own intrinsic reason: the disease of addiction itself.

Liver Transplant Review Board—Breaking Down Barriers

Traditionally, if someone had alcoholic-liver failure (as opposed to liver failure from cancer or Hepatitis C, for example) they would not even be considered as a candidate for a new liver transplant unless they stayed abstinent for six months. The reason for this dogmatic rule was not grounded in science, but in judgment. There's not a shred of proof in the literature that ties the arbitrary six-month waiting period with improved outcomes. However it's easy to see that for a disease many people consider to be a character flaw, a six-month waiting period can be seen as a type of punishment for being a bad person or doing bad things. Any way you spin it, the rule was cruel.

Alcohol is amongst the leading causes of liver disease worldwide with increasing comorbidity and mortality. Most centers have a 6-month abstinence requirement before transplantation is permitted to occur. Mortality rates for acute alcoholic liver decompensation approaches 80%.

Liver transplantation has recently been recommended for selected patients with alcoholic hepatitis. Concerns remain about recidivism after transplantation. 306 consecutive patients undergoing (OLT) between June 2011 and June 2015 were retrospectively reviewed by my colleagues at Methodist. Thirty-seven patients were found to have acute alcohol related hepatic decompensation and underwent transplant within sixty days of decompensation. Even patients with acute alcoholic liver decompensation with actively drinking achieved excellent outcomes post-liver transplantation. Relapse rates were similar to historical cohorts. The conclusion drawn attracted much attention because it shattered the traditional, punitive six-month waiting period:

"(select) patients presenting with acute alcohol related liver decompensation who have not met the six-month sobriety threshold benefit from liver transplantation."[51]

Chapter 3: The Nervous System and Neurons

I n order to understand the disease of addiction, it helps to be at least basically familiar with the nervous system. I will present what I consider to be an important general summary of not-so-basic concepts. This introduction will help set the stage for what we will be discussing in our search to further understand the disease in its entirety.

To begin with, our bodies are complex, but nothing in our body is nearly as intricate and complex as the brain. In fact, there are over 150 different known cell types within that one organ alone. Within the nervous system, there are over 100 billion nerve cells, or *neurons*. Neurons are the fundamental cells of the nervous system. Neurons are electrically excitable cells that process and transmit information. In general, the nervous system is an arrangement of neurons and other dedicated cells, or *glial cells* that relay data about our external and internal environments.

The nervous system processes environmental information in order to fulfill its role as the body's control center. The entire nervous system is divided into two sections, the *peripheral* nervous system and the *central* nervous system. The brain and spinal cord make up the central nervous system. All other nervous system structures make up the peripheral nervous system.

Neurons are the oldest and longest-lasting cells in the body. We have many of the same neurons throughout our entire lives. At one time we thought that once a neuron is dead, it is not replaced. In fact, we do have fewer neurons when we are old compared to when we were young. Yet we know that the brain can repair damaged neurons and grow new ones. This regenerative ability lies at the forefront of the concept of neural plasticity. Fortunately, the brain can heal and has a remarkable ability to also borrow from other areas to help compensate for lost function. This amazing ability explains why stroke victims have the potential to learn compensatory skills. Some stroke victims with lost brain function can teach the remainder of their brain to learn specific functions that were once only managed by the parts of their brain that are no longer working.

There are different types of neurons, sending information in different directions. For instance, *sensory neurons* respond to light, pressure, heat, and sound. Sensory neurons send their data from the periphery of the body to the spinal cord and brain. On the other hand, *motor neurons* transmit their information in the other direction, from the central nervous system out to the muscles and other glands in the body. There are also neurons that serve as connectors between motor and sensory neurons, and these are called *interneurons.*

The neurons of the nervous system have some unique characteristics. First, they communicate information via electrochemistry. Neighboring cells interpret these highly specialized electric and chemical messages. Second, they use special proteins, called *neurotransmitters,* to relay information and do their work. Neurotransmitters include dopamine, serotonin, norepinephrine, and

FIGURE I: NEURON

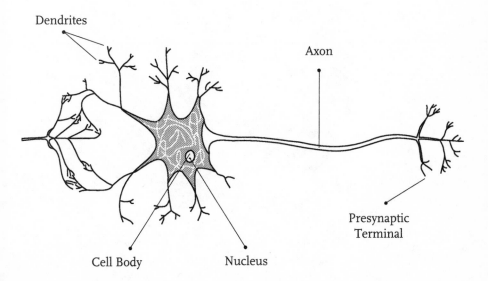

Dendrites

Axon

Cell Body

Nucleus

Presynaptic
Terminal

others. Many neurotransmitters make us feel good and motivate our behavior, and are at the core of understanding the disease of addiction. Drugs and addictive behaviors either mimic our natural neurotransmitters or facilitate their release. Third, neurons have specialized functional ends called *dendrites* that "listen," or gather information, and other long extensions called *axons* that "call out," or relay information. Neurons release their neurotransmitters at their *presynaptic terminals* into the space between neurons known as *synapses*. The dendrites of neighboring cells respond to the amount and type of neurotransmitters that move across the synapses onto their receptors. Neurotransmitters are stored in sacs known as storage *vesicles*.

FIGURE II: SYNAPSE

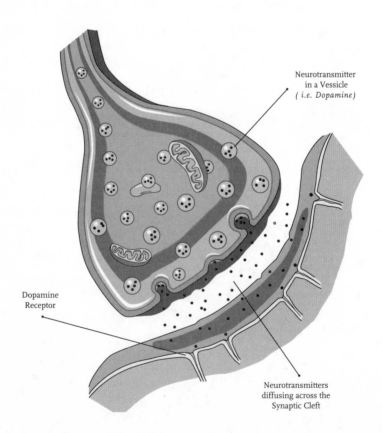

Neurotransmitter
in a Vessicle
(*i.e. Dopamine*)

Dopamine
Receptor

Neurotransmitters
diffusing across the
Synaptic Cleft

Neurotransmitters are synthesized in the *cell body* of the neuron; then they are moved down the axon to the axon terminal. Next, neurotransmitters are stored in vesicles, where they await release. Neurotransmitters are released from the axon terminal when their vesicles "fuse" with the membrane of the axon's presynaptic terminal, releasing the neurotransmitter into the synapse between neurons. After release, neurotransmitters attach to precise receptors on the postsynaptic membrane that fit with them so that they can cause an effect on the neighboring neurons. Substances that are abused either exacerbate the effect of our natural neurotransmitters or mimic their effects. Alcohol and other drugs can cause excessive release of neurotransmitters from vesicles, or prevent their breakdown.

The Connection Between Drugs and Our Nervous System

Survival requires that our control center have the ability to rapidly identify and respond to danger. Reacting to life-threatening situations requires lightning-quick responsive action. The survival control center in the brain is the midbrain, where we also find the "addiction center."

Survival instincts are called instincts because they are below the level of consciousness. If the survival center waited around to think about things for a while, we would be hit by the oncoming bus or attacked by the stalking mountain lion. Instead, any animal's drive to survive is a subconscious stimulus-and-response mechanism that does not waste precious time pondering. It simply acts decisively when it senses that survival is at stake. Addiction affects that same part of the brain that is not under our conscious control, where our instincts lie, known as the mesolimbic dopamine system.

The mesolimbic dopamine system, once activated by addiction, remains forever altered. A personal hero of mine whose work has benefited all of us tremendously, Dr. Nora D. Volkow, director of the National Institute on Drug

Abuse (NIDA) at the National Institutes of Health, demonstrated that in addicts, chronic changes occur in the pathways of the midbrain.[52] Once addiction is activated, it will always be present because it is a chronic disease. Even after someone has been in recovery for a decade or two, we can see by way of brain-scan imaging that visual exposure to very quick images of the person's drug of choice activates the "addiction center" of the brain. The drug image does not even have to be recognizable by the conscious mind for this to happen. It is not the thinking part of the brain that recognizes the image and decides to desire it. The activation of the addiction center is automatic, even instinctual. That is because the speed at which our midbrain operates is extremely rapid and out of our conscious control, as it must be for us to survive. Exposure to visual cues triggers an electrochemical process in our subconscious midbrain that motivates us to action. A beer commercial or picture of a syringe may be all that is needed for an addict to experience cravings to use.

Drugs of abuse either mimic our natural neurotransmitters or cause the release of a lot of what we already have stored. For example, pain medicine is very similar to our natural endorphins, which make us feel pleasure, decrease anxiety, and are good, natural painkillers. The medications are stronger and longer acting than the real thing, and when they fit on the endorphin receptors, a reaction takes place in the bodies of the predisposed and addicted, causing a heightened sense of reward and creating motivation to continue receiving that same level of stimulation. Cocaine, on the other hand, does not fit on our receptors, but causes the rewarding neurotransmitter dopamine to remain in the synapse for prolonged periods so it can continue to produce its effects at artificially high levels.

Normally, there are specialized transporters that keep the synapses clear and prevent the neurons from excessive exposure to neurotransmitters. This is fortunate, because too much exposure to neurotransmitters is harmful to the neurons. Also, our neurons do not have an endless supply of neurotransmitters, and the transporters' job is also to recycle these valuable chemicals. Dopamine would not naturally rise and remain at such high concentrations, but cocaine (among other drugs) increases dopamine tremendously, producing an intense feeling of euphoria. As a consequence, neurotransmitters are depleted after binge drug use, and the resulting emotional crash from a low neurotransmitter state causes intense depression. Specific drugs and their mechanisms are discussed in more detail in Chapter Four.

Let us explore how neurotransmitters can be deactivated under normal circumstances. First, they can diffuse, or passively ease out of the space between neurons where they can no longer fit on a receptor and exert their actions on other neurons. Second, they can be broken down and made inactive by "cleaner" chemicals, known as *enzymes*. Third, neurotransmitters can be removed directly by glial cells. Fourth, the process of *reuptake* involves the concept of recycling, because the neurotransmitter is reused. The catecholamines—dopamine, epinephrine, and norepinephrine—are commonly recycled in this way. Cocaine and amphetamines exert part of their action by preventing the reuptake of neurotransmitters, thus increasing the concentration and prolonging the action of these neurotransmitters, causing a magnified effect.

Functional Divisions of the Cerebral Cortex

The human brain is a three-pound mass of pink-and-gray-colored neural and supportive tissue that is responsible for our success at life on this planet thus far. We have evolved along a continuum that begins with simple, single-celled organisms with no brains, progressing through single-minded and purposefully driven reptilian brains to the more complex social mammalian brains, and ending with the incredibly inquisitive, adaptive, and intelligent primate brains. Our brains have functional divisions, or areas, that are specialized in carrying out certain tasks. The complexity of our brain can be understood by dividing it into three evolutionary parts: these can be thought of as the reptilian brain, the mammalian brain, and the primate brain.

The part of our brain that developed early in evolution is our reptilian brain, which controls some vital survival mechanisms like heartbeat, breathing, and movement. Our mammalian brains evolved later and include the mesolimbic system, where pleasure, defense, reward, appetite, and emotion are located. Finally, our primate brains, and then finely evolved human brains, provided us with our magnificent cerebral cortex. The cerebral cortex is what gives us our advantage. We are not the fastest or strongest animals on the planet. We are the smartest, though. Our cortex is so important, in fact, that without it we would be chased by lions while naked and filthy (because we would not know to wear clothes or make weapons or set traps for other animals). With our cortex, we can enjoy the comfort of air-conditioned, motorized vehicles while we take photographic images of lions while on safari.

The cerebral cortex is also the part of our brain in charge of various higher-order functions like problem solving, ethical thought, abstract reasoning, and language. It is the site that makes our final "thinking" choices. As a philosophy major and general fan of the human race, I am proud of this cerebral cortex. I think it's pretty cool and powerful. In the sections on the brain and brain disease that follow, I explain how addiction commandeers the subconscious and primitive areas of the human brain, thereby changing behavior and perpetuating the disease of addiction. Understanding how addiction hijacks the less evolved parts of our brains reflects that even though we may be highly evolved, self-aware, thinking, and logical beings, we are still capable of behaving as though we were no more evolved than a reptile. Despite our amazing cortex, we are not merely the sum total of our higher brain processes. The most difficult aspect of addiction for nonaddicts to appreciate is that we can be significantly controlled by parts of our brains that do not include awareness and choice. Our

FIGURE III: FUNCTIONAL DIVISIONS OF THE BRAIN

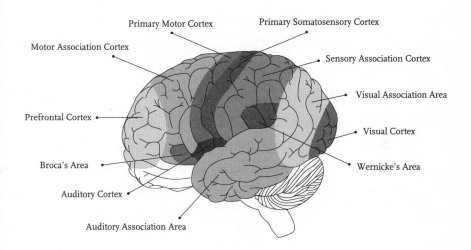

BRAIN AREA	FUNCTION
Broca's Area	Speech Center
Auditory Cortex & Association Area	Sound Center
Prefrontal Cortex	Impulse and Emotional Control, Thought Processing, Problem Solving
Motor Association Cortex	Complex Movement Coordination
Primary Motor Cortex	Voluntary Movement Initiation
Sensory Association Area	Multisensory Information Processing
Basal Forebrain & Ventral Tegmental Area	Included in Addiction Pathways & Sites of Action
Mesolimbic System	Survival, Pleasure, Salience, Motivation & Reward
Visual Cortex & Association Area	Visual Center
Wernicke's Area	Language Comprehension
Primary Somatosensory Cortex	Incoming Tactile Information Processing

*Note: Not all of these areas of the brain are visible in Figure III.

most recently evolved and intelligent cortex is neither as vital to our survival nor in as much control as the more ancient and instinctual parts of our brain.

Figure III shows where some of these specialized local cortex functions are and what purpose they serve. Our language centers are typically located only in the left cerebral hemisphere. On the other hand, don't forget that our brain has an amazing ability to learn its different areas' tasks and then reorganize itself in order to compensate, adapt, and overcome loss of function in one area. The *primary somatosensory cortex* is the specialized area of the brain that processes sensations corresponding to different body parts. Interestingly, brain imaging can demonstrate how addiction changes the brain. In compulsive overeaters, for example, the region of the brain corresponding to the mouth and tongue grows larger. This physiologic adaptation may be responsible for the development of tolerance in food addiction, because more food is required to satisfy the demands of the enlarged brain area.

Neuroplasticity

Scientists once believed that the majority of our brain was hardwired at a certain point in life and that any brain damage would leave us in a permanently weakened state. This would be a particularly troublesome vulnerability for those with addiction, because drugs do cause brain damage. However, we have discovered that the brain can adapt new functions through experience by growing new neurons and developing new neuronal pathways throughout our entire lives.

Neuroplasticity is the name given to our brain's lifelong ability to reorganize neural pathways. "Plasticity" refers to learning by adding or removing associations, or by adding cells. Learning new coping skills or abilities is actually made possible by our brain's ability to make functional changes in our hardware. Over time, our brains are actual reflections of our actions, knowledge, and skill set.

Learning strengthens the amount, type, and nature of the nerve cells' connections. I ask my patients if they would like sober brains. When they say yes, I ask them to describe how one acquires such a brain. That is, how do we develop the neuronal pathways that can reinforce healthy behaviors when faced with difficulties like resentment, loneliness, anger, and excitement? The answer is to stay in recovery. Although there is no cure for addiction, and nothing can absolutely protect against the possibility of relapse, staying abstinent gives us the foundation to enhance the brain changes required to help us stay in recovery.

Staying in recovery provides the brain with the means to make new connections and prune old habits. Because the brain is not fixed at childhood, it is possible for even the most self-defeating addict to make healthy lifestyle changes. "Once an addict, always an addict" does not mean anyone is doomed to a life of self-destruction, loneliness, and insecurity. You *can* teach an old dog new tricks. The reality is that people are never too old to achieve and maintain recovery. I have witnessed firsthand the miracles of change that result from a willingness to trust and make behavioral changes.

Neuroplasticity shows up in improved brain size and function as addicts find and stay in recovery. In active addiction, alcoholic brains experience atrophy, or a decrease in size. Multiple research studies have demonstrated that brains of alcoholic men early in recovery do, in fact, reverse brain size changes in a short period of time. After just three to six months in recovery, the brains demonstrated regrowth in volume.[53,54] Healing happens.

Coincidentally, there is a saying that addiction professionals adopted long ago in order to help guide those early in recovery: "ninety meetings in ninety days." It is aimed at helping guide the early recovering addict to attend ninety twelve-step meetings in ninety days. The truth is that it takes about ninety days for our brains to recognize new behavior as habit and make neuronal changes that help facilitate those changes. Often, the wisdom of experience shows up first and the science behind it comes later: recovering addicts recognized the inherent value of ninety continuous days of treatment long before NIDA did.

The human brain is a bit like clay and a bit like muscles. Shape it through experience and keep it active through action. "Use it or lose it" applies to our brains. When we exercise aspects of our brains, they are molded and developed. In addition, when we continue learning, or keeping a "beginner's mind," we prevent our brains from withering too much. Physicians now recommend activities that stimulate the brain and increase blood flow, like meditation, in order to slow the progression of Alzheimer's dementia once that ailment is diagnosed.[55] Furthermore, research has demonstrated that thinking not only activates the brain, but also produces brain development.

The great news for people in recovery is that healing happens. The brain is the target organ of addiction. Since the brain is the grand conductor organ, brain dysfunction causes emotional, physical, psychological, and spiritual dysfunctions that lead to overall pain and suffering. These dysfunctions are greatest while using and early in recovery. Without our brain's ability to redesign itself, we would forever be in a state of despair and loneliness. Addicts enter recovery after a long and hard road, but can start the process of healing the moment they start their recovery. Their brains follow, creating a new landscape in which to live. No matter how far down the ladder of despair and devastation someone falls, it is never too late to start the process of healing the brain and improving life and well-being.

The Brain

Addiction is a brain disease. Dr. Nora Volkow, Dr. Mark Gold, Dr. Daniel Amen, and many others have demonstrated that there are fundamental differences in the brains of those with the disease of addiction compared to those without it. Brain imaging studies by NIDA, Dr. Amen, and others have shown that addicted individuals have physical changes in functional brain areas corresponding to dysregulations in judgment, decision-making, learning, memory, and behavioral control. Dysfunction in the brains of addicts exists on several levels. The brains appear divergent on imaging, and when we examine their functioning on a microscopic level, we also find differences. There are different proteins that are made by the genes in the cells of brains of addicts.[56,57]

We see similar disease-specific changes in the sick organ systems in other diseases as well. Imaging reveals that differences in circulation, metabolism, and structure occur as a result of heart disease. We know that with specific heart diseases come specific dysfunctions that arise despite the patient's intentions, character, demographics, intelligence, faith, sex, or race. Heart disease does not result from or cause "bad behavior," as a rule. I have never heard of a heart disease patient getting arrested for exhibiting symptoms of the disease. The brain scans below demonstrate the visible changes that occur in the brains of addicts. These changes are a common and predictable reflection of what happens to the brain in that disease process. In addition, the one-year-abstinent scan reveals that healing does happen when the addict remains abstinent. We can see how much the one-year-abstinent brain has healed when compared with the other two scans. Even though more healing will continue to occur, that first year is a crucial time of healing and recovery.

The top left scan demonstrates what a "normal" brain looks like. By the way, I have never met a "normal" person in my life. Just when I think I have met the first "normal" person, he or she shows me a little of his or her craziness. That's not necessarily a bad thing, either. But the point is, the top left image is of someone who is not an addict. In contrast to that image, which shows uniformity and symmetry, the other images are not as "pretty." The top right and bottom left images are brain scans of people exposed to prolonged drug use—one relates to alcohol and the other to heroin, but it doesn't matter what the substance of abuse is. Fundamental changes occur in the brain as a result

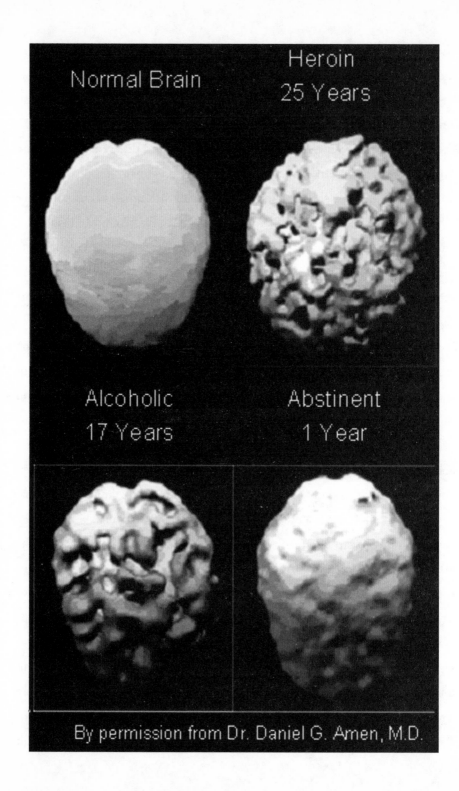

Normal Brain

Heroin
25 Years

Alcoholic
17 Years

Abstinent
1 Year

By permission from Dr. Daniel G. Amen, M.D.

of repeated exposure to all drugs of abuse. The effects of drugs on the brain involve many systems. Emotional, spiritual, motivational, and other pathways become dysfunctional as a result of repeated exposure to drugs. These images are visible evidence of these changes. They are also evidence of the adverse neurobiological processes that become manifest as the diseased state progresses.

Another remarkable aspect of these brain scans is in the bottom right image of the brain at one year in recovery. Look how much better it appears. This healing that occurs in the brain is due to neuroplasticity, described previously. The benefits of recovery are remarkable and physically evident. Due to neuroplasticity, the brain continues to grow and transform and heal throughout our lives according to what we do. A key point is that the brains of addicts look fundamentally different than those of nonaddicts. With time, the majority of the brain changes actually normalize. In addition to the reversal of brain atrophy found by Dr. Volkow, thinking and coordination improve within the first month of sobriety.[58] The image from Dr. Amen after one year of abstinence evidences that the brain is healing and functioning much better—it looks full and there is full blood flow and metabolism. Blood flow to the frontal lobe increases throughout recovery, returning to approximately normal after four years of abstinence.[59] It is generally believed that it takes about five years of recovery for the brain to fully heal to the point where it appears as if the person had virtually never used. Of course, there will be age-related changes. However, pathways in the mesolimbic dopamine system do not ever revert back to the predisease state. The addiction center remains forever changed.

What brain scans cannot demonstrate are the intricate details revealed under the magnifying power of microscopic analysis. Even at the smallest of microscopic levels, we can discern differences between the brains of addicts and those of nonaddicts. Genes, located deep within each cell of the human body, regulate all cellular and, ultimately, all life processes. Genes in the brain cells of addicts act differently. Animal studies reflect that "addict" rodents, for example, have genetic differences from normal rodents. There are more than thirty regions of the genetic code that correspond to alterations in increased drug use, tolerance, withdrawal, and drug sensitivity. Due to an evolutionarily shared ancestor, we share approximately 80 percent of our genome with rodents.

As a result, when we find genetic changes in rodents, we can then pinpoint our own changes with a probability of 80 percent. Obviously, humans have more in common with primates than rodents, and studies of primates exposed to cocaine demonstrate changes in the midbrain's genetic expressions as well. Overall, the changes observed and measured clearly demonstrate how active addiction creates a sick organ system. The brain and genetic differences between addicts and nonaddicts unequivocally substantiate the existence of a disease process.[60,61]

The Brain Disease

The brain is a complex organ that is difficult to study. There are few reliable tests for many diseases of the brain. Brain diseases are often diagnosed based on the presentation of the person's behavior, language, memory, thought processes, speech, and communication. Through these we can discern the presence of faulty thinking and abnormalities in perception. There is no test for bipolar disorder, depression, anxiety, schizophrenia, or addiction like there are tests for cancer, diabetes, high blood pressure, and heart disease. Addiction, like many other brain diseases, is diagnosed based on a set of clinical criteria. These criteria were reviewed in Chapter One. Even though we are far from establishing a single universal, reliable diagnostic test for addiction, we have nonetheless been able to uncover many disease-specific brain dysfunctions and changes that occur in addiction. These changes essentially help to establish the sick organ system in addiction, explaining its nature as a disease, just as sugar metabolism dysfunction helps to explain diabetes.

When the medical community began to search for the area of the brain where addiction existed or caused the most dysfunction, the first place that was examined was the prefrontal cortex (PFC), a specialized division of the cerebral cortex. The PFC is who we are: our choices, code of ethics, ego, favorite color, and so forth, because all these things lie in the PFC. It is the most evolved part of our brain; humans have the largest PFC, by far, of all the animals on Earth. The astonishing things that humans are capable of doing are due to our imagination, creativity, and adaptability—all of which are attributable to our incredible and highly evolved cerebral cortex. Without our PFC, we would not have computers, have been to the moon, or have invented the seedless watermelon. Who prefers to be spitting out seeds all day long?

The prefrontal cortex was the natural place to look for dysfunctional changes attributable to addiction because the assumption was that addiction was due to poor choices and character defects—and the prefrontal cortex is where those things occur. What research has demonstrated, however, is that the action of the disease of addiction is mostly concentrated in the part of the brain that is primitive and subconscious. Drugs of abuse mainly exert their effects, and dysfunction mainly occurs, in the part of the brain that is responsible for reward and survival, the mesolimbic dopamine system (MDS). Due to advanced brain imaging technologies, we can see that all drugs of abuse work in the MDS. All addictive substances interfere with the normal functioning of the MDS and its associated neuronal pathways.

The MDS does not operate in isolation from the rest of the brain, and researchers have uncovered other areas that are significantly involved in addiction as well. The MDS does have substantial pathways to the PFC, which plays a role in addiction, too. The strong emotional bond formed between the addict and his or her drug or behavior of choice owes its connection to the highways of neurons that connect the pleasure and survival center (MDS) to the center of human experience (PFC). Complex in nature, addiction affects more functional areas of the brain than merely the MDS and PFC, as noted in Figure IV. There are multiple pathways and other areas that are affected by and disrupted as a result of exposure to mind-altering substances. It is safe to say, though, that the MDS is the primary brain region that becomes dysfunctional in the disease of addiction.

The Mesolimbic Dopamine System (MDS)

The reward pathway that modulates our survival behaviors is hardwired to respond to dopamine release. When we eat food or have sexual intercourse (which is evolutionarily oriented toward procreation and survival of the

FIGURE IV: THE TARGET ORGAN OF ADDICTION

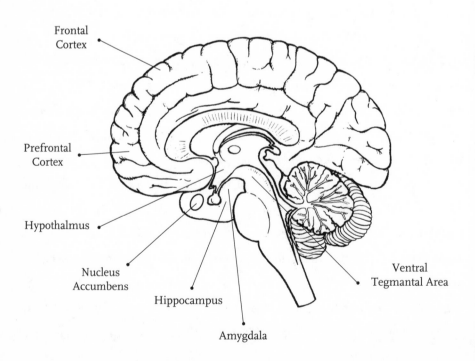

Frontal Cortex

Prefrontal Cortex

Hypothalmus

Nucleus Accumbens

Hippocampus

Amygdala

Ventral Tegmantal Area

species), dopamine is released, causing pleasurable feelings, so we intuitively know those behaviors are *good* things to do again and again. Dopamine makes us feel satisfied and content, and it gives us pleasure as well. Without any pleasurable or motivating stimulation, our MDS stays in a neutral, or baseline, position. Our "baseline level" of dopamine is another way of saying how many of us feel most of the time. It is our usual level of dopamine.

Food increases the dopamine level in the MDS by 150 percent over the normal baseline level. So, a good meal will cause a surge in dopamine over normal baseline levels and create the desire to repeat the experience. Sex (which rewards the survival of the species through the act of procreation) can increase the dopamine surge by 175 percent over baseline. That much dopamine gets the attention of the MDS. Drugs increase dopamine much more than sex. In fact, certain drug experiences are described by imagining the feeling that would accompany having multiple intense orgasms. Now multiply that feeling by a thousand, and you are close. For folks who have never done drugs or experienced the tremendous increases in dopamine they can produce, sex is often the most pleasurable activity in their hierarchy of experiences.

Let us now compare the surges in dopamine that occur in naturally rewarding and survival-benefiting activities with those that occur in the MDS with certain specific drugs of abuse. Researchers Gaetano Di Chiari and Assanta Imperato were able to measure the substance-specific surges in dopamine within the MDS.[62,63,64] I have adapted the graph below from their data.

Alcohol increases dopamine release in the MDS 200 percent over baseline, tobacco increases dopamine by 225 percent, cocaine increases dopamine by 300 percent, and amphetamines increase dopamine by over 1,000 percent. Such an enormous amount of dopamine surging through the MDS gives the brain higher reward recall and more motivation to recreate the experience. That much dopamine effectively smacks the MDS right in the face. In the merely one-millimeter-thick region of our limbic system, an explosion of dopamine

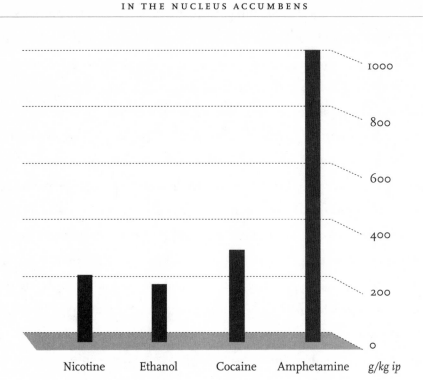

FIGURE V: DOPAMINE RELEASED
IN THE NUCLEUS ACCUMBENS

■ *dopamine released in the nucleus accumbens*

really grabs our attention. Our brains say, "Aaahhh . . . I like that! Let's do it again and again and again." Nothing natural causes quite the explosion that drugs can create.

Drugs of abuse not only increase the dopaminergic tone in the limbic system. They also stimulate our hippocampus, the primary site of memory; and the more advanced frontal lobes, where emotional value is assigned to the experience of using. In all these areas, our interest is piqued, our motivation is stimulated, and fond memories of using are created. In essence, the site of action may be in the limbic system, but the result—storage of euphoric memories and deeper meaning—is more pervasive.

We actually develop deep emotional bonds to drugs and drug use. It can be said that a love affair happens between the addict and the use of the drug. In fact, the same regions of the brain activate when people look at their lover's picture as are activated when addicts view images of their drug(s) of choice. Often, recovery only begins after a grieving process, whereby the addict mourns the loss of his or her chemical or behavioral companion. The midbrain's attention is truly and deeply captured by drugs.

The MDS consists primarily of the basal forebrain, amygdala, nucleus accumbens, and ventral tegmental area (VTA), in addition to pathways that extend into the frontal and prefrontal cortex. Neuroscientists have been able to localize these areas and demonstrate the chemical activities that occur both in the natural state and in addiction. Current understanding of the MDS includes its specialized functional divisions. For example, advanced neural imaging shows that the amygdala—a highly specialized area of the MDS involved in sexual response, anger, and fear—is actually more active when an addict is experiencing craving or when anyone is experiencing the fight-or-flight stress response. By producing acetylcholine, a major brain neurotransmitter, the basal forebrain orchestrates learning. In addition, the VTA—the origin of the dopamine system—is heavily involved in motivation and response to rewards. The nucleus accumbens has a specialized role as well. This area is the last stop on the pleasure pathway train. When drugs are used, addictive behaviors are carried out, or the rewards are anticipated, the nucleus accumbens charges with activity.

Drugs do not even need be ingested, or addictive behaviors actually carried out, for dopamine to rise in the MDS. The mere anticipation of the rewarding effects of drugs (or of the particular behavior) causes a measurable rise in dopamine levels.[65] Although the most crucial neurotransmitter with respect to addiction is dopamine, neuroscience has uncovered the roles that other neurotransmitters play. The other key players we know about include gamma amino butyric acid, which regulates inhibition; serotonin, which regulates learning, memory, mood, and sleep; acetylcholine, which helps in memory; endorphins, which are our natural painkillers and mood enhancers; and glutamate, which regulates learning and memory.

Actions that are beneficial to survival stimulate dopamine release in the MDS. Dopamine release in the MDS is pleasurable and therefore motivating. Drinking fresh water is innately pleasurable; no one has to convince thirsty people to refresh themselves with a glass of cool, clean water. That is because after such refreshment, dopamine is released in the MDS. Human beings will work extremely hard for water, food, and sex because they are so pleasurable. Not many people have good food or sex and then say, "Eh, not for me, I'd rather mop the floor." The natural release of dopamine in response to activities that help us and our species survive has been shaped by evolution to create a rewarding, natural, inborn mechanism for recognizing helpful survival behaviors and stimulating us to repeat them.

No matter what the cause, when our MDS experiences a surge in dopamine, it wakes up and says, "Pay attention, this is important; let's do it again." In other words, when ingested, addictive drugs powerfully but deceptively signal the brain that a survival fitness benefit has arrived. Subsequently, the brain is fooled into assigning vital significance to the experience of drug ingestion, and is motivated to repeat that experience. In this process, using drugs progressively supplants other, less pleasurable aspects of life like food and even sex, which the brain no longer considers as valuable.

Numerous animal studies have demonstrated how the survival instinct can become tricked into thinking that getting drugs is more crucial than other behaviors that actually benefit survival.[66] These experiments also explain that the "bad" behavior intrinsic to addiction is a function of subconscious MDS motivation—also known as "the hijacked brain." Actually, several studies have established that rats and monkeys will work incessantly to receive intravenous drugs and direct electrical stimulation to the MDS. They will ignore food and water to the point where they experience severe weight loss, dehydration, and death.[67,68] Normally, when they are hungry, the MDS will motivate animals to look for, acquire, and eat food. Remember, the MDS is in charge of survival, so it orchestrates the acquisition of food and water in order to ensure survival. Under normal conditions, even the sight of food will begin to send dopamine rushing through the MDS so that the survival task of nourishing the animal will be completed.

A study conducted on rats by Dr. Eliot Gardner and David James powerfully demonstrated how the MDS assigns higher priority to behaviors that stimulate greater pleasure than it does to behaviors that actually aid in survival.[69] Addicted rats that are deprived of food and water will forgo food, water, and safety in order to receive an electric impulse directly stimulating their limbic system—providing a degree of pleasure consistent with that provided by drugs of abuse. In this study, rats that were able to press a lever in order to stimulate their MDS directly and promptly acquired the habit of pressing that lever. Some rats would press the lever a remarkable 10,000 times an hour, and they would continue to press the lever to the exclusion of other pleasurable and survival-oriented attractions, such as sexually receptive rats of the opposite sex.

After several weeks, Dr. Gardner threw them a curveball by placing an electrified metal floor grid barrier that delivered painful shocks. When the rat attempted to reach the lever, it would feel the pain, yelp, and jump back. Next, it tested the whole floor. When it could not find a safe passage, it then tried to enlist the help of the lab technicians (more research humor). Remarkably, the desire to stimulate their MDS in the way they had become used to was so strong that the rats placed themselves in harm's way, crossing the electrified floor and subjecting themselves to painful shocks, in order to self-stimulate.

Other experiments have further demonstrated the remarkable lengths to which animals will go to self-stimulate their MDS.[70,71,72,73] Addicted rats that were starved of food and water for twenty-four hours were put into a cage, on one side of which there was food and water on a nonelectrified pad. However, there was a lever on the far side of the cage across an electrified bridge. Instead of remaining on the side of safety, water, food, survival, and no pain, the addicted rats endured the pain of crossing the electrified floor and ignored the food and water in order to inject drugs into their MDS by pressing the lever. What is even more remarkable is that addicted animals often self-administered stimulation to their MDS by pressing the lever repeatedly until they died. The reward and consequent meaning of stimulating their MDS had essentially trumped the importance of the food, water, and safety—the survival instincts of the addicted rats had been completely hijacked. Their "bad behavior" was beyond their control—they "chose" drugs over life.

In this way, the MDS, so crucial to survival, is actually changed. It becomes driven more by reward itself than by rewarding survival behaviors. Its pathways extend to the four corners of the brain, sometimes orchestrating fiendish behaviors intended to stimulate more dopamine activity in the MDS. That is, good people will be driven to do "bad" things. Furthermore, the limbic system cannot make an executive decision about whether or not to continue using drugs; only our cerebral cortex can. However, our prized cerebral cortex is not as instrumental in determining our behavior as we may like to think. In this regard, the MDS is the CEO.

When the MDS motivates us to act, we act. The MDS acting in survival mode can be nearly impossible to overrule. In essence, our subconscious brains exert more power over our actions in the active diseased state of addiction than our conscious brains do. Addiction is a disease that robs its host of volition. Again, addiction is not the result of poor choice, bad parenting, weak character, or any other archaic attack on the individual. Addiction is the result of a brain-changing process whereby our primitive brains make decisions based on stimuli and responses rather than logic or ethics.

Another way of explaining the different roles that functional divisions of our brains play in addiction is through a further comparison of the PFC and the MDS. I believe understanding the difference between these brain areas is crucial in appreciating the lack of choice addicts have while their disease is active.

The MDS is the part of our midbrain that controls survival. An ancient part of brain, the midbrain is focused on defense and survival. It must gather data and quickly process this information in order to determine the best course of action for our survival. As an example, let us explore what happens to our midbrains and frontal lobes when we are faced with danger. If an armed gunman were to enter your house and start screaming and shooting at you, the midbrain would instantaneously recognize DANGER and send out a cascade of hormones and chemicals designed to help you get moving out of harm's way immediately. It would not waste valuable time consulting your frontal lobe. It would act quickly and decisively so you have the greatest chance of surviving.

Through its pathways and chemical messengers, the MDS would send out commands to our more highly evolved motor cortex so that our legs would run the body to safety. If the MDS asked the frontal lobe for input, the frontal lobe might be curious as to what type of gun it was, where the bullets were purchased, what the motivating factor of the gunman was, where he bought his shoes, and so on, and valuable time would be wasted while the chances of survival dwindled exponentially. So when faced with survival decisions, the midbrain overrides intention and rationality, commandeering the body and changing behavior to meet its single-minded agenda.

The midbrain also cares about survival of the species. As mentioned earlier, sex is an activity that the MDS responds to by virtue of the fact that it raises dopamine levels and helps us to pass on our genes so the human race survives. The midbrain is only interested in passing on the genetic code. The frontal lobe is what is interested in romance and love. In contrast, the midbrain does not make love . . . it procreates. Making love is not necessary for survival. In fact, if it could be interviewed, the MDS would probably say lovemaking is a waste of valuable time. Our frontal lobes make love and assign emotional meaning and strive for higher goals. Our midbrain recognizes the survival aspect and dopamine surge, so the act itself, not the back story, has a value to the midbrain.

The midbrain pays attention to food. Food raises our dopamine levels and is also necessary for survival. Our frontal lobes, in charge of our decision-making, partake in highly selective eating ceremonies. Our frontal lobes care about food preparation, presentation, and table manners. Our midbrain, on the other hand, does not nibble delicately on crumpets; it engulfs, devours, and consumes. Consumption is essential, and so has value for the midbrain. The midbrain does not humanely dispose of an animal for consumption; it kills. The midbrain does not think; it reacts and does not care. The midbrain defends and drinks water and eats food and procreates to survive. That is all. The MDS does whatever it has to do to carry out its functions of defense and survival, blindly motivated by the stimulus-response mechanism hardwired through millions of years of evolution.

After repeated exposure to an addictive substance, the body becomes dependent. It will subsequently experience withdrawal when that substance is not available, and yet another disease-specific malfunction of the brain occurs. When the MDS becomes painfully depleted of its cherished neurotransmitters, its activity increases. Lower neurotransmitter supply and higher MDS activity have a significant uncomfortable effect on mood states and stimulate behavior aimed at acquiring more drugs. That is, an addict in withdrawal will have intense cravings and become irritable, restless, and discontented. The relief that comes with acquiring more drugs causes the addict to find and use drugs and avoid withdrawal at any cost.

In more ways than just seeking pleasure, alcohol and other drugs hijack the midbrain. The midbrain is fooled into thinking that drugs of abuse are part of the survival mechanism in another way because, in the state of withdrawal, drug use is associated with the removal of pain. This maladaptation of survival needs helps to explain why addicts often say they "need" to use. This can be taken one step further in that the "need" to use overrides the frontal lobe's input. Our frontal lobes offer objections to continuing to use, but to no avail. Protesting thoughts arising in the frontal lobes pale in comparison to the screams of *GO!* arising in the MDS. So, behavior that is fiendish or "bad" is merely an inevitable means to a necessary end. Good people will lie, steal, and cheat in order to continue using drugs because a changed, hijacked brain is leading them.

The addicted brain views the continued use of drugs as necessary for survival. As a result, human addicts will cross their own versions of an electrified floor in order to keep using, and, unfortunately, many will do so to their own demise. For some addicts, crossing that electrified floor translates to broken promises, manipulation, theft, or other "bad" behaviors. All the while, their motivation to do these "bad" things is not under their conscious control. They are being driven by their dysfunctional midbrains that are attempting to survive, albeit in a distorted way.

The majority of addicts feel so much shame and guilt over their own behavior that they may weep for days and weeks when they first enter recovery. Shame and guilt are among the hallmarks of early recovery. These emotions are only possible when there is a code of ethics. Most addicts have a code of ethics and typically are not bad people, although they certainly may do bad things. Addicts are wholly responsible for their behavior and for their recovery. It is important to understand that active addiction changes the brain, which in turn changes behavior in ways that can cause even the best of us to do the worst of things.

Addiction is more complex than merely hitting the dopamine bell. Pathways that extend from the MDS connect the highly evolved cortex to the primitive parts of the brain, creating an intricate and expansive network. Emotional and spiritual meaning becomes intertwined with the repetitive behaviors and stimulus-response mechanism at the heart of the addictive process. Recall how viewing images of a loving partner activates the same brain regions as those involved in addiction. Emotional and spiritual bonds add a profound depth to the relationship between the addict and his or her drug. Addiction is much more than a disease of pleasure. This is also evident in that the longer that addiction is active, the more the degree of pleasure experienced declines. At a certain point in the progression of active addiction, the pleasure is mostly gone and addicts will tell you they are just trying to survive, attempt to feel normal, or avoid the torture of withdrawal.

Even when the addiction causes outright wretchedness and pain, with a progressively expanding set of harmful negative consequences, addicts continue to use and act out. Too many patients I have treated desperately ask me in one form or another, "I know I shouldn't drink (or use) and I don't even like it! So why do I keep on doing it?" Addicts also routinely report that they cannot understand why they use when doing so significantly increases their chances of being incarcerated, losing a coveted job, or, even worse, losing their family and loved ones. Addiction is clearly much more than just trying to "get high."

Sick organ systems in other diseases have measurable changes in structure and function. In addiction, these disease-specific changes are most apparent in the MDS. The cells that make up the MDS undergo changes that can be seen and measured. The brain as a whole looks different, as seen in the brain scan images of Dr. Amen. Under the supermagnified detection of a high-powered microscope, the brain's smallest components also appear altered—the machinery in the neurons is changed. A slew of neurotransmitters besides dopamine—GABA, serotonin, endorphins, glutamate, and others—become affected and play a role in aberrant brain function. We also now know that even the genes in the brain are affected by prolonged drug use. Genes are responsible for synthesizing proteins and receptors, and managing every other facet of cellular activity. In other words, without our genes, our entire bodies would eventually come to a halt. Sustained drug use affects the molecular environment of genes, cell receptors, protein expression, and nerve pathways, altering how genes do their job. Over time, drug use changes the actual architecture of the brain circuitry.[74]

The molecular changes that occur create an environment that increases the potential for drug use and the development of addiction. Specifically, the brains of addicts can show lower levels of specific types of dopamine receptors. Lower levels of dopamine are highly predictive of increased drug use in animal models, and may help explain why some people born with lower levels of these receptors are predisposed to use drugs in order to feel "normal." Low levels of functional dopamine in their brains can also cause an overall lack of satisfaction and reward with normal daily activities. Life may not seem enjoyable, so drugs are sought to increase the dopamine levels, thereby "treating" the low dopamine state in order to feel better. Dr. Nora Volkow of NIDA comments on this phenomenon: "Brain adaptations such as this contribute to the compulsion to abuse drugs."[75]

As described above, research has taught us that addiction affects many systems in the brains of addicts. Changes like compulsive behavior and lack of impulse control have a more straightforward causal effect on perpetuation of drug use. Memory, coordination, motivation, mood, sleep, and concentration are also altered. In combination, the various elements of brain dysfunction can produce alarming amounts of damage. Dr. Mark Gold told me about an experiment where pathologists could not tell the difference on autopsy between monkeys that were using methamphetamine and those that were hit in the head with a hammer.[76] Some changes that occur are permanent and some are reversible. The image of the abstinent brain provided by Dr. Amen demonstrates that profound healing happens. I have seen many patients enter recovery with an enormous amount of dysfunction. Some appear to have so much cognitive damage that the treatment team will recommend a prolonged course of occupational therapy in order to help them with life chores. It is as though they need to repeat home economics and elementary mathematics in order to reenter the world independently as an adult. Yet the vast majority of them regain an incredible amount of their brain function even before discharge from inpatient rehab.

Research has shown that while some midbrain changes persist for a lifetime—which is why recovery is a lifetime process—the majority of the brain will heal over time. During the long period of healing, it is vital that we assist the dysfunctional prefrontal cortex. Poor decisions are often made due to disruptions in the PFC because that is where our ability to make rational and complex decisions lies. The impairments in our prefrontal cortex need time, patience, and practice to heal. Someone who is newly abstinent will have altered brain circuitry, neurotransmitters, genetic expressions, and moods. Therefore, it is helpful for the newly abstinent addict to have access to other healthy surrogate prefrontal cortexes, in the form of a recovery support system, to help mediate the brain dysregulations that show themselves through poor decision-making and lack of impulse control.

While medications can work in restoring certain chemical imbalances, they do nothing in terms of learning healthy coping skills and restoring health to the prefrontal cortex. What comprehensive recovery programs including twelve-step programs, faith-based recovery, therapy, and others do, in part, is provide a community of peers who offer their more functional prefrontal lobes as surrogates until the addict new to recovery achieves a healthy state of operational function in his or her own brain.

Our frontal lobes are normally used to override the primitive and base desires of the limbic system. Over time, the repeated exposure to drugs, pleasure gains from using drugs, the pain of not having the drugs, and the magnitude of emotional and spiritual meaning applied to drugs prevent our frontal lobes from doing their job. The brain gets hijacked when the limbic drive is in control, and the frontal lobes are ineffective in inhibiting the system. Fortunately, the brain does not have to stay hijacked, or no one could ever be in recovery. From a standpoint of brain structure and function, recovery can be said to occur when the frontal lobe can once again be effective in subduing the limbic drive.

In discussing addiction and brain dysfunction, some information specific to brain development is vital. Over the natural course of human maturation, brain development can be seen by an increase in the brain's size, although this is due primarily to increased myelination of the nerve fibers in the brain as we approach our twenty-fifth year of life. Our brains are most vulnerable while we are young. The earlier developing brains are exposed to mind-altering substances, especially when used with regularity, the quicker addiction develops. This phenomenon is also observed in animal models.[77,78] Adolescent rats exposed to cocaine will develop addiction much quicker than mature rats exposed to the same amount of the drug. Most often, human addicts begin their use early in life as well, when their brains are developing and most vulnerable.[79] Adolescents are essentially ideally primed to fall victim to behavior that increases the risk of developing addiction. Adolescents passionately desire to fit in and please their peers, are novelty- and risk-seeking, and lack as much impulse control as fully matured humans. Age matters. Using alcohol prior to fifteen years of age makes it four times more likely that someone will develop an alcohol use disorder at some point compared to those who first drink after nineteen years of age.

Most people who try marijuana for the first time are between twelve and seventeen years old. The same can be said for alcohol and prescription drugs. The brains of human beings are not fully developed until people reach their mid-twenties. That means that our prefrontal cortex does not have full control of judgment, decision-making, and our impulses until that time. Because the prefrontal cortex is one of the last areas of the brain to mature, adolescents tend to use other areas of the brain—emotional areas—when making decisions. NIDA also confirms that adolescent brains even react differently to drugs than do more mature brains.

Experimenting with drugs does more than speed up the development of addiction. Specifically, the brains of addicts who are exposed to substances of abuse become emotionally arrested at the stage of development at which they started using. In effect, if you began using at twelve years old and entered recovery at age thirty-five, you would have the central processing unit of a teenager. When faced with adversity, adolescents' brains will run, escape, and act out. These behaviors can be very distressing and lead to social isolation and further drug use. This may offer even more explanation of why so many addicts who relapse do so in their first year of recovery. With an adolescent coping skill set, life can be pretty harrowing. It takes time to allow the brain to heal and for addicts to learn a new set of healthy coping skills.

Dysfunctional brains contribute to the fact that addiction is the number-one public health problem in the United States. As reported by NIDA and elsewhere, drug-related deaths have more than doubled since the early 1980s. There are more deaths, illnesses, and disabilities related to substance abuse than to any other preventable health condition. In 2004, one in four deaths was attributable to alcohol, tobacco, or illicit drug use.[80]

For decades, vast evidence has indicated that drug users are more likely than nonusers to commit crimes, that those arrested frequently are under the influence of a drug at the time they commit their offense, and that drugs generate violence. For example, as long ago as 1991, a joint survey of federal and state prison inmates revealed that approximately 17 percent of state prisoners and 10 percent of federal prisoners reported committing their offense to get money to buy drugs; of those incarcerated for robbery, 27 percent of state prisoners and 27 percent of federal prisoners admitted committing their offense to get money to buy drugs.[81] Subsequently, the percentages of people incarcerated and serving time due to offenses related in some way to drug use and addiction have only increased.[82]

Estimates are that upwards of 25 percent of violent crimes are committed by people under the influence of alcohol and/or other drugs. Studies reveal that drugs and alcohol are implicated in many violent deaths by accident, homicide, and suicide.[83] In addition, people who are using or intoxicated are at greater risk of being victims of violent crime. They are more likely to be involved in accidents and fires, and to engage in self-harm.

There are serious consequences to the use of all mind-altering substances that users may ignore or assume will never happen. Accidents and self-harm happen all too frequently. A phenomenon that occurs when people are intoxicated is that the protective area of the brain that feels fear and controls impulses becomes silent. Without protective mechanisms in place, there is no impulse control, and while intoxicated, humans put themselves in harm's way by actions or words. This explains why people who are intoxicated are at increased risk for hurting themselves and others.

Chapter 4: Drugs of Abuse

Alcohol

A lcohol is classified as a sedative-hypnotic and is the drug of choice for our society. The active ingredient in alcohol is ethanol, a type of sugar. Expose many types of sugar to water and yeast, and alcohol will be formed. Ceremonial wine use is cited in the Old Testament, but alcohol use predates all written records. Alcohol has a strong social significance and is the oldest known drug in the world. In fact, fruit, honey, and grains have been fermented to make alcohol for thousands of years. Many of our forebears considered alcohol as a "gift from the gods." It has been an integral part of societies and religions across the globe and throughout history.

Alcohol, in and of itself, is not bad. However, having three or more drinks a day increases the chances of dying, and even moderate drinking can increase the chance of breast cancer in women. Overall, the production of alcohol is big business in our society because the demand is enormous. The abuse of alcohol is an unfortunate side effect of this demand, and it is also one of our nation's largest healthcare problems. Americans drink the equivalent of 500 million gallons of pure alcohol each year. People who have been drinking are at greater risk of being a victim of violent crime, and are also more likely to be involved in accidents and fires and to engage in self-harm. Nearly 8 percent of the US population, or 18.7 million people, abuse or are dependent on alcohol. Alcohol causes or is strongly associated with conditions that are responsible for more than 15 percent of all hospital admissions and is the third-leading cause of death. In 2013, 17.3 million Americans (6.6 percent of the population) were dependent on alcohol or had problems related to their alcohol abuse. This is a decline from 18.1 million (or 7.7 percent) in 2002.[84]

As a sedative-hypnotic drug, alcohol depresses the central nervous system. That means its primary mechanism of action is to slow things down in our brain and nervous system. Initially upon ingesting some alcohol, the good feelings we experience are due to its ability to cause an effect in the natural endorphin system in our brains, thereby producing a buzz of euphoria. Recall that a family history of addiction to alcohol or other drugs increases the chance that the buzz is a lot more pleasurable than in the general population, increasing the reinforcement and likelihood that more alcohol will be consumed. In large quantities, however, alcohol wreaks havoc on our nervous system and our major organs. In low doses, alcohol reduces anxiety. In those without the disease of addiction, it can be used to relieve stress and anxiety. In those with a family history of the disease, the stress-reducing effects can be greater than in the general population—again, increasing the reinforcement and leading to increased use.

In small amounts, alcohol can be calming. In small and controlled amounts, it may decrease anxiety and stress. Yet the opposite occurs with escalating use; alcohol causes more anxiety when overused. A vicious cycle ensues when people drink more in an attempt to reduce their anxiety, as escalating alcohol consumption and the need for it contributes to higher levels of anxiety, which then results in more drinking.

Alcohol lowers impulse control and inhibitions, decreases concentration, and slows reaction time. Even with moderate amounts, people's reflexes are diminished and the ability to operate a car is greatly compromised. Furthermore, moderate amounts can produce drowsiness, slurred speech, and dysregulation of emotional states. Higher doses can be lethal, with the potential to put someone in a coma and cause death. There are several dynamic factors that have an impact on how intensely we react to alcohol. These include our family history, age, health, gender, food in the intestinal tract, and the presence of other medications and drugs in our system.

Once absorbed through the small intestine, alcohol circulates through the body and reaches the brain, where it exerts its pleasurable and sedative effects. Since it is a small molecule and can travel easily in both water and fat, it gets into the bloodstream and into the brain very easily. It travels all over the body but eventually gets broken down, or metabolized, in the liver. Our liver is the organ that detoxifies the body, and alcohol is eliminated there through oxidation at a fairly steady rate of 0.5 ounces per hour. In the brain, alcohol affects several neurotransmitter systems, including the monoamines, acetylcholine, GABA, and endorphins.

While very moderate drinking can have some beneficial effects, there are many long-term medical consequences of chronic alcohol use. Over time, drinking can lead to physical dependence. This is seen when the body experiences physical withdrawal symptoms like tremors, anxiety, nausea, headaches, sweats, high blood pressure and heart rate, and even confusion and seizures. We have seen that chronic alcohol use can cause serious brain damage and can shrink the overall size of the brain. Alcohol also affects the cerebellum. This is the area of our brain that controls our coordination. The reason that field sobriety tests check our balance and coordination is precisely because alcohol exerts detrimental effects in the cerebellum that can be seen on brain imaging. Over time, alcohol abuse can cause permanent damage to our dexterity. Chronic drinking can damage the cerebellum to the point where people must walk with a wide-based gait so they don't topple over, due to a lack of balance.

Research demonstrates unequivocally that consuming alcohol can cause cancers in seven different body sites: liver, colon, rectum, breast, oropharynx, larynx, and esophagus. The relationship between alcohol and these cancers is strong and dose-dependent. Additionally, when alcohol consumption is reduced, research teaches us that risk decreases in some, but not all, of these cancers.

Excessive alcohol use led to approximately 88,000 deaths and 2.5 million years of potential life lost each year in the United States from 2006 to 2010. The lives of those who died were shortened by an average of thirty (yes, thirty) years.[85,86] Moreover, excessive drinking was responsible for one out of every ten deaths among working-age adults aged twenty to sixty-four. In 2010, the economic costs of excessive alcohol consumption were estimated to be $249 billion.[87]

While heavy drinking carries the most risk, even moderate to low drinking is risky. "But wait," you may ask, "isn't alcohol supposed to be healthy?" Perhaps you heard that moderate drinking can protect you against cardiovascular disease. Well, I hate to be the bearer of bad news. Contrary to popular opinion, moderate drinking is not as heart healthy as many people want to think it is.

The legal limit for the amount of alcohol in the bloodstream while operating a moving vehicle was historically established and has been progressively declining over time, because even small amounts of alcohol can significantly affect our reaction time. Despite the fact that some people are convinced they are not impaired, research has reliably shown otherwise when there is alcohol in our system. More than one drink can weaken our reaction time, coordination, fine motor skills, vision, comprehension, and concentration. Since alcohol is a depressant and slows down and disrupts the normal processes in our brains, our natural ability to react will be slower in all these areas, no matter what our perception of ourselves may be. Driving under the influence is dangerous, and drivers with high blood alcohol content or concentration (BAC) are at a significantly increased threat of motor vehicle accidents, injuries, and death.

It is a myth that coffee or showers help to "sober" someone up. If you bathe and give coffee to someone who is drunk, all you get is a clean, wet, and more awake drunken person. In addition, if there are other drugs in the system, the impairment and risk can be particularly dangerous. The unfortunate truth is that every case of injury and death due to alcohol and other drugs is unnecessary and preventable. We can do a better job of preventing alcohol and other drug-related injuries and fatalities. Quite frankly, although we have made progress, driving under the influence persists as a grave public health issue.

Driving under the influence is a difficult problem to eradicate. Specifically designated DWI or DUI courts can be effective tools in reducing the crime of driving while intoxicated by mandating education and treatment—in many cases, treating the underlying disease of addiction. Placing devices on cars that require blowing into a straw to detect alcohol before the car can be started also is effective at decreasing drunk driving accidents, and can assist in the treatment and recovery process. Simple incarceration does little to deter DUIs, although punishment remains wildly popular. Moreover, the era of Prohibition clearly demonstrated that the dramatic legal measure of making alcohol illegal was futile. The Constitution was amended twice over the issue of alcohol. Prohibition was a failed attempt at a war on the drug alcohol: the United States saw more crime, more deaths from bathtub gin, and the emergence of the joke that, when Prohibition was repealed, it was harder to get alcohol on Sundays. The fact is that people will use mind-altering substances, and alcohol reigns supreme as our mind-altering drug of choice.

Prohibition was a curious time in our history. The temperance movement should have been called the intolerance movement, as they were not seeking temperate drinking but were after total elimination of it altogether. And they won. Or did they? Prohibition highlights several important points about drugs. First, "wars" on drugs do not work. We continue to spend billions of dollars without making significant enough strides at accomplishing the goals of this war. Our current war on drugs is mostly a waste of time and resources; at least we had the hindsight to repeal Prohibition.

Today, drug cartel violence on the US-Mexico border is out of control and consistently deadly. Innocent civilians, including children, are regular casualties of the lucrative drug trade. Despite the drug laws and threats of serious legal consequences, millions of people continue to use drugs, which are widespread and available. During Prohibition, crime syndicates were that era's drug cartels that supplied an eager population with the contraband substance. The big bosses in these syndicates paid off police and routinely waged war with rival gangs. Violence was completely out of control then as well. Millions of people continued to illegally drink alcohol anyway. Law-enforcement spending was through the roof, much as it is today, and public outcry finally put an end to Prohibition in 1933, when the Eighteenth Amendment to the US Constitution was repealed. Sadly, the war on drugs today, with its various laws, policies, and realities, has many, many similarities to the corruption, crime, and death that existed during the era of Prohibition.

Barbiturates

Barbiturates are in the same class of drugs as alcohol: sedative/hypnotics. Like ethanol, barbiturates cause depressive effects on the central nervous system, and in moderate amounts cause an alcohol-like state of intoxication. For this reason, they have been used to induce sleep and reduce stress. The Bayer lab created the first ones in the 1860s, and in 1903 "barbital" was the first of the barbiturates to be used in the field of medicine. Since then over 2,000 different barbiturates have been synthesized, only fifty of which were available and marketed for human consumption. In 1912, a common barbiturate, phenobarbital, was introduced, and it is still used today, although only a few of the original barbiturates are used anymore. The "truth serum" used by the CIA is a barbiturate called sodium pentothal. Barbiturates are also responsible for taking Jimi Hendrix from us, as he died of a barbiturate overdose.

Barbiturates can produce pronounced effects on the brain because they are easily soluble in fat and can cross into the brain without difficulty. One problem with drugs like barbiturates that are fat-soluble is that they can accumulate in the body's fat stores and enter the bloodstream at unpredictable rates and amounts. As sedatives, barbiturates depress or slow down the brain and nervous system. It is thought that the mechanism of action is twofold. One is through decreasing the flow of sodium ions through channels on nerve membranes. This, in turn, slows down and can even totally block the messages, or action potentials, that travel down neurons in the nervous system. The second is by binding to GABA, the sedating neurotransmitter, and increasing the flow of chloride ions through channels on nerve membranes. This produces the same result in slowing down the nervous system. At low doses, the slowing down of the nervous system can decrease anxiety, heart rate, breathing rate, and blood pressure. With higher amounts, barbiturates can have a paradoxical effect by acting like a stimulant and increasing anxiety or agitation. But with escalating amounts, involuntary muscle reactions stop; people stop breathing and can be put into a coma and can die.

Today, barbiturates have fallen out of favor because a new group of sedative-hypnotics, the benzodiazepines, are preferred due to their comparative safety. In some cases, seizure disorders, alcohol withdrawal, and headaches are still treated with barbiturates. The small list of commonly used barbiturates today includes phenobarbital, pentobarbital, amobarbital, and secobarbital.

Like all drugs of abuse, barbiturates can cause tolerance, physical dependence, and withdrawal upon discontinuation. Withdrawal from barbiturates is similar to withdrawal from alcohol and other sedatives. People can experience profuse sweating, insomnia, severe anxiety, nausea, headaches, vomiting, seizures, hallucinations, and even death.

Benzodiazepines

Benzodiazepines, like alcohol and barbiturates, are sedative-hypnotics. These drugs were discovered in the 1930s by Leo Sternbach at Hoffman-La Roche laboratories and quickly became one of the most prescribed classes of medications. Since their discovery, benzodiazepines have been used for myriad conditions including alcohol withdrawal, involuntary movement disorders, muscle spasms, anxiety, seizures, insomnia, and night terrors, as well as for anesthesia.

As noted above, benzodiazepines are safer than barbiturates, and so have mostly supplanted them in medical applications. It is true that large doses of benzodiazepines are rarely fatal, unlike with barbiturates, but they have significant potential for abuse, are highly addictive, and can cause dreadful and potentially fatal withdrawals. Though benzodiazepines were initially marketed as safer *and* less addictive than barbiturates, the latter is unfortunately not true. Benzodiazepines account for approximately 30 percent of all prescriptions for controlled substances, and benzodiazepine addiction is very common, especially among young addicts.

Librium was the first "benzo" produced, followed by Valium, Xanax, and others. There are over a dozen different types of benzodiazepines available on the market today. The most common are Valium (diazepam), Xanax (alprazolam), Ativan (lorazepam), Restoril (temazepam), Versed (midazolam), Klonipin (clonazepam), and Librium (chlordiazepoxide). Xanax is a strong, short-acting agent that has become an increasingly abused drug among young people.[88]

Benzodiazepines are sedatives that slow down the brain and nervous system. This is accomplished by their binding to the GABA receptor. GABA is the primary inhibitory neurotransmitter in our bodies. GABA can be thought of as a chemical brake because it is responsible for slowing things down. When benzodiazepines bind to the GABA receptor, more GABA binds to it and so more inhibition or slowing of nerve impulses occurs. This happens because GABA facilitates more chloride entering the nerve cell and causes an overall increase in inhibition. This dampening effect, in turn, slows down and can even totally block the messages, or action potentials, that travel down neurons in the nervous system. This produces an overall slowing down of the nervous system, which can decrease anxiety and agitation and involuntary movements, decrease the chance of seizures, and slow down muscle twitching.

Benzodiazepines are divided into long- and short-acting agents. Short-acting agents are cleared from the body quickly, and the long-acting agents take more time. Benzodiazepines can be helpful with select indications, but they are generally indicated for only short-term use due to their side effects as well as their potential for abuse and dependency. Benzodiazepines can decrease anxiety, decrease muscle tension, decrease consciousness, and produce a generally relaxed state.

Unfortunately, too many people are prescribed too many benzodiazepines for too long a time period. Long-term use of benzodiazepines can actually aggravate anxiety, insomnia, and depression. Side effects also include sedation, drowsiness, fatigue, impaired coordination and thinking, visual changes, and slurred speech. These effects are compounded when mixed with alcohol and other drugs. Also, benzodiazepines are notorious for producing amnesia while the user is under their influence, so no new memories are formed, a phenomenon known as retrograde amnesia. Benzodiazepines can also cause blackouts, just like alcohol. Furthermore, too much benzodiazepine can even cause someone to stop breathing, and cause coma and death.

Like all drugs of abuse, benzodiazepines can cause tolerance, physical and psychological dependence, and withdrawal symptoms upon discontinuation. Benzodiazepines are most often abused with other drugs. In fact, benzodiazepine use among alcoholics and methadone-maintenance patients is higher than among the general population. Benzodiazepines are unique in that tolerance to the hypnotic effects seems to occur at a faster rate than tolerance to the antianxiety effects. Dependence occurs at a rate in proportion to the strength of the drug. Xanax, for example, is very strong and short acting, so physical dependence develops quite rapidly. Psychological dependence is particularly challenging to address in those who initially take these medications for anxiety because their self-confidence is already negatively skewed.

Withdrawing from benzodiazepines can be especially dangerous. Acute withdrawal from benzodiazepines is very similar to withdrawal from alcohol and other sedatives. People can experience severe anxiety, insomnia, nausea, depression, sensory hypersensitivity, muscle spasms, tinnitus, seizures, hallucinations, and delirium tremens. Benzodiazepines can have particularly troubling and prolonged withdrawal courses. Enduring depression, anxiety, and/or insomnia for weeks can be extremely frustrating and lead to feelings of hopelessness and despair. However, with the proper amount of medical management, engagement, and support, this too can be overcome.

Amphetamines

Amphetamine is a stimulant drug that was first synthesized by a German pharmacologist in 1887. A natural derivative, but not a precursor, has been around for centuries, as healers in China have been using ephedra from the ma huang plant to treat asthma. Later, ephedrine, a stimulant drug, was available beginning in 1920 to treat asthma. Amphetamines were first brought to market in Germany as a lung decongestant known as the Benzedrine inhaler. Soon thereafter, people discovered how to abuse the medication. Amphetamines quickly became the most abused prescription drug in the United States. In the United States, amphetamines were limited to prescription use in 1965, and in 1971 they became very highly monitored and controlled. Prior to that time, physicians believed that amphetamines were safe and effective in nearly forty medical indications and had liberally prescribed them.

Amphetamines are used to "rev up" the body with perceived boundless energy, to curb appetite, to help truck drivers and other workers stay up for days, and to feel euphoria. Its medical therapeutic properties allow it to be used under proper guidance for asthma, sleep disorders, brain injury, very short-term weight loss, and attention and hyperactivity disorders.

Historically, both sides during World War II gave their soldiers and pilots amphetamines to increase alertness and aggression, and to stave off fatigue. Experts agree that Elvis Presley was introduced to amphetamines while he served in the armed forces and continued using them (along with other substances) for the rest of his life. Kamikaze pilots used methamphetamines to increase motivation and acumen for their suicidal bombing missions. Hitler is believed to have been injected with methamphetamine five times daily, and it is generally accepted that Hitler suffered from an amphetamine-induced psychotic state toward the end of the war.

The public and social influences of amphetamines have been rather widespread. Several famous authors, musicians, mathematicians, and other professionals report that the use of amphetamines inspired them to produce their works and pieces and discoveries. Frequently, users claim to have enhanced creative thinking while using amphetamines.

It has been suggested that amphetamines have been one of the most widely abused classes of drugs in professional sports due to their attention-focusing and stimulating effects. Users' perception of their energy level is increased so that they believe they can play harder and longer, but these effects have not been consistently demonstrated in clinical research. Even for highly tuned athletes, the risk of using powerful stimulants during physical exercise can be very dangerous and even fatal. For example, the professional British cyclist Tommy Simpson collapsed and died at the Tour de France while using amphetamines in 1967. As a consequence, in 1968 the International Olympic Committee published its first list of banned substances. Major League Baseball banned amphetamines only as recently as 1996, but the drug still does not carry as significant a consequence for use as do other banned substances.

Amphetamines consist of MDMA (ecstasy), methamphetamine, and the N-methylated form. Ephedrine and pseudoephedrine are chemical precursors and may be found in over-the-counter (OTC) decongestant medications.

Since certain OTC products are used in the production of methamphetamine, increasingly states have implemented monitoring mechanisms and placed restrictions on the quantities that individuals can purchase. However, these constraints are far from foolproof. Moreover, meth manufacturing has begun to shift from US-based laboratories, often in rural areas, to superfactories located in Mexico and Canada.

Amphetamines are stimulants of both the central and peripheral nervous systems. The main action of amphetamines is to increase the synaptic activity of dopamine, but it affects the norepinephrine and serotonin neurotransmitter systems as well. Amphetamines cause an enormous release of dopamine from axon terminals, prevent the breakdown and recycling of this released dopamine, and prevent dopamine from being stored within the neurons. As a result, more of the rewarding dopamine floods the pleasure center of the brain, giving the user an intense feeling of euphoria. The release of dopamine in the pleasure center is more than five times that of the release experienced with orgasm, so it can quickly and powerfully grab the attention of our midbrain. The enormous amount of dopamine released is also toxic to the neurons, creating further dysfunction as the neurons stop working as efficiently. Tolerance to this class of drug develops so rapidly that the user must escalate the amounts used from the onset.

Because of their powerful and targeted properties, amphetamines activate the disease of addiction especially quickly. With alcohol, for example, the typical addict may have years of use before addiction becomes present. With amphetamines, the transition from experimentation to addiction is very rapid, and often happens in mere days to weeks. Amphetamines also are not usually used "safely" for years the way alcohol and other drugs may be. Instead, users often experience an ultrarapid and destructive course of addiction.

Prescription amphetamines include a group of medications commonly used for weight loss and to treat attention-deficit disorder (ADD) and attention deficit hyperactivity disorder (ADHD) in children and adults. Amphetamine medications are also used to treat symptoms of traumatic brain injury, the daytime drowsiness symptoms of narcolepsy, and treatment-resistant depression, as well as for short-term weight control. Brand names of the drugs that contain amphetamine include Adderall, Vyvanse, and Dexedrine. Methylphenidate (Ritalin, Concerta, Metadate, and Methylin) is also used to treat ADHD and similar indications and is structurally akin to amphetamines, yet it has a mechanism of action that is closer to cocaine, though it is weaker and longer acting. When these medications are utilized *properly*, they can have positive effects on concentration and impulse control. An underreported and alarming trend today can be seen in students at all grade levels who do not have a diagnosis of ADHD but who use and abuse amphetamines as a study and test-taking aid.

The ADD/ADHD medications can actually slightly increase test scores, so they have become very popular. I have personally witnessed an alarming trend among graduate students, many of whom take prescription amphetamines because of their effects of helping them study for longer periods of time and increasing test scores. Most of these graduate students do not need them and do not have a diagnosis of ADD or ADHD, but, as with performance-enhancing drugs in sports, when the competition is using them, the pressure to also use them is great.

Again, there are significant adverse physical side effects to amphetamines. Prescription amphetamines are not interpreted by the body as being safer. After all, they are amphetamines, too, and may cause reduced appetite, flushing, constipation, blurred vision, impaired speech, restlessness, dry mouth and skin, erectile dysfunction, rapid heartbeat, abnormal heart rhythm, increased breathing rate, increased/distorted sensations, hyperactivity, dilated pupils, increased blood pressure, fever, sweating, diarrhea, dizziness, uncontrollable movements or shaking, insomnia, numbness, and sudden (cardiac) death.

Such physical complications make using these drugs for a few extra points on a test risky business.

There are also many adverse psychological effects of amphetamines. Though a complete laundry list is beyond the scope of this book, commonly users will experience anxiety, insomnia, increased aggression, perception of increased energy, emotional instability, and even psychosis. Amphetamine psychosis most often occurs only with large doses, but it can also be an unfortunate result in children when they take even therapeutic doses for the treatment of ADHD.

While amphetamines can help focus attention and increase productivity under the right conditions, they can also lead to paranoia and hallucinations. Tolerance develops rapidly in amphetamine abuse, so users must increase the amount of drug needed to achieve the desired effect more quickly than with other drugs. Typically, users will have to escalate the amounts they use and may not sleep for days, compounding the problem. Amphetamine withdrawal can include agitation, extreme fatigue, suicidal thoughts, hypersomnia (excessive sleepiness), and hyperphagia (abnormally increased appetite). Amphetamines can also increase the risk of having a heart attack in every age group and state of health.

Cocaine

Cocaine is a powerful stimulant drug isolated from the leaves of the coca plant. Native South Americans have used coca leaves for thousands of years by either chewing or brewing them in order to stave off fatigue, hunger, and altitude sickness. They would take coca breaks in the same way we take coffee or cigarette breaks today. In its original form, the coca leaf is not dangerous. However, the same cannot be said of cocaine.

Albert Neiman, a German chemist, isolated cocaine from the coca leaf in 1860. He found that he could isolate cocaine by crystallizing the tropane derivative of coca through a process known as alkalization. It is a six-step process that starts with the coca leaf and ends with white crystalline cocaine powder. Cocaine works in the pleasure center of the brain, increasing mostly dopamine but also norepinephrine and serotonin. The effects are quite pronounced, as the surge in dopamine can easily be double the amount released during an orgasm.

Cocaine can cause a lot of pleasurable feelings, to be sure, yet it is highly addictive and dangerous. Its use is widespread throughout all socioeconomic and demographic levels regardless of gender, race, age, economic or social status, political or religious affiliation, or livelihood. In fact, cocaine is the second most popularly used illicit "recreational" drug (marijuana is number one). Tons of cocaine enters the United States every year, fueled by the demand of nearly two million addicts who perpetuate the trade of a drug that sells for nearly $200,000 per kilogram.

Cocaine has an interesting and colorful history. Native South Americans introduced Spanish explorers to chewing on coca leaves for their medicinal properties. Later, in the sixteenth century, the first actual medical writing on the subject was published. In the 1880s, the pharmaceutical giants Merck and Parke-Davis began marketing cocaine. Also in the 1880s, Angelo Mariani made a therapeutic tonic with alcohol and cocaine that became enormously popular and successful, and in the process also made himself a fortune. Other entrepreneurs would mimic Mariani's success by making tonics of their own. In fact, many medicinal potions sold as cure-alls during this era contained large amounts of alcohol and cocaine. These tonics were actually touted to cure alcoholism, opium and morphine addiction, colic, headaches, rheumatism, and everything else under the sun. Although unfamiliar with cocaine in its raw form, Americans ravenously consumed large amounts of these tonics. Cocaine was also available in cigarettes, candies, gums, and powders, and was easily obtained for intravenous injection. It was thought that cocaine could replace food and transform cowardice into bravery.

Many war veterans who were abusing alcohol and morphine were offered cocaine-laden tonics as treatments for their other forms of addiction. This practice of using cocaine therapeutically was brought to the attention of an Austrian physician, Sigmund Freud, who subsequently believed cocaine could literally cure nearly every affliction people faced. If one of his patients presented with symptoms of depression or neurosis, he would give them cocaine in his office. He would also use it himself, and quite often. Unfortunately for him and his patients, frequent use merely led to addiction and did not cure anything. Believing that cocaine made people more "normal," he published a landmark article venerating cocaine that would later be exposed as dangerously false, and it devastated his career until he changed his views and stopped using it himself.

A morphine-addicted pharmacist, Dr. John Pemberton, would launch the single most successful commercial product in the history of the world by using cocaine. Mr. Pemberton invented a nonalcoholic health tonic with cocaine that was aimed at treating his morphine addiction. His invention was Coca-Cola, and it had 60 milligrams of cocaine per serving. During Prohibition, this "temperance drink" capitalized on antialcohol sentiment. Unfortunately for the unsuspecting hordes, this temperance replacement would be just as bad as alcohol or worse. The cocaine was later removed from the tonic early in the twentieth century. It was Asa Candler, who bought the formula for Coca-Cola from inventor John Pemberton for $2,300, who actually made the drink wildly successful. By the late 1890s, Coca-Cola was one of America's most popular fountain drinks, due to Candler's aggressive marketing tactics. Asa Candler increased sales of Coca-Cola by over 4,000 percent between 1890 and 1900. Worldwide today, Coca-Cola is the single most recognized brand of any commercial product.

Cocaine was not even illegal until 1914 when the Harrison Narcotics Tax Act was passed. Despite the fact that it is illegal, it continues to be manufactured and distributed on an enormous scale due to its popularity and incredibly large profit margin. In its powder form, cocaine is frequently diluted in order to stretch the sellers' profits. This is called "cutting," and frequently impurities like anesthetics, other stimulants, baking soda, and sugars are added. In the early to mid-1980s, when the *crack* cocaine epidemic seemed to explode across the country almost overnight, users discovered on a large scale how much more powerful cocaine's acute effects are when it is smoked in its purer freebase form.

Cocaine can be ingested in several ways. It is snorted, smoked, or injected. The most common route of ingestion is snorting. About half of the drug is absorbed through the nasal mucous membranes. Over time, snorting cocaine can lead to a runny or bloody nose, loss of the sense of smell, infections, and a perforated nasal septum. Smoking cocaine is a rapid way to ingest it, as the drug reaches the brain quickly, usually within five seconds. The effects are shorter, though, lasting only minutes. Smoking crack can cause extensive lung damage that is known on the street as "crack lung." Symptoms of crack lung include fever, cough, difficulty breathing, and severe chest pain. Finally, injection delivers the highest serum concentrations of cocaine. The risks inherent in injecting drugs include spreading HIV, hepatitis, and myriad other infections; deep vein thrombosis; and pulmonary embolism.

After cocaine is ingested, it travels throughout the body and crosses quite easily into the brain, where it exerts its pleasurable effects. The liver is responsible for metabolizing cocaine. The main mechanism of action for cocaine occurs through blocking the reuptake of dopamine in the pleasure center. Cocaine tightly binds to the dopamine transporter on the presynaptic neuron and prevents it from recycling the dopamine. In this way, huge amounts of dopamine are left to bathe the synapses of the pleasure center. As more dopamine becomes available in the synaptic cleft, more dopamine binds to the postsynaptic receptors. Many users report that cocaine's effects are more pleasurable than an intense orgasm. Secondary mechanisms of action include elevating serotonin and norepinephrine neurotransmitters by preventing their breakdown as well. Cocaine exerts its effects as a powerful central nervous system stimulant rapidly, and these effects can last from a few minutes to a few hours. The vast majority of users do not experience its acute effects for more that forty-five minutes, however. Its acute effects include euphoria, excitement, hyperactivity, restlessness, increased heart rate, and increased blood pressure.

Chronic cocaine use depletes the brain's available supply of dopamine. This deficiency is believed to be responsible for the depression, irritability, and fatigue often experienced in users after prolonged use. Furthermore, the memory of the intense pleasure followed by the dysphoria of withdrawal and the negative emotional states associated with the drug's absence fuels the MDS to assign a high degree of importance to getting more cocaine. This is called *sensitization,* and, although it is not unique to cocaine, it happens rapidly with this particular substance. Cocaine's negative psychological consequences are not limited to depression, irritability, and fatigue. Many people also experience anger, restlessness, severe mood problems, hallucinations, and especially paranoia. In that vein, one of my patients reported that cocaine can cause the police to hide in your air vents.

Unlike withdrawal from alcohol and other sedatives, physical withdrawal from cocaine is not dangerous. Typically, when chronic users stop using cocaine, they "crash." Specifically, they feel anxious, irritable, depressed, hungry, lethargic, and dysphoric. However, cocaine use is extremely dangerous. Its physical consequences can include heart, heartbeat, and circulatory abnormalities that can be fatal. It also increases the chances of having a stroke. Cocaine causes an increase in the basal body temperature, and that, coupled with muscle contraction and blood vessel constriction, may lead to other fatal complications like hyperthermia (dangerously elevated body temperatures) and myoglobinuria, which leads to kidney failure. Cocaine use is not uncommonly fatal. Comedians Chris Farley and Jon Belushi and world-class athletes Ken Caminiti and Len Bias died as a result of cocaine overdoses.

Ecstasy

Ecstasy, or MDMA, is a drug with an interesting past and "dual citizenship." Ecstasy is a stimulant and a hallucinogen—related to mescaline in its psychedelic composite—that at one time was given to patients in psychotherapy until it became illegal to do so in 1985. Because it produces a great many effects, ecstasy is categorized as a psychedelic, a stimulant, and an *empathogen*—a substance that creates empathy and connectedness toward others. Ecstasy is unique in its capacity to generate a sense of intimacy with others and diminished ego for the user.

Merck initially developed ecstasy in 1912; it was passed to the Allies among other spoils of World War I from the Germans. Ecstasy was ignored for the most part until studies performed by the US government in the 1950s through the 1970s piqued the interest of a few psychotherapists. Due to the empathic effects, some researchers and clinicians suggested it might have therapeutic benefits in certain individuals.

Prior to becoming regulated as a drug with no medical value, ecstasy was actually used in couples and individual psychotherapy. It was also used to help treat clinical depression, as well as anxiety disorders. Early reports reflected the belief that ecstasy could reduce patients' defensiveness and increase communication and insight. Subjective reports also indicated an awakening of, and/or an increase in, the experience of empathy for others. However, research has failed to demonstrate convincing therapeutic benefits in the face of a growing amount of data pointing to the detrimental effects of ecstasy. Eventually, it was blacklisted by the Drug Enforcement Administration and currently is categorized as having no medical usefulness.

Ecstasy became readily available for recreational use in 1977, and the speed with which it caught on among users outside the psychotherapeutic realm was responsible for its regulation. Dallas and Austin, Texas, were two of the first cities where one could buy ecstasy over the counter at nightclubs and bars, and ecstasy would often bring in more sales than alcohol. Widespread use led to an increasing number of overdoses, deaths, and other major negative consequences until it became controlled in 1985. It has continued to be extremely popular in the United States and worldwide despite the fact that it became illegal soon after its introduction to the world's drug-using markets. In addition to claiming a popular spot in mainstream culture, it remains an integral part of the "rave" and other dance subculture scenes.

Ecstasy is usually swallowed in tablet form, although it has been known to be inhaled and even injected. Following ingestion, it travels to the brain where it acts mainly on the serotonin transporter system, causing the nerve cells to release their stores of that neurotransmitter and greatly increasing its amounts in the pleasure center. Ecstasy does not act on the serotonin system alone, however. It also increases the amount of dopamine. Together, serotonin and dopamine are responsible for making the user feel expansively good. However, when neurons release and are exposed to an overload of neurotransmitters, they can degenerate to the point where any major brain functions such as mood regulation and memory can become dysfunctional.

The onset of action is around forty-five minutes after oral ingestion and peaks at ninety to 120 minutes. Generally, users experience stimulation, hyperactivity, arousal, mood enhancement and euphoria, heightened empathy and inner peace, lessened fear and insecurity, and an amplification of sensations. On the other hand, users also experience a great many adverse effects, including jaw clenching and teeth grinding, extreme sweating, urinary retention, anxiety, paranoia, overheating, muscle tremors, rapid eye movements, elevated blood pressure and heart rate, insomnia, anorexia, memory impairment, blurred vision, and sexual dysfunction.

Users may feel too good to notice that they are overheated, dehydrated, exhausted, and perilously close to death. Chronic use has been shown in animal studies to cause neuronal damage. Human brain scans and cognitive tests suggest that the same effect happens in people, too. Chronic users report some fairly consistent long-term effects including suicidal thoughts, depression, memory disturbances, anxiety, irritability, agitation, and depression. A number of fatalities occur every year due to ecstasy when users experience the elevated body temperatures and dehydration that lead to either a heart attack or other major organ failure.

Caffeine

Caffeine is not a drug of abuse, but as one of the world's oldest known drugs and as its most popular stimulant, it deserves some attention here. Caffeine is delivered through the oral consumption of liquids, foods, and drugs. It is found in coffee, tea, sodas, energy drinks, drugs, cocoa, chocolate, and now even gum. Coffee is of course the most popular vehicle for caffeine, and today Americans ingest nearly forty-five million pounds of caffeine a year. More than 80 percent of Americans routinely ingest caffeine, mostly through coffee and sodas. While coffee drinkers account for the ingestion of over 350 mg daily, those who do not drink coffee still consume over 100 mg of caffeine daily.

Most sources credit coffee's discovery to an Egyptian herdsman named Kaldi who noticed that his goats became especially animated and lively after eating some red berries. Kaldi noted that they were dancing extravagantly and without reserve, so naturally he wondered if he could enjoy the same effect. As legend has it, he ate those berries and joined in the goat dance. The berries are bitter and eating them directly has never caught on, but coffee did become wildly popular over time. In short, that was because the monks at the nearby monastery perfected the roasting and brewing process of coffee, and their mastery spawned another one of the world's most enchanted beverages. Monks are apparently adept brewers of more than alcohol.

The caffeine found in food, drinks, and drugs varies widely. A small (5 oz) cup of coffee can contain anywhere from 65 to 150 mg. Even a cup of "decaf" coffee can have 5 mg. A small cup of tea can have around 65 mg of caffeine, and a small cup of cocoa or chocolate milk can have 6 mg. Sodas usually have around 30 mg of caffeine, while diet drinks can have twice that much, and the currently popular energy drinks have triple that amount! Chocolate-containing candy bars can have 10 mg of caffeine, while coffee-flavored yogurts and ice creams can have from 50 to 100 mg. Stay-awake medications carry up to 200 mg of caffeine, while the headache medicinal mixtures usually have around 30 mg.

Caffeine is a stimulant of the xanthine class. Caffeine is extracted from coffee beans, tea leaves, cacao pods, and kola nuts. In its raw state, caffeine is bitter and has no odor. By inhibiting another xanthine known as adenosine, caffeine produces its stimulation effects. When consumed in a beverage, caffeine enters the bloodstream and produces its effects rather quickly. It has a moderate range of action in that it sticks around the body for about six hours. Caffeine does cause physical dependence, because withdrawal symptoms like headaches and fatigue are experienced when someone suddenly discontinues its use.

Caffeine has several physiologic effects. It increases awareness and heart rate. In addition, caffeine can help relax the airways and allow some muscles to contract effortlessly. On the other hand, caffeine has negative side effects also, including headaches, anxiety, insomnia, and dizziness. Finally, it is possible to overdose on caffeine. In very large doses, caffeine can be lethal. One would have to ingest the equivalent of 100 cups of coffee very quickly, but stranger things have happened.

Opioids/Opiates

These are the painkillers and comprise the class of drugs and medications that fit on our opioid receptors. There are quite a few different types of opioid receptors, including the kappa, delta, and mu receptors. We have these receptors in the first place because our brains make our own opiates, known as endorphins. Endorphins are released naturally when we laugh, engage in pleasurable activities, or are in pain or under stress. Endorphins are also involved with hormones, respiration, nausea, and vomiting. Opioids that fit on our endorphin receptors vary widely in potency, but most often are stronger and longer lasting than those that we produce naturally. The result is that many people find them highly pleasurable and stimulating.

Opioids are ingested in three main ways: swallowed, smoked, or injected. Once ingested, they activate opioid receptors that are extensively spread throughout the nervous system in our body and brain. Opioids appear similar to our own endorphins, and once attached to the same receptors, produce pleasure and modulate pain.

As indicated by the title of this section, there are two closely related groups of pain-relieving, euphoria-producing drugs in this class: opiates and opioids. But the majority of these drugs, including those used for medical purposes, are actually opioids. There are only five opiates, directly derived from the opium poppy plant, *Papaver somniferum*: opium, codeine, thebaine, papaverine, and morphine. Codeine, morphine, and heroin are the most prevalent of the opiates. Opioids are synthetic or semisynthetic compounds derived from the naturally occurring opiates, and include methadone, oxycodone (Percocet, Oxycontin), hydrocodone (Vicodin, Lortab, Norco), fentanyl (Duragesic, Actiq), hydromorphone (Dilaudid), meperidine (Demerol), and buprenorphine (Subutex, Suboxone). Importantly, *opioid* or *opiate* is a distinction without a substantial difference from the standpoint of understanding these substances.

Although heroin is the most ill-reputed illegal drug in this class of substances, most opiates are available legally—prescribed by physicians as painkillers.

Found in Central and South America, Southeast Asia, and the Middle East, the opium poppy is a significant cash crop on the world market. Historically, the harvesting of opium by humans is thousands of years old. Opium was initially thought to be magical, "a gift from the gods," and was referred to as the "joy plant." Long ago opium was consumed by the Mesopotamians as poppy sap or baked into poppy cakes and eaten to enhance the pleasure of sex. First cultivated in Lower Mesopotamia in 3400 BC, it later spread to the ancient empires of Egypt, Greece, Rome, and China. Opium was used by the armies of Alexander the Great, whose soldiers could march longer and sleep better while under its influence. Trade routes made opium available in Europe. In fact, Queen Isabella of Spain was hoping Christopher Columbus could find a trade route to India to bring back, among other things, more opium. England waged and won a war against China in 1839 over the highly lucrative Oriental opium trade rights.

For centuries, opium was used medicinally as the only tool that could provide adequate pain relief during highly dangerous, essentially barbaric medical procedures that included amputations with saws and other crude blades. Thus, it was also known as the "flower of mercy." Opium would know many beneficent nicknames, but its widespread use beyond the battlefields would earn it more nefarious mottos. Hippocrates, the father of medicine who lived 2,500 years ago, dismissed the opium poppy's magical attributes, but did recognize its use as a painkiller. In AD 150, the famous Greek philosopher-physician Galen warned the world of the addictive properties and agonizing withdrawal symptoms that follow intemperate use of opium, evidence that knowledge of opiates' dangers is thousands of years old.

It was a seventeenth-century English physician, Thomas Sydenham, who is credited with introducing opium's medicinal properties to the field of medicine.

The first significant use of opiates in the United States occurred during the Civil War. Injured soldiers were given morphine for pain, often to moderate the pain of amputations and fatal wounds. Prior to morphine, soldiers' limbs were amputated while they were fully conscious with saws, butcher knives, or wire while several men helped to pin the poor soldier down. Without antibiotics, anesthesia, or other modern medical tools, morphine was the only relief soldiers would get from wounds inflicted during the ravages of war, and was therefore also known as "God's own medicine." Numerous soldiers were exposed to and continued using opiates, so in time many veterans became addicts. Subsequently, opiate addiction also became known as the "army disease."

Later in the United States and before regulatory control, countless potions and remedies were sold as cure-alls that contained laudanum, an opiate concoction. Some potions were up to 50 percent morphine, and so delivered on their promise to make the customer feel better. Many Americans had laudanum in their medicine cabinets and often would give it to infants for colic and other ailments. Unfortunately, people did not yet appreciate the dangers inherent in opiates, and many infants (and adults) would die as a result of unintentional overdoses. In adults, laudanum was extensively used for dental disorders, headaches, fevers, insomnia, cough, pain, boredom, menstrual problems, and many, many other indications. The price that would result from such liberal use of opiates was high, as more and more unsuspecting people became slaves to the drugs or died from overuse. In the early twentieth century, it is estimated that one out of every four hundred Americans was addicted to opium. Wyatt Earp's onetime companion, Mattie Blaylock, is one well-known historical figure who was addicted to laudanum.

Morphine, the most prevalent natural opiate, was first isolated by the German pharmacist Friedrich Wilhelm Sertürner in 1805 as a way to make opium more powerful. Like opium, it is a pain reliever, but it is ten times stronger than opium. Morphine, combined with the recently invented hypodermic needle, created an incredible drug epidemic in the United States. Originally, however, there were high hopes for Sertürner's discovery, as some thought morphine could cure alcoholism. Opiates are strong cough suppressants, and so Bayer marketed morphine as a nonaddictive cough suppressant in 1898. This seemed incredibly fortuitous because many people at the time were dying of tuberculosis and pneumonia, so many who stayed up all night with painful and relentless coughing spells were able to receive some desperately needed relief.

Because morphine made people sleepy or groggy, Sertürner named his discovery after Morpheus, the Greek god of dreams. Mythologically, Morpheus was the son of Hypnos, the god of sleep. Morpheus had two brothers, Icelus and Phantasus. In Greek mythology, dreams were sent out to man through one of two gates: a gate of horn from which true dreams came, and a gate of ivory from which passed dreams that were false. Icelus gave man dreams of birds and beasts. Phantasus gave man dreams of inanimate objects. Morpheus had the capacity to assume the form of any and every human being. His father Hypnos sent him out into the night to appear as a loved one in mortals' dreams. (This description makes it sound like the Greeks were already smoking opium.) Morphine is deadly as well. Sadly, Sertürner witnessed his wife die of an overdose of morphine and tried to warn others, but by that time it was too late.

Next to crack, one of the most vilified drugs is heroin. In 1874, a German chemist isolated heroin from morphine in the search for an even stronger painkiller. A stronger painkiller was indeed found, but it would ensnare many people in its forceful grip. Ironically, in addition to being marketed as a cough suppressant with minimal addictive properties, heroin was introduced to the market as a cure for morphine addiction! At the time, heroin was the strongest opiate ever produced, causing enormous physical dependence, negative global consequences, and horrific withdrawals. By the 1930s, heroin had supplanted morphine as the leading cause of hospital admissions for narcotic-associated conditions.

There has always been enough demand for heroin that attempts to control global poppy production have resulted in poppy fields closing in France and Turkey only to be opened in South America, the Golden Triangle in the Far East, and now the Middle East. Heroin use escalated in the 1970s as a result of the war in Vietnam, where heroin was readily available and cheap. Twenty percent of US soldiers there used heroin. Many soldiers became heroin addicts and brought their addiction stateside. President Nixon was deeply concerned about the spike not only in heroin use, but also in all drugs of abuse. Subsequently, he was the first president to implement mandatory drug testing of service members, and founded the Drug Enforcement Administration (DEA).

As described above, before heroin use became illegal and Nixon initiated the war on drugs, prescription opiate abuse was problematic in the United States. Again, there were many accidental overdoses as an unsuspecting public used opiates with impunity. Subsequently, opiates became highly regulated in the first half of the twentieth century, and many physicians were even arrested. Physicians, who used to freely prescribe opiates and even regularly administer morphine to patients out of their old-fashioned black leather physician house-call bags, were thus highly motivated to find alternative treatments. Prescription opiates were out of popular favor from the early 1920s for half a century. Opiates would see a resurgence in medicine as they again grew in popularity in the 1970s, when concerns over side effects and the potential for addiction were minimized when applied to the pain and suffering of cancer patients. It is important to note here that opiates can be safely prescribed by knowledgeable physicians for the treatment of pain and, when taken as prescribed, carry minimal risk. On the other hand, opiate abuse is an epidemic in the United States.

The recent high-profile deaths of celebrities such as Prince and Michael Jackson drew further attention to a national crisis exposed in a recent White

House study finding a 400 percent rise in prescription drug abuse between 1998 and 2008—400 percent! The national drug policy director at the time, Gil Kerlikowske, noted, "The spikes in prescription drug abuse rates captured by this study are dramatic, pervasive, and deeply disturbing." Hospital admissions, abuse, and deaths from prescription opioids have increased dramatically over the last decade.

Opioid abuse is easily the biggest curse of prescription practices. Many times these medications are overprescribed, leading to physical dependency, abuse, and addiction. People underestimate the dangers of taking any type of prescription medicine, falsely believing they are safer than illegal drugs. Many patients who eventually get referred my way became dependent on opioids during their course of treatment for a pain condition.

The most commonly abused prescription opioids are hydrocodone (Vicodin, Lortab), oxycodone (Percocet, Oxycontin), and methadone. Hydrocodone and oxycodone (though not Oxycontin, which is oxycodone in a high-dose, time-release formulation for serious pain conditions) are somewhat stronger synthetic replacements for codeine that do not have the same degree of side effects and so are preferred over codeine for mild to moderate pain.

Methadone, as will be described in greater detail in Chapter Nine, originated as a treatment for heroin addiction and is now used as part of an opioid-maintenance and harm-reduction treatment strategy. In addition, it has been increasingly used as a pain medicine in recent years. Like heroin, methadone is very powerful and long acting; for some addicts it is actually their drug of choice. Because Oxycontin is prescribed in extremely high doses due to its time-release capacity, its abuse quickly became widespread after it was introduced in 1996. People learned they could crush and snort or inject the pills to get a massive dose of opioid. This was such a serious problem that in 2010, Oxycontin's manufacturer reformulated the medication to prevent its abuse in these ways.

The use of opioids is so popular because they are powerful pain modulators. As discussed earlier, specialized neurons carry pain messages from the body to the spinal cord and up through other neurons to the brain. Opioids modulate pain by binding to receptors on these neurons and hindering the transmission of the pain signal. This blockading action of pain is known as *analgesia*. In the brain, opioids modulate pain via a different mechanism. Instead of blocking the pain signal in the brain, they bind to receptors in the brain and modulate the way in which pain is actually experienced. In addition to pain modulation, opioids produce another desirable effect: a euphoric high.

Initially when opioids are ingested, a brief charge is felt that corresponds with a strong release of dopamine in the limbic system. Following that initial sensation, the user enters into a sedated, relaxed state. Heroin users, for instance, will begin nodding off during the sedation phase, when they can essentially become semicatatonic. Opioids cause intense pleasure and major depression in the central nervous system. They can produce sedation, drowsiness, decreased coughing, nausea, and lowered body temperature. In higher doses, opiates can work directly in the brain stem to stop the breathing mechanism altogether, causing coma and death. Tolerance to the pleasurable effects of opiates motivates the user to ingest increasing amounts of the drug, but at higher doses opioids stop the breathing mechanism, and the user, who merely wanted to feel good, dies from an overdose.

Withdrawal from opioids is not life-threatening. However, the physical agony and psychological suffering are enormous. Withdrawal begins after the blood concentration falls. Users experience irritability, depression, runny nose, tearing eyes, yawning, body chills, goose bumps, sweating, stomach cramps, and diarrhea. The severity of these symptoms essentially keeps many people trapped in a vicious cycle whereby they live merely to not experience withdrawal. Once opioid addiction sets in, the pain of withdrawal keeps it going. No one dreams of one day becoming a heroin addict. It is especially ironic that prescription opioid addicts resort to using heroin as the cheapest and most accessible way to prevent the horrors of withdrawal.

Some addiction experts believe that there is a subgroup of opiate addicts who experience such intense craving and agony while attempting to achieve abstinence that they require long-term replacement opiate therapy—currently described as *medication-assisted treatment* and *medication-assisted recovery*—in order to live more normal lives. This position is supported, not surprisingly, by the pharmaceutical companies that manufacture these medications, and increasingly by some government policies.

I used to unabashedly disagree with this approach. For some the journey may be harder, but I do not believe the ultimate goal of abstinence is ever impossible. True, some recovering addicts experience incredible amounts of craving during their early stages of recovery. But craving is not the enemy, and learning to effectively manage it and other triggers without resorting to the use of mind-altering substances is a fundamental part of addiction treatment and essential to the process of recovery. Today, I don't argue this point (as much). While I still firmly believe and continue to experience it to be true that anyone can achieve abstinence in recovery, the fact is that the seemingly ever-escalating rate of opioid overdoses due to both prescription opioids and heroin is unacceptable and requires a variety of potential solutions.

There are no maintenance medications for alcohol, marijuana, cocaine, meth, or hallucinogens like there are for opiates. This also separates opiate treatment from the treatment of all other substances. When an addict of any variety relapses, we should not throw in the towel. Relapse alone is not a sufficient reason for opiate-maintenance therapy, but too many overdoses warrant more use of indicated medications to decrease not only misery and suffering but also avoidable fatalities. Maintenance is an appropriate option for some. In fact, based on observation, I cannot differentiate addicts who are working a recovery program on maintenance from those who are working a recovery program based on total abstinence, because the group on medication is neither sedated nor otherwise impaired in any way.

Opioid replacement medications can be effective tools, but they are best utilized as a bridge to help people make the transition from active addiction to abstinence-based recovery. Ongoing, long-term maintenance with these medications is such an easy option for both doctors and patients that it may be used too often, too easily, and for too long, depriving opiate addicts of a chance to experience the benefits of true abstinence. This is an issue that is likely to continue to create controversy in addiction treatment and recovery circles for the foreseeable future.

Inhalants

Inhalants are a class of substances in the gaseous state that can be ingested in order to achieve an altered state of consciousness. Their effects are most pronounced when absorbed through the lungs, so these chemicals are nearly always inhaled—hence, the name of the category. Most people may not be familiar with inhalants as drugs, but they are cheap and can be found anywhere. There are a great many different chemical compounds that can be inhaled and abused.

These chemicals are found in many of the most common household products used every day, such as deodorizers, pens, cleaning fluids, glue, hairspray, gasoline, computer duster, shoe polish, laughing gas, lighter fluid, paint, paint thinner, and nail polish. Inhaling is also known as "huffing," and those who huff are affectionately known as "huffers." Of especially great concern is that the largest at-risk age groups for abusing inhalants are children and adolescents, because inhalants are cheap, can be easily found at home or in school, and can be purchased easily and cheaply over the counter. In recent years, computer duster has become an increasingly popular abused inhalant across all age groups.

Inhalants are ingested by sniffing through the nose, or breathing in through the mouth, the vapor fumes of the chemical from a container, bag, balloon, aerosol spray can, or soaked rag. The gaseous vapors are inhaled and quickly get absorbed through the lungs. The chemicals coat the inside of the lungs and prevent oxygen from entering the body. They then get pumped through the heart to the brain and the entire body, where they produce their intoxicating effects. The intoxication produced by inhalants, however, is of very short duration—only a few minutes, at most. The mechanism of action is mainly as a nervous system depressant, but inhalants can affect the brain and body in many ways.

Nitrous oxide, or laughing gas, is the first well-known inhalant. It was first produced in 1772, but was not inhaled until 1779. Thomas Beddoes, an English chemist, opened the "Pneumatic Institute" and offered the public nitrous oxide as the "gas of paradise." Nearly fifty years later, nitrous oxide found its way into America's popular culture, where its use became a kind of public amusement. Interestingly, one night a man who paid twenty-five cents for a shot of nitrous oxide fell and sustained a deep laceration in his leg without feeling any pain. This was witnessed by a dentist, Horace Wells, and the dental and anesthetic application of the gas was born. Thereafter, nitrous oxide was used in tooth extractions, surgery, and childbirth. Its surgical and obstetric applications have since disappeared due to side effects. Users abuse this drug for its mirth-inducing, hallucinogenic, and painkilling properties. Currently, we do not fully understand nitrous oxide's mechanism of action. Due to its availability, dentists are the largest group of chronic abusers.

Users of inhalants experience dizziness, euphoria, confusion, sedation, slurred speech, lack of coordination, nausea, vomiting, and hallucinations. Inhalants can be fatal when users accidentally aspirate contents of the stomach into their lungs, suffocate, or experience heart failure. Over time, chronic use of inhalants is detrimental to the mind and body, as users can experience brain damage through the destruction of neurons, mood disturbances, memory and learning problems, lack of fine and gross motor coordination, visual disturbances, heart damage, lung damage, bone marrow damage, and kidney failure.

Hallucinogens

Not surprisingly, hallucinogens are the class of drugs most notable for causing hallucinations or alterations in one's perceptions and senses. Hallucinogens can bring about physical, auditory, and visual hallucinations, surreal and trancelike states, and paranoia. Natural hallucinogens are found in plants and mushrooms, and synthetic hallucinogens are their chemical relatives produced in the laboratory. Hallucinogens include LSD, marijuana, peyote, mescaline, psilocybin mushrooms, PCP, ketamine, and dextromethorphan, among others.

We have an incomplete understanding of how this class of substance exerts its effects in the body and mind. Most hallucinogens contain nitrogen and are molecularly similar to natural neurotransmitters. Hallucinogens appear to interfere with the natural effects of neurotransmitters or to block neurotransmitter receptor sites. The only consistent aspect of the effects of hallucinogens is their high degree of unpredictability—that is, different effects are produced in different people at different times. Hallucinogens are also known as psychedelics, from the Greek *psyche,* or "soul," and *delein,* "to make manifest."

Users may experience an initial elation, followed many times by an intensification of sensations and internal perceptual awareness. The experiences are very diverse, so it is difficult to generalize on the effects. Many artists like Ken Kesey and Aldous Huxley have credited the use of hallucinogens as their creative muse, while others have experienced gut-wrenching, horrific events, so-called "bad trips" that left them mentally and emotionally scarred. Proponents assert that psychedelics help spread harmony and nonviolence, while others question the sanity of chemically inducing temporary "insanity." In any case, psychedelics are illegal and can be abused.

Hallucinogens have been used for thousands of years, in religious and communal ceremonies and healing rituals. Initially, tribal healers would summon intuitive or extracorporeal (out-of-body) powers through a trancelike state they would enter either naturally or through the assistance of hallucinogenic substances. In fact, an LSD-like substance, ergot, was used for over 2,000 years in the ancient Greek Eleusinian Mysteries, an ancient secret society's rites of passage involving entering into a mind-altered state that was part of a ritual thought to secure a favorable afterlife.[89]

LSD

The first major hallucinogen to enter the drug culture in the 1960s and gain widespread popular attention was LSD (D-lysergic acid diethylamide), commonly known as "acid." LSD is one of the most potent mood-changing chemicals ever synthesized. It can cause life-changing experiences that can last for extremely long periods of time. In the laboratory, LSD is isolated from the fungus ergot, and LSD is also structurally related to the woodrose and morning glory plants' active hallucinogenic chemicals.

Dr. Albert Hofmann, a chemist at Sandoz Pharmaceuticals in Switzerland, became the first to synthesize LSD in 1938. Interestingly, he accidently became exposed to it in his lab one day and reported that "colors became more glowing," and when his eyes were closed "there surged upon me an uninterrupted stream of fantastic images of extraordinary plasticity and vividness." Instead of reporting that his accidental exposure was dangerous, he actually let others know how appealing it was.[90]

The US military and the Central Intelligence Agency (CIA) sponsored many early experiments on the effects of LSD on humans in the 1950s and early 1960s, due to their interest in potential use of LSD related to espionage activities and its application during interrogations. However, LSD was not a reliable extractor of information, and the CIA did not count on the many cases of psychotic reaction that would occur during these experiments. Prior to its classification as having no medical therapeutic benefit, LSD was used for a time to treat alcoholics.

In an excellent example of unintended consequences, those early military experiments with LSD provided the first exposure to the drug for someone who would go on to popularize the use of hallucinogenic drugs and lead the "counterculture revolution" of the 1960s—Timothy Leary, a psychology professor from Harvard University. Leary's first experience with LSD kept him speechless for five days and made such an impact on him that he reported that LSD was more important than Harvard. He essentially became the poster child for "better living through chemistry" and coined the influential phrase "tune in, turn on, and drop out." He thought LSD could expand the mind, and encouraged our youth to use it in order to develop a sense of what it meant to follow their own path in the world instead of unquestioningly following the conventions, authority, and dogma of previous generations.

Today, LSD is usually ingested orally via liquid-infused paper squares, caplets, or liquid droplets. Physical effects may include an increase in heart rate, dilation of pupils, and rise in body temperature. The user experiences a prolonged effect, known as a "trip," which may last up to twelve hours.

LSD's effects are related to the user's mood and expectations, as well as to the amount of the drug taken. The user may experience dramatic shifts in space and time, personal identification, life and object salience, and spiritual breakthroughs. The effects are entirely unpredictable. In general, it is difficult to explain the effects of any hallucinogen. Brain pathways that do not ordinarily cross or communicate begin to have extraordinary relationships. Users sometimes describe such incredible and terrifying experiences as being able to "see smells, taste sounds, hear colors, and touch noises." LSD use may cause a "bad trip," whereby the user may experience profound terror and paranoia, delusions, intensely negative hallucinations, or panic.

LSD users find that they develop a rapid tolerance, and so must increase the amount taken to achieve the desired effect. Furthermore, some users also find that even after not having used the drug for months or even years, they may have flashbacks—a phenomenon whereby they experience vivid recurrences of certain features of their "trip."

Peyote

Peyote is a slow-growing, spineless, acrid cactus. Popular myth credits the discovery of peyote to a lost and starving unfortunate man who ate the plant and heard a voice saying that the plant should be eaten and brought back to his tribe as a divine gift to bring peace and courage to the people. People in northern Mexico and the southwestern United States have used this plant for thousands of years for divination in shamanic services, for treatment of illness, and as a part of religious ceremonies. Bona fide religious use of peyote in ceremonies of the Native American Church is legally protected under the First and Fourteenth Amendments to the US Constitution.

The main active ingredient in peyote, mescaline, was isolated in 1897 and first synthesized in a lab in 1919. Peyote tastes bitter and usually induces nausea and vomiting after the plant is ingested, usually by soaking or brewing the root in liquid and drinking it. As mescaline courses throughout the body, the user experiences an increase in sweating, salivation, body temperature, heart rate, and blood pressure. There is also dilation of pupils. As with LSD, the effects are lengthy and can last up to twelve hours. Peyote users consistently report experiencing visions and profound realizations while under the influence of the drug. While long-term effects are poorly understood, users may experience flashbacks.

Psilocybin

Psilocybin (4-phosphoryloxy-*N,N*-dimethyltryptamine) and psilocin (4-hydroxy-*N,N*-dimethyltryptamine) are the primary active hallucinogenic molecules found in certain kinds of psychoactive mushrooms that are indigenous to North and South America. For thousands of years, Central American natives used psychoactive mushrooms in tribal ceremonies to achieve visionary altered states of consciousness.

It was not until 1955, however, that R. Gordon Wasson and his wife, Valentina, discovered that the chief supply of natural hallucinogens comes from this class of mushrooms. Sandoz Pharmaceuticals patented these molecules and sent doses to Timothy Leary in the 1960s for the Harvard Psilocybin Research Project. However, the synthetic forms were too cost-prohibitive, and so the more widespread use that blossomed in the 1960s involved the natural, organic psychoactive species of mushrooms. Anti-LSD propaganda also helped to fuel interest in discovering natural ways to experience mystical phenomena. This led to greater experimentation with psilocybin mushrooms, known more commonly as "magic mushrooms," or simply "shrooms."

There are over two dozen species of psychoactive mushrooms known thus far. Psychoactive mushrooms are usually eaten raw, incorporated into other foods, or brewed in teas. The effects of psilocybin, which appear within twenty minutes of ingestion, last approximately six hours. Research subjects in studies conducted in the 1960s and 1970s could not discern the differences among psychoactive mushrooms, LSD, and mescaline. Users of psilocybin may also experience changes in sensations, perceptions, behavior, and autonomic and motor function. As with LSD and peyote, hallucinations, anxiety, panic, and psychosis may occur. Long-term effects such as flashbacks may also occur.

PCP

PCP (phencyclidine) is another drug in the hallucinogen class. It was actually developed in the 1950s as an anesthetic and was only used in that capacity until 1965, because by then there had been too many patients who experienced intense agitation, anxiety, and psychotic reactions. As an anesthetic, PCP is a dissociative type because it causes a mind-body split whereby the user has an out-of-body experience or feels detached from his or her environment. Today, PCP is an abused substance, often made clandestinely by home chemists who do not have a vested interest in producing safe or equipotent doses. Users may get a hazardous, weak, or dangerously strong batch. Due to the high incidence of intense psychological reactions, even many addicts report that PCP's benefit is not worth the risk. PCP is known by many street names, including "rocket fuel," "DOA," "hog," and "angel dust."

PCP is a white crystalline powder with an acrid taste. On the streets it is sold in a variety of different-colored powder or tablet forms. Normally smoked, swallowed, or snorted, PCP is often added to other herbs like tea, mint, or oregano, or to drugs like marijuana. When added to marijuana, it can be known as "wet" or "fry," although the latter term usually refers to either cigarettes or marijuana that have been dipped in embalming fluid. The effects of PCP can be felt within a few minutes to an hour and can last approximately five hours.

PCP is like other hallucinogens in that it has very different effects on different people. However, the effects of PCP are distinct from those of LSD and psychoactive mushrooms. Specifically, PCP has a better-known mechanism of action. We know that it inhibits glutamate by blocking NMDA receptors and it inhibits the reuptake of dopamine, norepinephrine, and serotonin. PCP also interacts with some opioid receptors in the brain.

PCP can produce depressant, stimulant, pain-relieving, and hallucinogenic effects. However, instead of producing visual hallucinations, PCP effectively distorts one's body image. Users experience a delusional sense of invulnerability and strength. While "bad trips" are possible with LSD and psychoactive mushrooms, PCP more often causes intense and disturbing hallucinations, paranoia, confusion, agitation, terror, and despair. PCP can cause increased blood pressure and heart rate, shallow breathing, nausea and vomiting, blurry vision, seizures, coma, and death. PCP is associated with some long-term negative consequences as well, including depression, cognitive impairment, and memory loss.

Ketamine

Like PCP, ketamine is a dissociative anesthetic hallucinogen. It was developed in 1962 and is used today as a pediatric anesthetic and in veterinary medicine. It has a rapid onset of action and has very few side effects except in older people who report accounts of hallucinations and out-of-body experiences. It is known as "K," "vitamin K," "super K," and "special K" (no relation to the cereal) on the streets and is popular as a club drug. It is abused for its effects of dissociation, feelings of floating, stimulation, and hallucinations. Some users take enough to have complete out-of-body experiences, but the amount required is dangerous as it can stop breathing and cause death. It can be injected, snorted, or swallowed. Ketamine has a short duration, lasting only up to thirty minutes. Physical side effects of ketamine include confusion, impaired coordination and thinking, delirium, blurry vision, and muscle weakness.

Dextromethorphan

Dextromethorphan is yet another dissociative anesthetic that, at high doses, produces similar effects to ketamine and PCP. Dextromethorphan's intended use is actually as a cough suppressant. It is found in a great variety of over-the-counter cough and cold medicines and is the active ingredient when "DM" is found on the label. At low doses and used as directed, it is relatively safe. It was initially removed from the market soon after its introduction when it was found to be abused and dangerous. In a rational move to discourage abuse, it was reintroduced in preparations that were intentionally designed with bad-tasting syrup flavors. Later, however, in a less-than-rational move, dextromethorphan was again put in syrups that were more pleasant tasting. Naturally, abuse resumed.

Dextromethorphan is among the most dangerous and abused over-the-counter medications. For example, in 2006, nearly three million youths aged twelve to twenty-five reported using over-the-counter cough and cold preparations to get high. It is known on the streets as "dex," "poor man's ecstasy," and "robo," among other names. Rap songs extol its abusable effects. At high doses, it induces potent hallucinogenic effects ranging from stimulation, euphoria, and visual hallucinations to out-of-body experiences. The duration of the effects ranges from thirty minutes to six hours. Abuse of dextromethorphan has been particularly troublesome in the past decade, and the danger is compounded by its use in conjunction with other drugs like alcohol, GHB, and ecstasy.

Negative effects of dextromethorphan include dizziness, nausea and vomiting, sweating, confusion, impaired body temperature control, rapid uncontrolled eye movements, high blood pressure and heart rate, lethargy, slurred speech, paranoia, and psychosis.

Marijuana (Cannabis)

Marijuana is grouped with the hallucinogens, yet does not cleanly fall into any one category of abused substances. It can be considered to have similarities to hallucinogens, stimulants, opioids, and depressants. After alcohol, marijuana has the highest rate of dependence or abuse among all drugs. In 2013, 4.2 million Americans met clinical criteria for dependence on or abuse of marijuana in the past year—more than twice the number for dependence on or abuse of prescription pain relievers (1.9 million) and nearly five times the number for dependence on or abuse of cocaine (855,000).[91]

Marijuana has a unique and ambiguous status. Under federal law, it is illegal to possess, use, buy, sell, or cultivate marijuana, since the Controlled Substances Act of 1970 classifies marijuana as a Schedule I drug, claiming it has a high potential for abuse and has no acceptable medical use. However, increasingly, states have created exemptions for for medicinal marijuana and even legalized it for recreational purposes.

Marijuana may be one of the world's oldest "medicines." Records of its earliest use come from ancient China and India. Indian mythology claims that the god Shiva bestowed humankind with the plant as a gift from the gods. It has been used medicinally for stomachache, pain, fever, insomnia, nausea, malaria, and tuberculosis. Marijuana was brought to Europe from the Middle East after Napoleon's army found it more attractive than alcohol because there was not as much of a hangover. When the Spanish conquistadors came to the New World, they brought marijuana to the Americas. In the Americas, cannabis fiber was also used to make paper, clothes, and ropes. Strangely, there are no records of inhaling cannabis in the United States until after 1876. Maybe folks were too stoned and "forgot" to write?

Marijuana was once entirely legal in the United States. It became more popular during Prohibition when alcohol was illegal for thirteen years, but the

Great Depression was causing many Americans to be out of work, and concerns over immigrants who could be taking jobs away from citizens catalyzed an antimarijuana campaign aimed at eliminating immigrants because they were the cause of a "dangerous marijuana epidemic." Other concerns, including crime and health issues, fueled the reclassification of marijuana from legal to illegal on October 1, 1937. At the time, a hugely distorted propaganda campaign aimed at vilifying marijuana—most potently exemplified in the 1936 exploitation film *Reefer Madness* (originally released as *Tell Your Children*)—helped to convince Congress to pass the Marijuana Tax Law, thereby criminalizing possession of marijuana without a license. It is particularly interesting to note that one could not obtain a license without first illegally possessing marijuana, thereby incriminating oneself. Timothy Leary brought this legal quagmire of sorts to the attention of the US Supreme Court in the 1960s, and the Marijuana Tax Law was overturned. However, marijuana (along with most other drugs) was again banned in 1970 through the Controlled Substance Act. Since 1937, it is estimated that over twenty-two million people have had legal trouble in relation to marijuana.

Marijuana comes from drying the flowering buds and leaves of the cannabis plant. Although, as noted above, humans have used marijuana for thousands of years, its main active ingredient, THC, or delta-9-tetrahydrocannabinol, was only discovered in 1964. To date, we know of over 400 different chemicals in marijuana. THC works directly on our natural endocannibinoid receptor system and, like other substances of abuse, also increases dopamine release in our mesolimbic dopamine system. THC actually has been shown to affect several neurotransmitters. There are other active ingredients in marijuana whose mechanism of action remains unclear. Hashish is a form of concentrated THC, formed from the resin collected from the cannabis plant. In contrast, hemp is a fiber produced from low-THC varieties of cannabis that are cultivated by industry for rope, clothing, and so forth.

Worldwide, marijuana is one of the most popularly used mood- and mind-altering substances. In the United States, marijuana is the most frequently abused illegal drug. Marijuana is often grown in large fields, but there is an increasing number of smaller-scale and indoor growers who adeptly use the latest horticultural and illuminant technology in their efforts to avoid detection and arrest. Law-enforcement agencies use thermal imaging and other advanced technologies to identify growers. Authorities report raids that have uncovered incredibly intricate and advanced growing techniques. Over the years marijuana growers have applied scientific advancements in botany and genetic manipulation to facilitate the breeding of more potent and popular strains and crops of cannabis. Marijuana plants can vary widely in THC concentration, but today's crops are frequently more than four times more potent than the strains that were grown during the height of the Woodstock era.

Marijuana is most often inhaled. It can be rolled into a cigarette (joint), vaporized, or smoked through a pipe or specialized water pipe known as a bong. Absorption is quickest following smoking, and the effects last up to three hours. Marijuana can also be brewed in teas or eaten, usually by being mixed in with foods like cookies or brownies. Absorption is slower when it is digested, but its effects can last up to an hour longer.

As with other hallucinogens, we still have much to discover about the exact mechanisms of action of marijuana. Interestingly, like nicotine to our muscarine nicontinic receptors, one of the main ingredients in marijuana fits on our naturally occurring endocannabinoid receptors. Certain areas of the brain have a high density of these endocannabinoid receptors, like the functional units of the brain responsible for memory, coordination, sensations, involuntary muscle movements, concentration, and pleasure.

After THC binds to its receptors, users experience euphoria and perceptional, temporal, and sensational enhancement or distortion. One common perceptional distortion occurs by heightening the sensation in the taste buds, causing foods to be highly pleasurable. THC stimulates one's appetite, which, combined with the enhanced pleasure derived from eating, commonly causes a ravenous desire for certain foods, colloquially referred to as the "munchies."

The bloodshot eyes so characteristic of marijuana users are produced by the action of THC dilating blood vessels in the eyes. Coordination can be impaired, as can concentration, memory, and learning. Marijuana is notorious for causing "cotton mouth," a sensation where the user's mouth becomes very dry. After the initial "high" passes, other effects like sedation or depression may dominate. At other times and in certain individuals, there may not be as much of a euphoric high as paranoia and anxiety. Marijuana affects the heart by increasing heart rate, and as such may exacerbate anxiety and panic. High doses of marijuana can even cause significant disorientation and hallucinations.

Like other substances of abuse, ongoing marijuana use can lead to addiction. Because it is routinely viewed as more benign, many people continue to be unaware of marijuana's addictive potential. Many daily marijuana users, including those who smoke several times a day, will deny that marijuana is addictive—even as they light up their next joint. Yet marijuana can indeed activate the addictive cycle of obsessive thinking and compulsive using. In turn, this leads to increasingly harmful negative consequences including physical dependence, tolerance, and withdrawal. Once it was rare for treatment programs to admit people solely for addiction to marijuana. That is no longer the case, as it is now not uncommon for people to receive inpatient and outpatient addiction treatment specific to their use of marijuana.

There is a group of general symptoms that characterize marijuana withdrawal, which start on day one and can last for weeks. These include craving, nausea, appetite changes, boredom, insomnia, anxiety, and irritability. A study demonstrated that animals in withdrawal from cannabis had an increase in their stress-response system. The most helpful way to understand how this stress-response phenomenon works in humans is to recognize that it contributes to making the user feel that the only way to decrease his or her stress and anxiety is to use more of the drug.[92] In this way, marijuana creates many of the same reactions in the brain and body as many other substances believed to be more addictive.

In early 2017, the California Society of Addiction Medicine (CSAM) posited several basic facts the public should know about marijuana and the brain to be adequately informed about the potential public health implications of legalizing marijuana.

Chemically, marijuana mimics the brain's natural molecules, and frequent use significantly disrupts the brain's delicate chemical balance. Marijuana is addicting for approximately 9 percent of people who begin smoking it at the age of eighteen or older. Because the brains of adolescents are still in the process of developing, smoking marijuana before the age of eighteen results in increasingly higher rates of addiction (up to 17 percent within two years) and disruption to an individual's life. The younger the user, the greater the risk.[93] Moreover, CSAM further reports that among near-daily users of marijuana the rate of addiction is estimated to be 35 to 40 percent.[94]

Even in terms of marijuana's medicinal value, we need more research and evidence to draw definitive conclusions. A massive (more than 450 pages) report released by the National Academies of Science, Engineering and Mathematics in January, 2017, *The Health Effects of Cannabis and Cannabinoids: The Current State of Evidence and Recommendations for Research,* examined a broad array of evidence regarding the health effects of using cannabis.[95] Among the report's findings: cannabis or cannabinoids appear effective for the treatment of chronic pain in adults, for alleviating nausea caused by chemotherapy, and for improving spasms associated with multiple sclerosis. Cannabis or cannabinoids also may help improve fibromyalgia, chronic pain, multiple sclerosis, and short-term sleep outcomes for obstructive sleep apnea.. The researchers found only limited evidence that "cannabis or cannabinoids are effective for increasing appetite and decreasing weight loss associated with HIV/AIDS and improving symptoms of post-traumatic stress disorder (PTSD)." Contrary to the popular myth around the association between marijuana and glaucoma, there is actually some limited evidence that cannabis or cannabinoids are ineffective for improving the intraocular pressure associated with glaucoma.

The adverse health effects of smoking marijuana include chronic coughs, intense respiratory symptoms, and frequent chronic bronchitis episodes. Smoking marijuana increases the amount of tar and carbon monoxide inhaled to levels much greater than those of cigarette smoking. Smoking cannabis may increase the risks of developing chronic obstructive pulmonary disease (COPD). Importantly, for chronic users, there is moderate evidence of a statistical association between stopping smoking and improved respiratory symptoms. And yes, marijuana smoke contains carcinogens, although it is unclear at this time whether or not there is a direct correlation between smoking marijuana and respiratory tract cancers. In states where cannabis is now legal there is an increased risk of overdose injuries, including respiratory distress, in pediatric populations. Many of the overdoses in children relate to ingesting edible forms of cannabis.

Not surprisingly, this study found that there is substantial evidence that cannabis use increases the risk of getting into a motor vehicle accident. Marijuana use can cause memory loss and difficulty concentrating, can impair learning, academic achievement, and educational outcomes, and can lead to a motivational syndrome characterized by extreme lethargy and apathy. The effects of marijuana on individuals with preexisting psychiatric disorders were also examined. Although there is moderate evidence that among individuals with psychotic disorders using marijuana may improve cognitive performance, individuals diagnosed with bipolar disorder often experience increased symptoms of mania and hypomania. A somewhat increased risk for the development of depression and social anxiety disorder was also noted, as well as an increased incidence of suicidal ideation and suicide attempts and completions among heavy marijuana users.[96]

Nicotine

"Giving up smoking is the easiest thing in the world. I know, because I've done it a thousand times." —Mark Twain

Human beings are arguably the smartest animals on the planet . . . yet why are we the only animal that does not intuitively run from fire? No, instead, an incredible number of us selectively inhale fire while smoking cigarettes and other drugs. Other nicotine-containing products are dangerous as well. Personally, I also wonder how history will remember this period of human existence when we fostered the death machine that is the tobacco industry. In the United States alone, tobacco is responsible for over 1,100 deaths per day.[97] It remains one of the chief unnecessary and completely preventable causes of death.

Tobacco products are prepared by drying the leaves of the nicotiana rustica or nicotiana tabaccum plant. These plants were named after their earliest primary exporter, Jean Nicot, and are native to North, Central, and South America. Tobacco was used in native tribal religious ceremonies for thousands of years before Europeans colonized the New World. The first Europeans exposed to smoking tobacco were among Christopher Columbus's crew, and they loved the stuff and quickly became addicted to it. After its export to Europe, smoking tobacco quickly grew in popularity, as did its trade value. In fact, it was used as currency in the New World for a time. The big tobacco companies, R. J. Reynolds, Philip Morris, and J. E. Liggett, grew very quickly after opening their shops in the mid-nineteenth century. Tobacco was soon one of the most lucrative crops, not only for those big producers, but also for the government. So important was tobacco that overseas trading routes were designed according to their proximity to major areas of tobacco farming. The Lewis and Clark expedition was also initiated, in part, to look for suitable tobacco-cultivating lands.

It took the United States Congress decades too long to issue the surgeon general's health warning on every pack of cigarettes and even longer to hold the tobacco industry accountable for the morbidity and mortality they are directly responsible for causing. The link between lung cancer and smoking was evident as long ago as the 1930s and 1940s. There were television advertisements in the 1950s, however, that exposed Americans to actual doctors espousing the health benefits of smoking particular brands of cigarettes. The tobacco industry shamelessly targeted youth in their advertising campaigns as well. Adolescents preferentially purchase the most heavily advertised brands.[98] At one point, more children were able to recognize "Joe Camel" than Mickey Mouse. More than 4,000 American children between the ages of twelve and seventeen try their first cigarette each day.[99] The form of addiction most likely to be established in adolescence is cigarette smoking.[100]

Today, the tobacco industry openly acknowledges that cigarettes are addictive and that there is no health benefit to smoking. In fact, the link between smoking cigarettes and heart, lung, and other serious diseases is undeniably clear. Yet the industry continues to operate and profit handsomely at the expense of the health of their consumers and the overall public. As a physician, I have zero tolerance for this industry. Having the freedom of choice to smoke is an inadequate justification in my opinion when the consequences include thousands of deaths and billions of taxpayer dollars spent treating preventable smoking-related illness.

While tobacco is used in several different forms, smoking remains the most popular form in the United States and worldwide. The World Health Organization reports that there are 1.1 billion smokers worldwide,[101] and the US Centers for Disease Control reports that there are over forty-six million adult smokers in the United States, accounting for over 150 billion dollars in economic costs to society via medical expenses and lost productivity.[102] Tobacco is smoked mostly through cigarettes, cigars, pipes, and water pipes mixed with flavorings. Tobacco can also be absorbed orally when chewed or nasally when snorted. No matter what the route of administration and absorption, nicotine exerts strong effects in the brain.

E-cigarettes or vaping, electronic alternatives to traditional cigarettes, exploded onto the market around 2005. E-cigs can differ in terms of shape, size, and flavors, but they all share three common components: a heating element, a place to hold a vial of nicotine-containing liquid, and a battery that drives a heating element to vaporize the liquid. The nicotine-containing liquid includes not only addictive nicotine, but also chemicals like aldehyde and flavorings such as cinnamon, fruit, and even cocoa.

A significant public health concern is that the use of e-cigs is growing much faster than our understanding. Vaping has quickly become a six billion-dollar industry. Since vaping is still relatively new, there is little research on the long-term effects compared to those of traditional cigarettes. However, although this new technology does seem to be a step in the direction of harm reduction, as time and experience progress, we are discovering that e-cigs do contain toxins and act to suppress the immune system. Early research is beginning to dispel the myths that vaping is "safe" for the respiratory system, that it is not addictive, and that bystanders aren't affected by secondhand vape smoke.[103] Moreover, there are accounts of e-cigarettes causing burns. The liquid vapor can contain toxic chemicals such as aldehyde and propylene glycol or ultrafine particulates of heavy metals, and even carcinogens such as acrolein, that get inhaled deep into lung tissue.[104]

The good news is that fewer Americans are smoking. In 2013, an estimated 55.8 million Americans aged twelve or older, or 21.3 percent of the population, were current cigarette smokers. This reflects a continual but slow downward trend from 2002, when the rate was 26 percent. Teen smoking is declining more rapidly. The rate of past-month cigarette use among twelve- to seventeen-year-olds decreased from 13 percent in 2002 to 5.6 percent in 2013.[105]

All tobacco products contain nicotine, a mood- and mind-altering substance that can behave as a stimulant and a sedative. More than one hundred chemicals are added to tobacco to make cigarettes. Some of these chemicals include hexanoic acid, ammonia, ethyl acetate, tolualdehydes, benzaldehyde, butyric acid, 3-methylbutyraldehyde, methylcyclopentenolone, and decanoic acid. Ammonia is added to cigarettes by the tobacco industry because ammonia effectively causes the nicotine to be freebased, which causes its concentration to peak faster and higher in the brain. This quick and powerful increase in the concentration of nicotine is responsible for the enhanced addictive pull (and higher sales) of cigarettes. In tobacco smoke, nicotine also connects with tiny elements of tar.

Tar is the result of the tobacco companies' strategic design for their cigarettes. On the one hand, they want each cigarette to burn fast enough so that the addicted smoker has to light up another more quickly, leading to faster purchases of more product. On the other hand, the tobacco companies know it's not in their best interest for their cigarettes to burn up too rapidly, so binders and additives are added to this end. It is more pleasant to hold a slowly but continuously burning cigarette than one that burns into ash too quickly. The solid matter in cigarettes does not burn completely; it is inhaled with the smoke and settles on the lung tissue as tar. In addition to causing irritation and cough, tar causes cellular damage and leads to the formation of cancer. Smoking so-called *light* cigarettes does not lead to inhaling less tar.

Smoking tobacco releases over 4,000 different chemicals and hundreds of known cancer-causing agents. When the smoke with this nicotine/chemical/tar mixture reaches the lungs, it is quickly absorbed, and the nicotine reaches the brain within fourteen seconds when smoked. Nicotine reaches the central nervous system in about three to five minutes when tobacco is chewed. Absorption here is much slower than with smoking because the drug must be taken in through the veins of the mouth before it circulates to the heart and lungs before reaching the brain. When nicotine reaches the brain, it combines with the pleasure center's high density of nicotinic acetylcholine receptors that cause stimulatory and euphoric effects. As indicated earlier in Figure V, pleasure-inducing dopamine is released in the limbic system at a higher concentration than when it is released with alcohol. Nicotine acts on the nicotinic acetylcholine receptors in both the central and peripheral nervous systems. Moreover, nicotine addiction develops very rapidly, and the brain dysfunctions can last several months, even after short-term use.

The ordinary effects of smoking tobacco include increases in blood pressure, respiration, and heart rate; constriction of the circulatory system; lung damage; cough and bronchitis; receding gums; gum and mouth disease; tooth decay; and stained teeth. Long-term exposure to tobacco, whether by direct or secondhand smoke, has many grave health risks, including heart disease, heart attacks, high blood pressure and heart rate, strokes, impotence, menstrual abnormalities, miscarriages, stillbirths, low birth weight, sudden infant death syndrome, emphysema, chronic bronchitis, premature skin aging, impaired senses and cognition, intestinal ulcers, immune system dysfunction, bladder cancer, mouth cancer, lung cancer, pancreatic cancer, kidney cancer, and throat cancer.

Nicotine has proven to be one of the most addicting and difficult-to-stop substances known. Lab animals addicted to both nicotine and other substances will preferentially withdraw from all other substances first. Nicotine addiction often exists in conjunction with addiction to other substances. In fact, many people in recovery from other substances, including some with years of abstinence from all other drugs, continue to smoke cigarettes. Nicotine withdrawal symptoms include headaches, anxiety, lethargy, irritability, hunger, and depression. There are an increasing variety of medical and behavioral strategies and treatments available for tobacco cessation, including behavioral modification therapy, aversion therapy, nicotine replacement therapy, antidepressants, and other medications. Even though the quit rate remains low, the more time and energy one puts into quitting, the better the chances of being successful.

Gamma Hydroxybutyrate (GHB)

Gamma hydroxybutyrate, or GHB, is a central nervous system depressant. Developed in 1960 as a general anesthetic, we discovered soon afterward that it was a naturally occurring substance in the human brain during the synthesis of gamma-aminobutyric acid, or GABA. In the brain, natural GHB is concentrated in the thalamus, hypothalamus, and substantia nigra. Since GHB causes a small increase in human growth hormone during sleep, many bodybuilders use GHB to build muscle. There is no proven correlation between GHB and increased muscle mass, yet it remains popular despite negative consequences. GHB was also used in the 1970s as a treatment for narcolepsy, but this was discontinued due to its euphoric side effects. GHB is still used in Europe today to treat alcohol dependence and withdrawal.

GHB is a chemical that is structurally similar to GABA, our primary inhibitory brain neurotransmitter. Our understanding of its exact mechanism of action is incomplete. It is thought that GHB binds to specific GHB receptors, thereby inhibiting, or slowing down, neurotransmitters in the dopamine and GABA neurotransmitter systems. We have discovered that GHB activates both GHB and GABA receptors, increasing acetylcholine levels and serotonin levels.

The 1980s saw GHB's use expand as it was sold over the counter as a muscle-building agent and a fat burner. When GHB was found to be responsible for an increasing number of fatalities, it was outlawed. GHB has been linked to dozens of deaths, tolerance and dependence, and thousands of overdoses. The overdoses that present in hospital emergency rooms are difficult to treat because detecting the drug can be difficult. Moreover, many producers continue to manufacture two precursors of GHB, BD and GBL, which are converted to GHB after consumption. BD and GBL are used as industrial cleaning chemicals and floor strippers and have no approved use for human consumption.

On February 18, 2000, President Bill Clinton signed HR 2130, making the possession of GHB illegal. However, in July 2002, a form of GHB was designated a Schedule III controlled substance (possessing some medical utility). GHB cannot be sold, distributed, or provided to anyone other than for its prescribed use. However, since it is also frequently made in clandestine labs, the strength and purity of GHB can vary widely.

GHB is a common "date rape drug." It is colorless and odorless and easy to conceal in drinks or food. It is used by sexual predators in many cases of date rape because of its rapid onset of action and its ability to powerfully sedate the user. On the street it is known as "G," "salty water," "growth hormone booster," "sleep," "soap," and "liquid ecstasy." It continues to be popular in certain circles, including among some bodybuilders, in clubs, and in the "rave" party culture.

One GHB user whom I interviewed reported that GHB made him feel "ten feet high and bulletproof." Its onset of action begins within fifteen minutes and can last a few hours. As a sedative with a rapid onset of action, it can cause the user to lose consciousness in just a few minutes. Due to inconsistent concentrations, the same dose can produce variable effects in different individuals. In addition, alcohol and sedatives can significantly exaggerate the sedative effects of GHB. Like alcohol and opioids, GHB can cause euphoria and decreased inhibitions. As a substance of abuse, GHB causes tolerance and withdrawal symptoms, including anxiety, insomnia, psychosis, and tremors. GHB also causes drowsiness, muscle relaxation, dizziness, nausea and vomiting, decreased heart rate and breathing, disorientation, impaired thinking and coordination, headaches, seizures, hallucinations, and coma or death.

Anabolic Steroids

Anabolic steroids belong in a class of drugs and hormones that are chemically related to the major natural male hormone, testosterone, which increases protein synthesis and promotes muscle growth. Anabolic steroids also are responsible for the development and preservation of masculine characteristics like a deep voice, body hair, and muscle mass.

Anabolic has Greek roots meaning "to build up and produce man." These drugs have been considered a Schedule III controlled substance and have been banned by all major international and national sports governing bodies as performance-enhancing substances since 1990, yet they are still widely used in competitive athletics. There are myriad legitimate medicinal uses for these hormones, but it is estimated that illegal diversion and black market use top $400 million annually in the United States. The majority of users are noncompetitive athletes and those who desire the cosmetic benefits of the drugs. On the streets, steroids are known as "roids" and "juice."

Testosterone was first identified in 1935. It was initially used to treat men who were otherwise unable to produce their own testosterone, in order to normalize their development, growth, and sexual maturation. This and other steroid hormones and compounds that were synthesized soon after the discovery of testosterone were used in athletes in the 1940s and 1950s, first in the former Soviet Union and what was then East Germany, and later in the United States. When unfair performance advantages and medical consequences were discovered, the International Olympic Committee banned these compounds in 1975. Over the past several decades, athletes in the sports of bodybuilding, football, and baseball, among others, have been suspected of using steroids and human growth hormone (HGH) to enhance their performance and give them a competitive advantage.

After seeming to ignore this issue for years—as players became noticeably bigger and stronger, hitting many more home runs, and raising disquieting questions—Major League Baseball conducted an extensive investigation that implicated dozens of players, including some of the best and most famous. Overall, the implementation of protocols to test athletes for the presence of these performance-enhancing substances has significantly decreased, though definitely not eliminated, their use in professional and Olympic sports.

There are merely a few natural steroids. However, over 100 different synthetic anabolic steroids have been developed—with only a small minority providing legitimate and approved medicinal value to either humans or other animals. Steroids are used in medicine for low testosterone, increasing muscle mass and appetite in chronic wasting syndromes, improving libido, gender identity disorder, initiation of male puberty, growth stimulation, and hereditary angioedema. Steroids increase muscle mass and bone growth, cause growth of select internal organs and male glands, deepen the voice, and increase facial hair growth.

Steroids are most often injected into the veins or muscles, but also can be swallowed or rubbed onto the skin. When they are used for their nonprescribed purposes, the doses are several times higher than those used for medical conditions. Moreover, the users apply highly intricate preset patterns of ingestion over several weeks that are known as "stacking," "pyramiding," or "cycling." Once inside the body, steroid hormones circulate until they bind to specific receptors on cells that, in turn, internalize them into the main "brain" of the cell, the nucleus. Inside the nucleus, the steroid influences the genes to orchestrate signals to other cells or directly stimulate protein synthesis. In turn, muscle mass increases and recovery time decreases. In effect, the user can build more muscle bulk as well as decrease the time required for rest between periods of strenuous physical activity.

Steroids produce many negative biological and psychological consequences. In both men and women, biologic adverse effects of steroids include heart and liver damage; blood clotting dysfunctions; bone density loss; muscle, tendon, and ligament damage; elevated blood pressure; swelling; headaches; stunted growth in adolescents; cholesterol and blood sugar abnormalities; and acne. Other negative medical consequences include development of breasts in males and male characteristics in females. Steroids can also decrease sperm count and testicular size in males, and reduce breast tissue in females. Furthermore, males may experience impotence, infertility, and urinary abnormalities, and women may experience abnormal menses and an enlarged clitoris. There is evidence that anabolic steroids are reinforcing in the mesolimbic dopamine system, produce euphoria, and so can be addictive. Many use steroids excessively and develop compulsive use, despite negative consequences.

Lyle Alzado was a former star National Football League defensive lineman who was twice named All-Pro and won a Super Bowl with the Los Angeles Raiders in 1984. Throughout his pro career he used anabolic steroids, and he died from brain lymphoma, a rare form of cancer, at the age of forty-three. Although there is no medical link between steroids and brain lymphoma, Alzado was certain the drugs were responsible for his cancer. Before he died he told his story publicly and tried to discourage others from using steroids. He became a tragic and cautionary tale, a symbol of the dangers of steroid abuse. Mental and behavioral side effects of steroids in both men and women include aggressiveness, depression, irritability, insomnia, paranoia, and delusional thinking. Withdrawal symptoms exist and include depression, decreased appetite, craving, insomnia, lethargy, decreased libido, and mood lability.

Kratom

Kratom is found on the leaves of tropical trees native to Thailand, Malaysia, and other areas of Southeast Asia. Since the active ingredient is destroyed by heat, it is not smoked; rather, it is chewed. Now illegal in Thailand and Malaysia, kratom was traditionally used for its medicinal properties to combat fatigue and increase mental acuity by day laborers and during religious rituals.

Pharmacologically, kratom is a mu-opioid receptor agonist, which means it acts like a painkiller. Indeed, it is used in Mexico and Canada to ease signs and symptoms of opioid withdrawal, but it is not indicated for any use in the United States, as it has no proven healthful effects. Kratom can produce anorexia, weight loss, insomnia, skin darkening, dry mouth, frequent urination, sedation, and constipation.

Chapter 5: The Addiction Cycle

A ddiction is defined as a brain disease and habit-forming process that creates negative behavioral, psychological, emotional, and spiritual consequences. Addiction does not spontaneously emerge out of nowhere. Rather, it is activated over time in response to the interplay among the agent, host, and environment. Once addiction has been activated, there is a set of disease-defining behaviors and a specific brain dysfunction in the mesolimbic dopamine system. Science is able to objectively explain the chemical and genetic changes that occur physically to the brain. Addiction's behavioral characteristics can be explained through a model known as the addiction cycle. The addiction cycle delineates four phases along the continuum of a disease characterized by self-propulsion. Left untreated, an addict who is caught in this addiction cycle becomes as trapped as a hamster running in a wheel, hoping to escape its cage.

People use drugs for many reasons. In fact, name a reason, and it is likely that it was behind someone's use of drugs at some point. Drugs are used because of their ability to make us feel good—or at least different. Drugs are powerful, predictable, and easy agents of change. Addicts use drugs for many reasons *plus one*. Addicts use drugs for all the reasons nonaddicts do, and also because they "need to." The *need* to use stems from the activation of the disease, hijacking of the midbrain, and dysfunction created in the body, mind, and spirit of the addict. The addiction cycle is a behavioral representation of the various systems affected in the addict, driven by a need.

What Addicts Tell Themselves Within the Cycle

The addiction cycle is, as its name suggests, cyclical. Like a windmill, when it is in motion there are no specific starting or stopping points. For the sake of simplicity, it can be thought of as starting once the addict is triggered. Triggers are stimuli that evoke a response. Addiction is a stimulus-response mechanism because addiction is a disease existing primarily in the subconscious, automatic recesses of the brain. Such deep structures are primitive and without thought; deep-brain structures are stimulated and respond in a straightforward and linear fashion. When the brain is stimulated, the addict's response begins with a **preoccupation** about using. Addicts use for every reason plus the need to use. Examples of triggering factors may include boredom, a fight with a partner, financial concerns, viewing the drug of choice (e.g., a beer commercial), being on vacation, or running into a drug-using buddy. These and many other stimuli can kick-start the process of preoccupation wherein the addict starts to entertain the prospect of using. In that process, obsessive thoughts cloud the addict's brain, prompting an inner dialogue such as this:

"I am feeling really uncomfortable right now. This is not pleasant at all. In fact, I'm anxious and angry and lonely and hungry and tired. Wow, it would be really good to have a drink or get some dope. I know I shouldn't do that. Just one won't hurt. But last time we did that, we didn't make it home for three days. Yeah, but this is different. I'm really mad right now and I can't think straight, so if I have a drink or some dope, I'll calm down enough to think straight. Plus I've been on my best behavior for so long, I deserve it. Yes, I do deserve a reward. One won't hurt . . . but we have to pay the bills. Okay, so I'll just spend twenty bucks. Man, I shouldn't. No, it's fine. This time will be different. This time I will control things better. Maybe I'll just pop into the bar to see how all the guys are doing. That never works. I'll go straight home and be responsible. Well, I have thirty minutes, so I can just have a taste and then go on my way. If I drink (or use drugs), I will feel better."

The internal dialogue that preoccupies the mind can completely entrance the addict. When the addict is lost in obsessive thoughts during this phase of the addiction cycle, relationships suffer, and work and family responsibilities are neglected.

Forming a Habit

The preoccupation phase feeds into the ritual phase of the addiction cycle. A ritual is a set of actions performed mainly for their symbolic and emotional value. The purposes of rituals are extremely diverse, and can include

- to satisfy the spiritual or emotional needs of religious practitioners;
- to strengthen social bonds;
- to demonstrate respect, dominance, or submission;
- to demonstrate one's affiliation;
- to obtain social acceptance or approval for some event; or
- sometimes just for the pleasure of the ritual itself.

Rituals can also be thought of as habits or behaviors that are automatic. Rituals become deeply ingrained within the fabric of the repetition and habituation of use. A common ritualistic action is putting our clothes on in the morning, when most of us automatically put the same foot first in our pants every day. Another example is how students, when observed in a classroom with no assigned seating, tend to sit in the same place each day. There are rituals woven into nearly every aspect of the addiction cycle: in checking the day's drug supply and planning the day's events from that information, in how drugs are procured, in how they are prepared for use, and in how they are used. The rituals that constitute the addiction cycle are triggered by the preoccupation phase. For instance, active addicts would not dream of going away for a week without making sure they had an adequate supply to bring with them. Their supply is their lifeline, and so there is an ongoing preoccupation with it.

Rituals in chemical addiction do not need to be elaborate. The routine stop at a convenience store on the way home to purchase the first six-pack is a ritual in the cycle. Some rituals are elaborate, though, including diabolical concoctions designed to construct "valid" reasons to use. For instance, an addict may start a fight with his or her partner in order to create resentment and a "real" reason to go get drunk or high. In this case, it is the fighting itself that becomes part of the ritual in the addiction cycle. Fabricating justification to use may be clever, but it is still driven by addiction's dysfunctional interruption of the unconscious part of the brain.

Stockpiling supplies in several "safe zones" is ritualistic, too. Never knowing when the *need* to use will strike, addicts will stash their supply like industrious squirrels storing acorns for the winter. That is, whenever possible, addicts will have multiple hiding places or easy-to-access spots where they know what they need is safely and conveniently waiting for them. This strategy serves to protect the all-important supply, as any one stash can be discovered and emptied.

Rituals assist in the process of stimulus-response leading to obsessive thinking of the preoccupation phase. Rituals help provide relief from the preoccupation because rituals are routines leading up to actual use. Rituals resolve anxiety created during the preoccupation phase. Rituals signal to the brain that a reward is coming soon.

Brain imaging studies demonstrate that addicts' pleasure centers explode with activity when there is merely the anticipation of a reward. Further, when anticipation of a reward is followed by the reward itself, then that reward is more pleasurable than a reward received without the addict knowing it was coming. Thus, rituals enhance the excitement and experience of the addiction and become part of the self-propelling system.

Rituals, which are carried out without thought and are rewarding for their own sake, remove the addict from awareness and being "present" in their lives. If preoccupation is a trancelike state, rituals enforce and deepen that trance. As in the preoccupation phase, rituals perpetuate the addict's absence from his or her life. While engaged in the obsessions and rituals, the addict is not "present"—other areas of his or her life and any non-addiction-supporting goals are disregarded, and the drive to seek relief is fueled. While engaged in

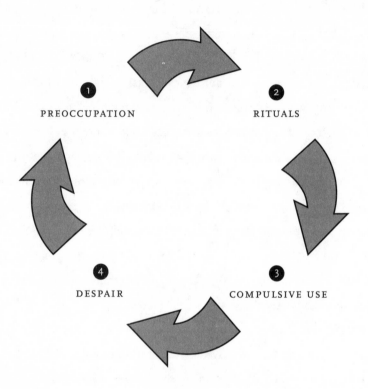

FIGURE VI: THE CYCLE OF ADDICTION

rituals, the addict is not present or attuned to his or her needs and self-care and will ignore sleep, work, family, commitments, and health.

One Thing Leads to Another

The third phase of the addiction cycle is compulsive use. After the addict spends time moving through preoccupation and rituals, the cycle moves into actual drug use. Addicts may not use compulsively every time they use, but at some point compulsive use occurs. Compulsive use does not necessarily mean that the addict uses daily, for example. He or she may have one to two drinks a night for days or even weeks at a time, but then the dam breaks. Any form of loss of control characterizes compulsive use. This translates into the inability to stop, stay stopped, or predict what will happen once drug use has started. Compulsive use often leads to unpredictable behaviors like using more than you intended, staying out all night, getting into fights, getting arrested (also known as *breaking out in handcuffs*), getting harmed, harming others, spending too much money, waking up in strange places, losing your car, or even losing your clothing.

Consequences mount as preoccupation, rituals, and compulsive use are mechanically followed to avoid whatever stimulus started the process. Shame and guilt are frequently experienced by the addict who is out of control. Continuing to use despite the desire to quit and despite negative consequences can be an enormous source of grief. It is said that the worst place to be is out of control. Remaining in the cycle of addiction is a subconscious strategy to avoid the pain and anxiety experienced over strained relationships, stress at work, financial difficulties, or the loss of control.

The avoidance mechanism of the addiction works for a time, but it then leads to greater pain and even more despair, the last phase. Negative consequences begin to build. The lower bank account, tumultuous relationships, and police record cause even more pain and suffering. Both the lack of control and the addiction cycle itself are huge sources of strain for this and other reasons. For example, the discomfort felt as a result of behaving in opposition to one's integrity is also incredibly painful. Regret, shame, and despair are not easy emotions to cope with, especially while under the strain of many other stressors. The despair phase further propels addicts through the addiction cycle, because these undesirable emotions are triggers in themselves. The cycle provides relief from pain caused by the addict's own hand by numbing most feelings. Like a windmill's blades exposed to just a hint of momentum, the addiction cycle can continue to spin from any one of its phases to the next to the next to the next, for a long time.

Chapter 6: The Development of Addiction

Finally Feeling "Normal" and Other Contributing Factors

Why do people get addicted, and how? We have reviewed how certain contributing factors, like genetics, predispose certain people to develop the disease. We know that our neurochemistry, our reactions to drugs, our environment, our past, our personality, and the drugs we choose also have vital roles in who gets addicted and how they get that way. Most people who use drugs do not become addicted. Over the years scientists have been able to recognize that a higher percentage of certain groups of individuals become addicted when compared to the general population. None of the higher-risk groups has a 100 percent certainty of developing addiction. Discussion is nonetheless helpful in understanding the disease and in concentrating effective prevention and treatment efforts.

Shyness, anxiety, depression, low self-esteem, and trauma are all risk factors for developing addiction. Personality disorders and other mental illnesses are risk factors as well. People who have difficulty learning from mistakes or have trouble controlling their impulses are likewise at higher risk. Thrill seekers and sociopaths are also more at risk. A lifelong feeling of general malaise can be a risk. Many addicts say that they never felt "normal" until they began using drugs. The shy teenager who finds liquid courage to socialize is a clear example of someone who has found a pharmacological coping skill. Others who live with debilitating anxiety or depression may find that certain drugs quiet their minds, and so they are apt to continue repeating the experience. Trauma victims are often subject to horrifying memories that cause them to relive the traumatic event, and this pain also may be dampened with the mind-numbing effects of mood-altering substances.

Again, drugs are powerful and rapid-acting agents that can change the way we feel. Until addiction develops, drugs can be the coping tools of choice for many people. The problem with using drugs as coping tools lies in their long-term harmful consequences. Yet to those who have not developed different ways of coping, they provide an immediate, tempting, and easy way out of short-term discomfort.

Agent + Host + Environment = Recipe for Addiction

If we recall the story of the three blind men and the elephant, we can see that addiction is an entity with many parts. We can use current science to simplify the answer to the question "How does addiction arise?" Updated research explains that the development of addiction depends on interactions among three main variables. The elements that interact in the development of addiction are agent, host, and environment. As a result of the interactions among them, one or more of the following take place: (a) no use, (b) some use, (c) substance abuse, or (d) addiction. Several factors may weigh in favor of no use, while others may predispose someone to use. Some genetic variants predispose people to use, while others are protective against use. Certain environments are likewise protective, while others may heavily predispose individuals in those environments toward addiction. Finally, some agents are intense and spur the development of abuse and addiction early and rapidly, while others have a more gradual and insidious effect in activating addiction.

The "host" refers to the individual. How can the host influence what will happen? Again, we know that addiction has a fairly strong genetic component similar to type 2 diabetes, which is approximately 40–60 percent genetic. Schuckit, Cloninger, Goodwin, Heath, Kendler, and other researchers have all provided the data to support the genetic component.[106,107,108,109] If one has a genetic predisposition to addiction, there is an increased likelihood of developing the disease. We also know that some people actually have a protective genetic makeup. For example, many Asians lack a crucial enzyme that breaks down a toxic by-product of alcohol. Thus, due to the higher-than-normal concentration of a toxin, they experience an imbalance of negative consequences early on, and the reinforcement to not use is greater than the reinforcement to use.

Imagine experiencing the worst hangover you have ever felt after drinking your first half a beer, and the same thing happens every time you drink. How likely would you be to continue repeating that awful experience? You can see, then, how this negatively reinforces continued use and why someone with this genetic predisposition would choose not to drink alcohol. Further studies have found genetic protective factors against abuse of other drugs like nicotine and codeine.[110,111]

Other host factors have reinforcing effects that predispose people to use, and to use more. The studies by Schuckit and others demonstrate that those with family histories of addiction can have more anxiety, enjoy more stress-relieving effects from using, and experience more euphoric effects from using. Other genetic predisposing factors were found in studies of genes encoding receptors for the neurotransmitters dopamine and GABA, which are intricately connected to the brain chemistry of addiction.[112] Research shows that the age of the host is an important variable in the onset of the disease. When I educate others about addiction, I emphasize that addiction is a young person's disease. Not only is it present in young people, but the onset of the disease is greatly affected by the age at first use. The younger your brain is when exposed to mind-altering substances, the quicker addiction develops. Young hosts have a higher likelihood of developing addiction than older hosts. This phenomenon is seen in laboratory rats as well. There is a robust risk of developing substance problems when drug use begins in adolescence versus adulthood. Recall that the brain does not fully develop until after twenty-five years of age. The immaturity of the brain is believed to influence the speed of the onset of addiction. On the other hand, delaying exposure to mind-altering substances has a protective effect. So, if we could somehow delay experimentation until after age twenty-five, we could prevent the onset of addiction in millions of people.

Moreover, certain groups of people, or hosts, exhibit a higher incidence of addiction. It is crucial to appreciate that these risk factors are NOT prerequisites for developing addiction. The existence of risk factors creates a predisposition, meaning that the odds are increased; it does not mean that addiction is inevitable. However, we do know that among people with certain other illnesses (comorbid conditions), the percentage of those with addiction is higher than in the general population. So, those with depression, anxiety, antisocial personality disorder, borderline personality disorder, high risk-taking behaviors, poor impulse control, low stress tolerance, difficulty learning from negative experiences, anxiety, bipolar disorder, and post-traumatic stress disorder all have a higher probability of developing addiction.

That notwithstanding, risk is not fate, and obviously not everyone with those illnesses or conditions will develop addiction. Furthermore, there are plenty of people with addiction who have no underlying coexisting illness. A host can have no risk factors and still develop addiction. When I assess patients, I have my antennae up, vigilantly looking for comorbid illnesses, but what I discover is that there are many cases without any other illness. Addiction is a primary illness that can affect anyone; every one of us is vulnerable to varying degrees. When people do suffer from addiction with other co-occurring disorders, unless they can become abstinent, any attempts to help them with their other issues will be in vain. Active addiction makes psychological and spiritual growth impossible.

Returning to the host variable of genetics, like type 2 diabetes, addiction is 40 to 60 percent genetic. Importantly, there are other genetic variants that can affect the development of addiction. Dopamine is the primary "feel-good" neurotransmitter. Without enough of it, our moods and dispositions can be bleak. We know that not all human beings have the exact same type, ratio, and amount of dopamine machinery in the brain. There are some who have less than the normal functional dopamine systems in their brains. They have less feeling of reward with everyday life because their reward center is not functioning optimally. They are said to have what is called *reward deficiency syndrome* and are at higher risk of self-medicating the doldrums that are more common in this group of individuals. This physiologic difference is experienced in animal models to some extent; strains of alcohol-preferring rats show evidence of less dopamine and serotonin from birth.

Clinically, I encounter many patients who fit into this category. Many addicts I treat claim that initially drugs actually made them feel "normal." They report that until they were exposed to mind-altering chemicals, they lived their lives feeling generally miserable and uncomfortable in their own skins. One addict remarked, "It was as if everyone else had the guidebook to life, and I was left out. I always felt like I was trying to function on an uneven playing field." For many people like this, life before drugs was monotonous and without flavor. Once they discovered the effects of drugs, they began to experience life as being more worth living, filled with meaning and inspiration, and whole. Studies of nonhuman primates demonstrate that more highly stressed animals within a group have less functional dopamine machinery than animals that experience less stress. The same genetic difference in dopamine receptors that helps explain why certain groups use more and others use less can also help to explain the phenomenon of addicts who report that drug use made them feel "normal."[113]

Since this group does not experience the normal and adequate sense of reward from everyday activities, they search out and may even "need" a boost from chemical enhancement to elevate their quality of life to what others may experience as normal. Over time, this process of self-medicating directly contributes to the development of the disease of addiction. The original normalizing effect progressively and paradoxically makes the users' lives worse. The coping mechanisms that were initially effective no longer work; however, often the addict continues to operate under the delusion that they still do. Insanity is loosely defined as *doing the same thing over and over and expecting a different result.* Here, it could be defined as *doing what used to work, expecting a result long since extinguished to reemerge.* This group is no longer chasing the initial high; rather, they are chasing the experience of what has become, to them, feeling "normal."

How can the *environment* influence the potential development of addiction? Environmental factors essentially refer to all the influences external to or outside of the host. These include family relationships not attributable to genetics, peer associations, geographic locations, demographics, exposure to stress, academic performance, and community and spiritual/religious involvement. The risk of addiction within families is related to genetics and the stress of environmental influences.[114] Sibling and environmental friendships and interactions play a significant role in substance use.[115] However, studies show that while environmental forces appear to have a large role in affecting how often an individual may experiment with drugs, these forces take a backseat to genes in affecting who will progress to addiction.[116,117] In households, neighborhoods, and social groups where drugs are readily available, there is greater access to drugs and more opportunity to use for "newbies." Yet the likelihood that those newbies will then go on to develop addiction is determined in larger part by their genes.

Some environmental factors increase the risks of developing addiction, while others have a protective influence against its onset. Families, communities, or cultures that impose grave consequences for substance abuse witness a lower incidence of addiction. Moreover, where alternative opportunities for pleasurable activities are readily available, there is less addiction.

In general, high drug availability, low demographic status, and poor parental support are the environmental factors that elevate risk for developing addiction. Some environmental factors are clear-cut. In communities that lack alternative youth programs, we find more drug use, more deviant behavior, more truancy, and more crime. Moreover, the peer groups that one associates with can encourage or discourage substance use, as well as influence which substances are permissible to use and which ones are not.

We know that in geographical areas where there is high drug availability, there are high rates of addiction. The price of drugs also affects their availability. Cheap gin in England once caused an epidemic of alcoholism. When mood-altering substances are cheap and plentiful in the environment, they are often used enough to activate addiction. For example, the easy availability of cheap heroin in Vietnam caused an enormous amount of heroin addiction among American soldiers during the Vietnam War. Ironically, soldiers in Vietnam under the age of twenty-one found it much more difficult to acquire alcohol than heroin.

Environmental cues assume an enormous role in the development and maintenance of active addiction. We have learned from multiple studies that the environments in which substances are used can trigger mental and emotional associations sufficient to change behavior. For instance, the sight of the drug dealer's car in the driveway or the case of cold beer in the store produces brain changes almost equivalent to the brain changes that happen when drugs are used. The addiction center of the brain, the MDS, actually fires a shot of dopamine when exposed to cues that signal the probable onset of drug use.[118] This is an important consideration concerning the role of environment and the extent to which someone's environment puts them at increased risk for relapse or supports their recovery from addiction. It also speaks to how fundamentally vital it is to remove oneself from high-risk environments and change the people, places, and things associated with using in order to achieve and maintain recovery.

The nature of the *agent* (the mood-altering substance or behavior), as well as how and where the agent exerts its effects, is also a crucial element in the development of addiction. First, the agent must be reinforcing enough to cause repeated use, known as *habituation*. Agents that do not stimulate continued use do not cause addiction. On the other hand, agents that are highly rewarding and reinforce their continued use do.

The site of action is also key. All agents that are abused have at least some effect on the brain's mesolimbic dopamine system. Drugs of abuse are rewarding when they come in contact with the brain's MDS—the primary site of their action. As described earlier, lab animals will continuously self-administer drugs to stimulate their MDS. However, if this self-administration mechanism is altered so that the drugs avoid the MDS, the lab animals will stop self-administering.

The agent can also affect how quickly addiction develops. The chances of developing addiction are increased along with the speed at which the agent reaches the brain and the intensity of the pleasurable response the agent produces. Agents that are available in rapid-acting forms are more self-reinforcing and easily abused. Heroin injected into the veins leads to addiction more quickly than swallowing opioid pain pills. Injecting or smoking any drug makes the concentration reach the brain much more quickly and affects it more powerfully than does swallowing it. The agent's delivery system is thus crucial as well. The tobacco industry capitalized on this relationship when they began to add ammonia to cigarettes. The nicotine is effectively freebased, and as a result the speed of the delivery of the drug is much more rapid. Quick delivery with rapid onset of mood-altering effects translates to "highly addictive." The nicotine patch has a very, very low risk of abuse because it provides only a slow and gradual release of nicotine through the skin into the bloodstream; it takes some time for that small amount to even reach the brain.

The agent's nature, speed of delivery, and site of action all play essential roles in the development of addiction. Hence, the host, the environment, and the agent are all fundamental considerations in understanding how addiction develops. Trying to explain addiction merely by looking at what substance is used or how long it is used is like explaining what an elephant is by describing only its tusks (and some elephants don't even have tusks). The unique interactions among these different variables—the host, the environment, and the agent—determine whether someone develops addiction.

Co-occurring Disorders

The host has a specific variable that is prevalent enough to warrant its own section, even though I covered it briefly above. Those with other mental or behavioral illnesses are at a higher risk of developing addiction than the general population. Nearly 70 percent of people who seek addiction treatment in the United States have a co-occurring illness.[119,120] Keep in mind that this figure applies to the population selected out—those whose issues are more severe.

There is a curious awareness surrounding the frequent pairing of mental illness and substance use, abuse, and addiction. Each of these disorders is primary and chronic and may exist without the other. There are some patients with depression who drink but who are not alcoholics. Also, there are some addicts who have low moods but do not have depression. Mental illness and addiction are separate conditions and have independent courses. However, when present together, as they are frequently, they can greatly influence each other's progression. The exact nature of the relationship between mental illness and substance abuse/addiction is frequently debated among professionals. Some common questions that arise include these:

- Do those with addiction develop mental illness as a result of their substance use?
- To what extent do those with mental illness use substances to self-medicate?

People who suffer with mental illness—for example, mood disorders like anxiety, depression, or bipolar disorder; post-traumatic stress disorder; or psychotic disorders such as schizophrenia—have a higher prevalence of substance abuse when compared to the general population. And it is also true that those who suffer with addiction have higher rates of mental illness when compared to the general population. When a substance-use disorder and mental illness are present in the same individual, then that person is known to have *co-occurring disorders*. This is also known as *comorbidity*. The terms are used to describe the phenomenon of two diseases present in the same patient. The close association between addiction and mental illness can be explained by shared genetic, environmental, and host factors. Patients with co-occurring disorders are a challenging and vulnerable group with intricate needs. The presence of mental illness with addiction can be an especially dangerous mix. There are difficulties in determining which disease may be masking the other. Further, there are certain questions that only time abstinent from substances can answer, such as:

- Are presenting symptoms of addiction, including intoxication or withdrawal, covering up a psychiatric illness?

- Are symptoms such as anxiety, depression, and poor hygiene or self-care evidence of mental illness that needs to be treated in its own right, or are they emotional or behavioral effects of active addiction?

- Has the patient's substance use been an attempt to self-medicate preexisting anxiety, depression, post-traumatic stress, or other psychiatric symptoms?

- Has untreated addiction contributed to a psychiatric illness?

The combination of mental illness and addiction is associated with an increase in negative physical, emotional, psychological, and social consequences. Patients with co-occurring disorders have higher rates of relapse, increased rates of self-harm, increased rates of homelessness, more social exclusion, higher rates of denial, increased rates of HIV transmission, increased risk of violence, and more contact with the legal system. In addition, they are more likely to experience prejudicial treatment and even exclusion from care in the healthcare system. There are many healthcare workers who are not well prepared, and in some cases not even willing, to treat this group. Even within addiction treatment settings, those with co-occurring disorders are challenging to manage and less responsive to treatment.

Mind-altering substances are extremely easy to access for anyone. For mentally ill patients wishing to take matters into their own hands, it is very easy to use marijuana, alcohol, nicotine, or other drugs to change the way they feel or control their mood. Psychiatric conditions can cause extreme anxiety, depression, stress, and other painful, uncomfortable feeling states. You can see, then, how tempting it might be to self-medicate. Who wants to suffer? However, while under some circumstances self-medication may be understandable, that doesn't make it advisable. Mind-altering drugs of abuse are dangerous in general, but they can make mental illness considerably worse, and sometimes trigger psychotic episodes or lead to fatal outcomes.

Naturally, confusion exists when an individual self-medicates with substances for a time prior to getting properly evaluated for a mental illness. Even experienced and skilled professionals cannot always decipher whether the substance use came before the mental illness or the person was self-medicating a mental illness that was already present or in process. Sometimes psychiatric treatments themselves can lead to drug use. That is, some psychiatric medications dampen a patient's dopamine system. Antipsychotics block dopamine receptors in an effort to stop hallucinations, paranoia, or racing thoughts. Recall that dopamine is a key player in the brain's reward system. So, less dopamine can cause less overall pleasure in life, and this may explain why so many patients on these medications smoke. Recall that inhaling nicotine can boost the dopamine in the pleasure center more than even alcohol. Therefore, the treatment for mental illness may inadvertently influence those patients to use cigarettes or other drugs in order to counteract certain of the effects of their medications.

Another reason why mental illness predisposes people to addiction is that mental illnesses are chronic. The relentlessness of any chronic disease makes it difficult to accept. There are multiple losses, constant limitations, and ongoing reminders of the disease. It may often seem as if everything in life gets filtered through the lens of the chronic disease, and any chronic disease is associated with higher rates of anguish. Those with mental illness may use self-medication to temporarily relieve themselves of the anguish, upset, and grief related to having such an illness. The physical and emotional distress of any chronic medical condition can lead someone to self-medicate, and those who continue to do so are prone to developing addiction.

On the other hand, substance abuse and mental illness may be a two-way street. It is believed that substance abuse increases one's vulnerability to mental illness. We know that substance use can lead to psychiatric symptoms, even after the first use. Intoxication can present with psychiatric symptoms and can make preexisting mental illnesses worse. Also, physical dependence is associated with psychological symptoms, and continued use may cause psychiatric syndromes. Addiction causes an enormous amount of the physiologic changes responsible for anxiety and depression. Substance use may activate a preexisting or dormant mental illness or contribute to the formation of one, and, in turn, lead to more drug use.

Although there is a clear, established relationship between mental illness and substance abuse, that relationship may be extremely complex and confusing to delineate. They are often present in the same individual, and each exacerbates the problems of the other. When mental illness is overlooked, merely treating the substance abuse will have little effect on the individual's well-being. On the other hand, many times substance use fails to be identified and mental illness is incorrectly diagnosed. So, as with anyone with addiction, but even more so, the intricate needs of those who suffer from co-occurring disorders must be addressed with a comprehensive treatment plan.

Adolescents

I am frequently approached by parents and schools with questions about teens, such as "What's the best way to prevent addiction?" "How do we know if our Johnny has a problem?" or "What type of treatment works on teens?" The truth is that very little is known for sure. There is relatively little good empirical data out there on the topic. But federally funded research on adolescents guides us in several effective interventions on risky teen behaviors.

In order to be effective, prevention programs should follow these recommendations to the maximum extent possible:

- Be long-term[121] and comprehensive in addressing any and all forms of alcohol and other drug abuse, including illegal underage use of legal drugs.[122]

- Include a community approach with parents, teachers, law enforcement, social scientists, and other related personnel all working together on a unified message,[123] and locally via an ethno-appropriate approach (i.e., race, gender, age, etc., should be matched to intervention efforts).[124]

- Family members and other key support systems should receive concrete relationship and parenting skills training.[125,126]

- Early intervention is key; as is true with diabetes or addiction, early intervention on risky behavior, such as poor self-regulation and truancy, is more effective than waiting until the problem is larger.[127,128]

- Prevention programs are most effective when they are interactive, including role-playing exercises, rather than relying heavily on classroom, didactic-style lecturing.[129]

- Prevention programs need to focus on the dual goals of decreasing risk factors, such as risky behaviors or dangerous attitudes, and increasing positive protective factors, such as healthy role models and activities.[130]

A frequent challenge I encounter when working with parents of teens with a substance abuse or behavioral issue lies in the key role parents must play in their children's lives. In session, a fairly large number of parents turn to their child after I say something about firm boundaries and consequences and say,

"Do you hear that? Listen to him." I then have to remind parents that I cannot be the parent, I cannot go home with them, and boundaries with consequences are theirs and theirs alone to set and enforce.

Chapter 7: Addiction Treatment Works

T reatment for addiction is effective. Treatment catalyzes change in the individual and the community. Treatment decreases substance use, improves overall health, decreases hospital admissions, reduces crime, decreases social costs, decreases unemployment, and improves overall social functioning.

Psychosocial Treatments

There are many psychosocial and medical treatments available and currently in use for the treatment of addiction. First, psychosocial treatments may include intensive residential twenty-eight-day-and-longer programs and twelve-step groups, but there are other forms that are less well-known. For instance, another example of a psychosocial treatment is a brief and frank discussion aimed at eliciting change, known as a "brief intervention." Other treatments include individual and group therapy, cognitive behavioral therapy, recovery/sober living communities, intensive outpatient treatment, partial hospital programs, family therapy, social and occupational skills training, acupuncture, hypnotherapy, hydrotherapy, motivational interviewing, motivational enhancement therapy, and others. These psychosocial treatments are designed to empower the individual in relation to his or her psychological well-being and social functioning. Some will be defined later in this chapter.

Medical Treatments

The second broad category includes medical treatments. Medical treatments refer to physician-guided approaches that consist mostly of pharmacological interventions such as those used during detox, relapse prevention, maintenance programs, and nutritional supplementation. There are only a handful of FDA-approved medications for addictive disorders, yet even these are not fully embraced or used. The future holds promise, though: several medications (and even a vaccine) are currently being investigated for their beneficial application in addictions and compulsions.

Medical management for addictive disorders is complicated by a lack of consensus among addiction professionals. Among other fundamental issues, doctors disagree on optimal prescribing practices. While some physicians use medications that I and many of my colleagues would deem unsafe for addicts, other physicians may view our philosophy as being overly rigid. On one hand, some practitioners believe that the only way to help addicts is to medicate them and give their brains "something it wants," even when that "something" may be mind-altering. Others feel the opposite—that the only good treatment is to keep the recovering addict "off of everything." This extreme may lead to undertreating in some cases.

I have heard stories from older members of Alcoholics Anonymous about the use of certain medications among the members in their groups. They observed that many who went to doctors and were prescribed Librium (a sedative), for example, looked and behaved as if they were drunk. Oddly enough, Librium was once marketed as a cure for alcoholism. It was initially misunderstood to be nonaddictive. However, as was soon found out, people were becoming physically dependent on it, having seizures, overdosing, and withdrawing. It caused the same types of problems that alcohol caused. Over the years, similar stories have created a culture of distrust among many in the recovery community. However, there are those who need medical management for many legitimate medical and psychiatric conditions, and there have been many people in recovery who have been helped thoroughly with the oversight of skilled physicians. Thus, a growing number of both professionals and recovering people accept the prudent use of certain medications. I am in agreement with them—the best practice lies somewhere in the middle. Some treatments help some people some of the time, and no single approach is appropriate for every person all the time.

It is important to appreciate that the twelve-step community formally has no opposition to medications, and officially they do not claim that the Twelve Steps are a replacement for professional therapy or medical treatment. Twelve-step programs are one way to interrupt the cycle of addiction and facilitate the process of recovery. When other modalities are useful, they should be utilized.

The overall problem of reactivating the disease of addiction or switching addictions is real. There is always a risk in prescribing a medication that can be abused that the medication will be abused, and that its use or abuse will trigger abuse of the original drug of choice. It is important for medical prescribers to recognize that similarities among substances of abuse are much greater than any differences among them, whether the drug being abused is alcohol, Valium, Vicodin, or heroin. When put into the body, all drugs of abuse essentially work in the exact same place in the brain and can trigger addictive thinking, even when that substance is not an addict's specific drug of choice. When misused, all mind-altering drugs create the same essential components of the addiction cycle. The drug itself is only a symptom within the overall larger context of the disease of addiction.

Even the Big Book of Alcoholics Anonymous states that alcohol is only one symptom of alcoholism. The belief is that an alcoholic's use of other mind-altering drugs, including those that are medically prescribed, will usually create the same type of unmanageability in his or her life as alcohol. So, while no doctor would intentionally (one would hope) harm someone, many physicians can, out of ignorance or ideology, put someone at high risk for relapse by prescribing medications that have the potential for abuse and that work in the same part of the brain as all drugs of abuse.

On the other hand, many medications have been used successfully with recovering persons. There may be a fine line between hurting and helping, and again, optimal medical management is individualized. What we have been learning recently due to the burgeoning work of science in the addiction field is that we have a growing arsenal of medications that can help the person suffering with addiction. We have medications that can counteract the mood-altering effects of drugs. We are even working on vaccines as medicinal tools to treat addictions. There are medications that can diminish the substance-related cravings and others that are helping to restore imbalances in receptors in the brain and thus can assist the recovery process.

These leaps forward notwithstanding, the lack of consensus as to what constitutes gold-standard addiction care is a continuing concern. There are clear guidelines for most other major diseases. For instance, if you have chest pain and significant blockage in your coronary arteries, it would be crystal clear that you should have an invasive procedure. If you have acute appendicitis, you would get the appendix surgically removed. Both of these medical maladies have clear-cut interventions and have uniformly agreed-upon treatment regimens. This is rarely the case with addiction treatment—such standardization does not yet exist, especially on the same large scale as in other fields. My intent is not to imply that addiction treatment is like the Wild West. The majority of reputable treatment centers and professionals have essentially similar standards for care, based on their licensing, accreditation, and other regulatory mandates. Most of us employ a group and individual dynamic process infused with supportive communal care, because it is a very effective therapeutic system. But due to problems in defining *treatment* and *success,* our field still has a long way to go to match the rigor and clarity in other areas of medical practice. Treatment is effective, as we shall discuss, but how do we define success? Is success only total abstinence? That is not a standard we use for other chronic diseases. Is success less crime and more people working and paying taxes? That is not how we define success in treating disease, though it may be an important definition of success with social problems. "What are we treating?" and "Why are we treating it?" will be answered next. Then, in Chapter Eight, we will explore the question "What is treatment?"

What Are We Treating?

Not an Acute Illness

In addressing whether treatment is effective, it is vital to appreciate that addiction is not an acute illness. What does "acute" mean? It refers to a condition that is sudden or quick. If you were to have sharp pain in the bottom right side of your abdomen with some nausea and fever, you might have an appendix that is inflamed or burst, diagnosed as appendicitis. That would be an acute illness. You would be admitted to a hospital, where a surgeon would remove the appendix and that would be that. You would not need to worry about a recurrence of appendicitis, you would never need to worry about fulfilling your potential as a human being, and you would not need long-term psychological counseling to live out the rest of your life sans appendix. In the end, you had an acute illness that was treated by an appropriate one-time interventional procedure and were cured.

Addiction causes brain changes that are lasting, and so must be viewed as a disease that requires long-term treatment. Addiction is *not* an acute illness. Neither is high blood pressure, for example. Addiction and high blood pressure are chronic, long-term diseases. As such, they are not cured by the brief courses of treatment we employ for acute and short-term disease processes. If you try to treat a chronic condition as though it is an acute illness, you get into major trouble. Chronic diseases cannot be treated effectively by one-time interventions.

For example, let us say that "Jon" has chronic high blood pressure that is well controlled with medication after he has attempted to improve diet, exercise more, and practice stress relief. Let us imagine Jon is doing well—his two blood pressure medications are working so effectively that his risk for heart attack and stroke is equivalent to that of someone without high blood pressure. Now let us remove his medications. What will happen? His symptoms will come back. His blood pressure will go back up, his health will deteriorate in the long run, and the uncontrolled state of his disease will return.

High blood pressure is a chronic disease that requires ongoing, "chronic" management. Similarly, substance use is a chronic disease requiring long-term management. If you remove disease management from someone with addiction, you will have a resurgence of symptoms of that chronic disease as well—namely, use of alcohol and/or other drugs will resume and, with reactivation of addiction, all the horrid consequences of that disease will resurface, too.

Addiction is a chronic disease with long-term brain changes.[131] What we have witnessed is that relapses occur much more frequently when people do not continue their treatment and fail to work a program of recovery. In fact, those who only enter detox but do not receive further treatment have the same success rate of long-term recovery as those who do not enter detox at all. Addiction is a lifelong condition, so as treatment providers we attempt to get people ready to engage in a lifelong process of recovery, one day at a time. No one can live the rest of his or her life all at once, so maintaining a recovery plan, one day at a time, will effectively sustain a recovery plan for the rest of his or her life. Of course, there are no guarantees, but the point is that, when treated appropriately like the chronic disease that it indeed is, addiction can be managed effectively. If addiction is treated for only a short period of time, there most likely will be a relapse and reactivation of the disease process at some point afterward.

Why Are We Treating Addiction?

Treatment *Is* Effective

There is an enormous degree of misunderstanding about the effectiveness of treating addiction. Contrary to yet another misconception that addiction is resistant to treatment, we know that treatment is indeed effective. In spite of the absence of consensus on a gold standard of care, research confirms that addiction treatment is as effective as treatment for other chronic conditions such as asthma, diabetes, and high blood pressure.[132] Medical visits related to alcohol and other drugs decline 53 percent following treatment.[133] If relapse occurs, it is *not* due to treatment's ineffectiveness. Instead, ongoing medical and psychosocial interventions are directed to strategize and better individualize the treatment. We may look for environmental clues to enhance medical and therapeutic compliance and facilitate better outcomes, or we may utilize other modalities that are typical in managing a chronic disease—where fluctuations in treatment compliance and the recurrence of symptoms are the norm.

Too frequently, though, we do not have the opportunity to treat addiction adequately. That is, we are forced to curtail treatment length due mostly to lack of understanding and to financial constraints. I believe that this dilemma stems in large part from both the overwhelming standardization pitfall and the widespread misconception that addiction is not an effectively treatable disease. If addiction outcomes were universally measurable and if all of us demanded equal consideration, then we would treat addiction appropriately as indicated with the proper level of care for the right length of time. It has been demonstrated that for every dollar we spend treating addiction, we can save society between seven and twenty-three dollars. When we do not treat it, we are subjecting individuals and society as a whole to catastrophic expenditures and negative consequences. Bottom line: treatment works for this chronic disease.

Furthermore, research shows that patients who received less-than-recommended levels of care used nearly twice as many hospital beds over the next year for substance-abuse treatment than those who were treated appropriately.[134] Our unwillingness as a society to treat addiction as a disease has implications that affect all of society and individuals alike, because when we do not treat substantial diseases, society bears the brunt of the cost. Billions are spent every year in lost wages, costs related to healthcare, law enforcement and the criminal justice system, and lost productivity due to untreated addiction. Those individuals who go untreated suffer. Their families, loved ones, and communities suffer.

Not only does ongoing addiction treatment work generally, but so do more targeted, time-limited treatment approaches. Brief interventions, discussed later in this chapter, have reliably produced reductions in alcohol and other drug use. In fact, nationwide brief interventions of adults in need of treatment could save nearly $2 billion a year.[135] It is important to remember that as a chronic disorder, addiction requires long-term treatment, and that treatment should be measured in months and years.

Still, even suggestions are helpful in planting the seeds that will one day help the addict in long-term recovery. Several research studies have shown that when healthcare professionals briefly and gently engaged in conversations about the risks and benefits of continued use of alcohol and other drugs, hospitalization costs were cut by $1,000 per person for those screened prior to discharge from the hospital, with a savings of four dollars for every one dollar invested in trauma center and emergency room screening. A study from the state of Washington found that brief interviews reduced Medicaid costs by $185 per patient per month.[136] So while more intensive treatment for addicts is still optimal, even brief interventions can make an important and positive difference. The overall take-home message is that treatment is effective, and it is effective in many forms.

Treatment, Recovery, and Success

Let us examine further what is meant by *treatment* and what constitutes *recovery*. These are not easy tasks. The lack of a foolproof diagnostic test for addiction, combined with the absence of consensus as to what recovery actually means, puts us in a quandary of sorts. We have no way of accurately knowing how many people have addiction and what percentage of that population is in recovery. The US government, with the help of a nonprofit third-party research institute, surveys a wide and representative swath of American households, asking questions via telephone. From that official survey we make an informed guesstimate of the incidence of addiction. The National Survey on Drug Use and Health (NSDUH) provides national and state-level data on the use of tobacco, alcohol, and other drugs (including the nonmedical use of prescription drugs) and mental health in the United States. NSDUH is conducted under the auspices of the Substance Abuse and Mental Health Services Administration (SAMHSA) within the US Department of Health and Human Services (DHHS).

Another issue clouds the picture. While there has long been a plethora of anecdotal evidence that twelve-step programs and traditional residential treatments work, we have only recently begun to scientifically verify that certain treatment modalities produce better outcomes than others. Research demonstrates that twelve-step programs work; the problem is that we do not know exactly *how* they work. There are also significant inherent challenges in attempting the scientific study of programs in which the participants are, by formal tradition, anonymous. We just know that these programs are an effective method for helping many people recover from addiction and other compulsive behaviors. Not knowing the specifics of the *how* creates a vacuum in which confusion and criticism can flourish.

When referring to the end goals of treatment, we also often face mixed or conflicting messages. Depending on the ideology of the treating professional or institution, what constitutes success can be defined quite differently. Do you believe that success is achieved only by total permanent abstinence? Do you believe that any degree of harm reduction represents success? Do you believe that medication-assisted treatment and medication-assisted recovery represent success?

No matter what ideology or definition of success with regard to treatment and recovery you may have, there is yet another fundamental issue to consider. Addiction is a relapsing disorder, as is any chronic disease. This notwithstanding, many people have the unrealistic expectation that treatment should permanently *cure* addiction. Other diseases measure success in variants of total control and are considered successful in considerably smaller time increments than "forever."

It would be impossible to find a single doctor whose patients with diabetes, high blood pressure, asthma, epilepsy, cancer, and so on, had 100 percent perfect control of their illnesses from the moment they were diagnosed and treated, for the rest of their lives. The reality is that people with any of these chronic diseases are also prone to relapse. Relapse can be due to factors beyond personal control, like genetics, or to factors within our control such as the choice to diligently adhere to treatment recommendations. It is not uncommon for any patient with a chronic condition to become at least occasionally noncompliant with his or her treatment regime—the result of which is that the disease can once again become active.

Continuous abstinence is great and remains the number-one goal, but it's not the only indicator of success in terms of addiction treatment and recovery. With any relapsing disease, defining and measuring success in ways that don't resemble real life and ignore other valuable indicators of health and well-being such as meaning, relationships, and engagement is neither accurate nor helpful.

The difficulty of attempting to scientifically measure success in addiction treatment and recovery is further complicated by the large number of variables that must be accounted for and controlled when doing research. For example, there are different treatment structures, models, and approaches, different types of therapists/counselors, different spiritual approaches, vastly different home environments and living situations, and very different individual circumstances that frequently include combating a variety of other significant challenges—such as co-occurring mental disorders and/or medical conditions. Interestingly, the one variable that makes just about any type of "talk therapy" effective is trust. If you trust and have good rapport with your therapist, the chances are that he or she will be much more effective in helping you than another therapist who might have more education, training, and experience.

It's important to be careful when reading about extremely high rates of treatment success. Occasionally, there are incredible claims of success that call for magnified scrutiny. For example, the levels of success claimed by some treatment centers could stem from the fact that they only accept relatively well individuals over the age of twenty-five from the higher end of the socioeconomic spectrum—thus intrinsically skewing their results. This particular subpopulation has the best chance of success before they even start treatment, especially since they are most likely to have access to both financial resources and a good support system.

Other common practices for measuring outcomes rely solely on phone calls to track postdischarge client status. Many times I have heard my patients report that they were abstinent and in recovery during such follow-up interviews when, in fact, they had relapsed and were too ashamed to admit the truth. Moreover, such follow-up surveys tend to be limited to six months, one year, or eighteen months following discharge. Virtually no treatment programs, to my knowledge, have the capacity or willingness to invest the resources needed to track and evaluate postdischarge outcomes over the long term.

The Betty Ford Institute convened a panel in 2007 that developed a helpful preliminary definition of recovery as a starting point for enhancing communication and developing professional standards. Recovery was defined as a voluntarily maintained lifestyle characterized by abstinence, personal health, and citizenship. Abstinence involves alcohol and all other nonprescribed drugs. Personal health relates to improved quality of personal life in the areas of physical health, psychological health, independence, and spirituality. Citizenship relates to living with regard and respect for others.[137]

Defining recovery is such a necessary ingredient for progress in addiction treatment that the US government is now involved in this process. In May 2011, the Substance Abuse and Mental Health Service Administration (SAMHSA) published their working definition of recovery: *a process of change through which individuals work to improve their own health and well-being, live a self-directed life, and strive to achieve their full potential.*

SAMHSA then expands this further into categories of life necessary for a comprehensive life in recovery:

- *Health: overcoming or managing one's disease(s) as well as living in a physically and emotionally healthy way;*
- *Home: a stable and safe place to live;*
- *Purpose: meaningful daily activities, such as a job, school, volunteerism, family caretaking, or creative endeavors, and the independence, income, and resources to participate in society; and*
- *Community: relationships and social networks that provide support, friendship, love, and hope.*[138]

Simultaneously, SAMHSA also published their *Guiding Principles of Recovery,* a list of ten guiding principles that support recovery:

1. Recovery is person-driven: self-determination and self-direction are the foundations for recovery.

2. Recovery occurs via many pathways: recovery pathways are highly personalized and are characterized by ongoing growth and improved functioning that may involve setbacks, a natural, though not inevitable, part of the recovery process.

3 Recovery is holistic: recovery encompasses an individual's whole life, including mind, body, spirit, and community.

4. Recovery is supported by peers and allies: mutual support and mutual aid groups, including the sharing of experiential knowledge and skills, as well as social learning, play an invaluable role in recovery.

5. Recovery is supported through relationships and social networks: through these, people leave unhealthy and/or unfulfilling life roles behind and engage in new roles that lead to a greater sense of belonging, empowerment, autonomy, social inclusion, and community participation.

6. Recovery is culturally based and influenced: culture and cultural background, including values, traditions, and beliefs, are essential factors in determining a person's journey and unique pathway to recovery.

7. Recovery is supported by addressing trauma: this includes, but is not limited to, physical or sexual abuse, domestic violence, war, and natural disasters.

8. Recovery involves individual, family, and community strengths and responsibility: each of these has strengths and resources that can contribute to laying a foundation for recovery.

9. Recovery is based on respect: community, systems, and societal understanding and acceptance of people affected by addiction and mental health problems are crucial in achieving recovery.

10. Recovery emerges from hope: the belief that recovery is real provides the essential and motivating message of a better future—people can and do overcome the internal and external challenges, barriers, and obstacles that confront them.[139]

What, then, should the goal of recovery be? Can we ignore the fact that recovery is a process and not just a goal? In the treatment community we often speak of a turning point in our patient's recovery when "the light bulb comes on." Recovering individuals themselves often report that something intangible happens as a result of maintaining their course of recovery. How do we accurately measure such intangibles or the totality of the other criteria described by the Betty Ford Consensus Panel and SAMHSA—citizenship, physical health, psychological health, independence, purpose, community, and spirituality? How do we account for the deeply personal aspects of recovery—cultural differences, religious or spiritual beliefs, abstinence-based versus medication-assisted recovery, trauma-driven responses, and the myriad forms that personal growth can take?

As I suggested above, the success rates dwindle if the only outcome we consider is 100 percent perfect long-term control of this chronic disease. By that measure, we could only claim success if the person is totally abstinent without any slips, forever, from the moment he or she is diagnosed. In limiting ourselves to equating success only with 100 percent perfect long-term abstinence, we shut ourselves off from looking at other measures of success, like personal growth and the minimization of suffering. Although abstinence remains the ultimate goal, whenever an addict achieves weeks, months, and especially years of recovery, he or she has achieved a degree of success and gained experiences of considerable value.

As I have argued, the field of addiction treatment is in great need of a widely accepted set of definitions and standards against which we can measure treatment efficacies. Abstinence from all mind-altering abused substances still remains the ultimate goal of recovery for most treatment programs in this country. The reality is that total abstinence is difficult to achieve—it takes an average of seven attempts to quit before someone can stop smoking,[10] drinking, or even using heroin. In my experience, seven attempts at quitting is fairly consistent no matter what substance my patients are trying to stop using.

A measuring stick that takes into account multiple real-life variables is required in order for any outcome evaluation tool to be truly effective. Most diabetics cannot get their diabetes under perfect control during the initial few months postdiagnosis, and sometimes even years following it. In fact, some may never attain perfect control during their entire lives. Yet we do have ways to measure how well treatment for diabetes is working, as well as the status of someone's diabetes at a specific point in time: we measure the sugar in their blood. The question remains, what do we measure in addiction and recovery? Some argue that drug screens are the answer. Since we began utilizing them on a large scale, we have been able to identify folks who need more help earlier, and I feel more people avoid relapse because drug screens are such an effective deterrent.

I do not believe that only important variables in life can be measured. Love is the best example of a vital life element that defies objective measurement. However, the development of commonly accepted standards that can be utilized in addiction treatment and recovery necessitates use of such measures, and as such this remains our task. I am optimistic that in the near future we will continue to move toward collaboration on a genuine consensus on outcome measures that become widely accepted within the field of addiction treatment, our healthcare system, and our general culture.

Chapter 8: Treatment 101

There continues to be a large "treatment gap" in this country. In 2013, an estimated 22.7 million Americans (8.6 percent) needed treatment for a problem related to alcohol or other drugs, but only about 2.5 million people (0.9 percent) received treatment at a specialty facility.[140]

In addiction treatment, one size does not fit all, and treatment for addiction is offered in a variety of ways. There is a range of types and intensities of treatment, and no one type of treatment is considered the best fit for all addicts. Optimal addiction treatment is individualized. Whether the treatment plan is purely psychosocial or a combination of psychosocial and medical approaches, decisions should be guided by an individualized assessment of each person's needs and goals. It is also crucial that the needs and goals—identified through the formal assessment and operationalized within the framework of the treatment plan—be continually reassessed throughout the course of treatment to ensure their continuing relevance and maximize the addict's participation.

Again, there are many inpatient and outpatient treatments available. Studies that have examined which kinds of treatment are most effective have yielded important results. We now know that the best chance for success is achieved if we can initially treat patients for a minimum of ninety days.[141] This magic number for length of stay means that when an addict is engaged in ninety days of continuous treatment, he or she has a better chance of maintaining recovery. However, it does not mean that the addict must be in an inpatient residential treatment program for ninety days. Instead, it means that outcomes are improved if he or she engages in some form of treatment continuously for ninety days.

Essential elements of any treatment approach are empathy and trust between the provider and the patient. When there is a trusting relationship between the patient and his or her treatment staff, therapist, and doctor, success is more likely than when trust is absent. Of course, there are certain programming elements that also positively affect outcomes, such as encouraging participation in twelve-step groups. Most importantly, when addicts can be engaged in a treatment process for an extended period of time with caring, compassionate addiction professionals, their chances of establishing and maintaining recovery are significantly enhanced.

Insurance Issues

Unfortunately, many people cannot afford the length and/or type of treatment that they need. This is true even when they have health insurance, and it is a topic worth touching on here. When insurance is used, insurance companies dictate our patients' level of care and length of stay. Tragically, it is often only when patients have the means to pay for the entire length of recommended treatment that we are able to keep them engaged long enough to maximize the likelihood that they will attain maximum benefit. One cynical, though not inaccurate, explanation is that insurance companies are in the business of making money. Insurance companies often deny care, approve only very limited lengths of stay, or dictate the specifics of the care they are willing to reimburse for.

There are obvious problems when financial concerns trump health needs. It adds insult to injury when people work hard to make a living and pay their health insurance premiums only to have their insurance companies deny payment for the care they need. While denying or limiting care saves insurance companies money in the short term, we all pay for it in the long run. The disease of addiction left untreated accounts for nearly $600 billion annually in lost wages, criminal justice and healthcare costs, missed work, and so forth.[142] In contrast, when we treat addiction, we save society money. When we don't properly treat a costly disease, the consequences are immense.

When insurance companies deny my patients the care they need, I sometimes participate in peer reviews, in which I discuss the case with one of my peers in the medical profession. Through such reviews, I have seen that many insurance companies have their own versions or interpretations of what constitutes appropriate criteria for admitting people into treatment, and for continuing that treatment. In my view, these selective criteria are strategically designed to deny care.

When insurance companies do use standardized admission criteria, it appears to me that they creatively interpret them in order to deny coverage and, in the process, save money. The American Society of Addiction Medicine has established an excellent set of admission criteria that are logical and advocate for recovery and patient care. The widespread acceptance of these criteria by the insurance industry would serve their customers and our society well.

Advocating with insurance companies to admit patients or continue their care is usually an uphill battle. In my experience, doctors who work for insurance companies often seem to have their minds made up to deny or minimize care before we even begin our review of the case. This is consistent with a fundamental aspect of their role, which is to save their employer money. Once I was even called a "wanker" simply because I asked the insurance company doctor what he would do if the case we were reviewing was that of his son. These experiences notwithstanding, I have had meaningful reviews with insightful and empathetic doctors and insurance professionals. However, in my experience, such positive, collaborative encounters have been the exception.

I know that healthcare spending is out of control and efforts must be made to contain healthcare costs. It is also important to emphasize that managed care is not the enemy. However, the fact remains that, in every case, addiction is a serious, life-threatening condition that responds to treatment, which, in turn, saves money and lives.

A Variety of Options for Treatment

Treating addiction utilizes many of the same strategies used during the treatment of other chronic diseases. We employ individual therapy of varying types, group therapy, education, behavioral therapy, medication management when indicated, family therapy, or a combination of these services. In order to tailor treatment to meet an individual's needs, we often must be multifaceted—that is, a one-dimensional approach would not be effective because of the complex nature of individuals and of the disease of addiction. While adolescents especially benefit from more intensive family therapy, older adults benefit from esteem-building and nonconfrontational methods. But individual differences can also make the reverse true. Some addicts need extra hugs in treatment, and some need more of a push.

There are a few new addiction medications that have received a lot of media attention lately. I will review specific medications in much more detail in Chapter Nine, but a brief overview is called for here. Medications can be useful, but they are just one aspect of the treatment of addiction. Medications have a narrower application than behavioral treatment options. Some medications target only alcohol cravings, while many behavioral approaches apply to cravings for all substances. Medicines used to treat addiction are as varied as medicines for other chronic diseases. There are medications for alcohol abuse, opioid/opiate (including prescribed painkillers) abuse, stimulant (cocaine and speed) abuse, and others. Some medications target craving, while others target the specific receptors or parts of the body with which substances interact, and other medications help restore a balance in the body.

The skilled clinician can decipher the needs of the addict, and treating addiction as a disease with a set of defined professional guidelines will yield the best outcomes. Nearly three decades of scientific research have yielded thirteen fundamental principles that characterize effective treatment. These principles are detailed in NIDA's *Principles of Drug Addiction Treatment: A Research-Based Guide:*[143]

1. No single treatment is appropriate for all individuals.

2. Treatment needs to be readily available.

3. Effective treatment attends to multiple needs of the individual, not just his or her drug use.

4. At different times during treatment, a patient may develop a need for medical services, family therapy, vocational rehabilitation, and social and legal services.

5. Remaining in treatment for an adequate period of time is critical for treatment effectiveness.

6. Individual and/or group counseling and other behavioral therapies are critical components of effective treatment for addiction.

7. Medications are an important element of treatment for many patients, especially when combined with counseling and other behavioral therapies.

8. Addicted or drug-abusing individuals with coexisting mental disorders should have both disorders treated in an integrated way.

9. Medical detoxification is only the first stage of addiction treatment and by itself does little to change long-term drug use.

10. Treatment does not need to be voluntary to be effective.

11. Possible drug use during treatment must be monitored continuously.

12. Treatment programs should provide assessment for HIV/AIDS, hepatitis B and C, and tuberculosis and other infectious diseases, as well as counseling to help patients modify or change behaviors that place them or others at risk of infection.

13. Recovery from drug addiction can be a long-term process and frequently requires multiple episodes of treatment.

It is important to stress that treatment outcomes are optimized when we provide individualized treatment. One inherent requirement is that treatment providers have enough time to accurately see what they are dealing with. Remember that many people with addiction also have a co-occurring disorder such as depression, anxiety, post-traumatic stress disorder, bipolar disorder, or schizophrenia. Treatment, when customized for the individual and combined with an appropriate length of stay, can screen those patients who also have a co-occurring or other underlying disorder.

Time is a key element in treatment because addicts are quite "out of it" early in their recovery process. There can be problems with concentration, attention, mood, memory, and sleeping. People are commonly anxious, irritable, and depressed, and have intense cravings early in their recovery process and thus exhibit some behaviors that can be confused with a mental illness. It is crucial that we have the opportunity to see people through this early phase so we can make informed clinical decisions about their needs and how best to tailor their treatment.

For example, "Joe" was a middle-aged businessman who was confused and lethargic. He cried nearly all the time in his first two weeks of treatment. His insurance company wanted us to hurry up and discharge him to a lower level of care. However, I was not comfortable with his state of mind, and I was also uncertain whether he had depression or another form of mental illness besides addiction. He was clearly not ready to leave after five or ten days; it would have been irresponsible and disastrous if we had "stepped him down" to an outpatient level of care when his insurance company wanted us to. It also would have been premature to start him on medications for depression, yet that mistake is often made because patient presentation in early recovery can mimic mental illness. As it turned out, Joe finally began to turn around as a result of our inpatient programs and, through his processing, we learned that he needed grief counseling and treatment for codependency. He did not need medications. Joe needed treatment and time. He is doing well today in therapy and is still in recovery. Further, he does not exhibit any evidence of depression or anxiety.

Time in treatment and patience with regard to progress were essential to his success—as they are for so many people seeking recovery allies.

When to Start?

Another question that comes up in the arena of treating addiction is when to start treatment. There is another widespread misconception that an addict must "hit rock bottom" before treatment can be effective. What is "rock bottom," and how do you know when you've hit it? The problem is, things can always get worse. I thought that I had hit rock bottom 100 times before I got into recovery. We know from years of experience that interventions work. Surely, if left alone, things would have gotten worse, but the opportunity to treat should be seized whenever possible. We do not have to wait to make a positive impact. Medications can help us intervene more aggressively at points of maximum catastrophe.

With appropriate pharmacotherapy, it is even possible to begin treatment for alcoholism while the individual is still actively drinking heavily and at the point of maximum crisis. Although abstinence remains the ultimate goal in treating individuals addicted to alcohol, it is generally understood that reducing the severity and frequency of drinking decreases alcohol-related consequences and improves quality of life.[144]

Research increasingly supports the benefit of intervening at any point in the course of addiction. Quite simply, it is a myth that an addict has to hit a bottom on his or her own before treatment should begin. Medications can be effective interventions and can be utilized prior to waiting for an addict to hit a lower bottom. Help is warranted at any stage of the addict's path because it can be beneficial.

In many circumstances, medications are necessary for safe detoxification. But detoxification alone is not treatment. Safely detoxifying someone is but one aspect of addiction treatment, and not everyone who comes into treatment needs detoxification. Some people we treat believe that once they are done with detoxification, they are cured and ready to begin the journey on their own. Nothing could be further from the truth. In fact, it is sad to see people leave treatment early, because most often they fail, as they leave with exactly the same limited set of coping skills that they came in with. If tolerance and withdrawal were the only elements of an addictive illness, treatment would consist simply of detoxification, a process that allows the body to cleanse itself of the offending substances while receiving decreasing doses of medication to reduce withdrawal symptoms. We now know that achieving a drug-free state is not the most significant accomplishment; the real key is maintaining it.

Medication Management Is One Piece

In addressing the best practices for treatment, it is imperative that we treat the whole person, the whole picture. My favorite quotation is from Sir William Osler, the first professor of medicine and founder of the Medical Service at Johns Hopkins University Hospital:

> *"It is more important for us to get to know what kind of patient has the disease rather than know what type of disease the patient has."*

This is a priceless nugget of insight. Too many times in my training, this perspective was largely ignored. The healthcare system is overwhelmed, and physicians are trained to think of the worst-case scenarios in order to avoid untoward complications. I understand the roadblocks, but whatever the case, we need to dig deep in order to best serve our patients. Identifying addiction is merely the starting point. We must look for sources of trauma, impaired thinking and coping skills, emotional dysregulation, mood disorders, and process addictions if we are to adequately help those on the journey toward recovery. Again, there is no single way to treat everyone with addiction; we are all different.

What is constant is the nature of the disease and its progression and devastating effects. It becomes the job of a skilled and adaptable clinician to find the right treatment approach designed for the individual. We do not recommend that everyone live in a recovery/sober living community after residential treatment, but there are many people who desperately need a structured, supportive, and safe recovery-oriented environment. Moreover, I do not believe everyone needs medication, either. My job, again, is to recognize what type of person has the disease and to formulate an individualized treatment plan to best support his or her journey in recovery.

We have made enormous strides in the field of addiction medicine. There are new medications that are specific, relevant, and effective. This was not true seventy-five years ago when Bill Wilson founded Alcoholics Anonymous. A modern nuance is the magnitude with which prescription and illicit drugs have affected the recovery and treatment culture. The average age in most treatment centers today has dropped two or three decades since the 1950s, 1960s, and 1970s because the substances that became widely abused caused the disease to progress much faster than alcohol alone. Younger addicts are experiencing quicker devastation, and there are now treatment programs designed exclusively for adolescents.

Drugs (this time not including alcohol) have changed the milieu, and they have changed treatment approaches. Moreover, in previous years up to the 1970s, there were not many treatment options with scientific merit. There were treatments back then, but none with nearly the scientific validity of treatments that we use today. Past treatments like lifetime institutionalization and sterilization would be considered abhorrent by today's standards and ethics. Great strides have been made over the last few decades, and I anticipate that this progress will continue.

Addiction has an enormous behavioral component, but it also has strong emotional, spiritual, physical, and psychological aspects. Despite the wonderful novel medications that are helpful in augmenting traditional behavioral approaches to therapy, there will never be a pill to cure addiction or replace behaviorally focused treatment approaches. A pill or an injection cannot give someone coping skills, and media attention that suggests otherwise is foolish and irresponsible, in my opinion. Too often, patients present to me after they have seen a TV commercial or read an advertisement about a new magic-bullet cure for addiction, expecting a quick fix. Any behavioral disease requires time, patience, hard work, and dedication in order to be treated. Staying on the path of recovery is an action that cannot be replaced by mere medicine.

A medication that works for some will not work for all, because treatment approaches and plans must account for individual variability. Not every patient with the same diagnosis needs any one medication or any one treatment. Furthermore, the same medication can work very differently in different patients—one patient may have an extremely positive response, while another might experience no effect or have a negative reaction. Moreover, the absence of medication does not indicate the absence of treatment. We must not lose sight of the fact that medication is merely one possible treatment option. It is crucial to avoid jumping on board the "magic-bullet train" every time a new medication hits the market. Addiction is best treated by a comprehensive and systematic approach that continues to maximize behavioral therapeutic modalities, alone or with medication management—based on a comprehensive assessment of each patient's individualized needs and a multimodal treatment plan to help the patient achieve his or her identified goals.

A Higher Level of Complexity

As an example of the benefits of behavioral interventions and the pitfalls of medication management alone, let us say I am treating "Joe" for heartburn, or gastroesophageal reflux disease. Let us also imagine he drinks a few alcoholic beverages daily. He also smokes half a pack of cigarettes daily. Furthermore, he eats a lot of chocolate and drinks five cups of coffee daily. Let's go even further and say he loves very spicy foods and frequently eats the "Diablo Fire" hot sauce on his jalapeño-infused enchiladas. If Joe comes into my office complaining of heartburn, I can give him a strong prescription antacid and proton pump blocker to relieve his symptoms and make his life more comfortable. If that is the only thing I do for him, I have not optimally served him.

Let us explore another scenario: he comes in to see me for heartburn, and I spend time discussing his behaviors that are leading to the pain. We explore the possibility of making some difficult changes in his behavior in order to improve his condition and avoid more serious risks that may transpire if he continues on his present course. I offer him hope and reassurance in his journey and continue to stay involved in his life by frequent monitoring through follow-up visits.

In the second scenario, he is more likely to develop healthy habits, as well as develop into a healthy human being. If he can change his behaviors, it is more likely he will not need medications. If he can learn to live without coffee, cigarettes, and spicy foods, he will have to adapt his way of life and in the process develop a different set of coping skills that are healthier and more balanced. In the long run, he will be better off. In the first example, the "prescription" was to numb him from the experience of his own behaviors. In the second, the treatment gives him greater awareness of how his choices affect his health and his life, giving him more control of his choices and lifestyle in order to create the healthiest Joe possible.

We can actually draw analogies from this vignette to a majority of diseases. When I was in training, I was amazed at the sheer number of diseases that have their basis in behavior. Yet I received precious little training in exploring the dynamics of supporting behavioral changes. The point is that in the case of patients with the disease of addiction, we must not forage only in the forest of pharmaceuticals. Medication is only one piece of a considerably larger puzzle.

Detoxification

Detoxification is frequently the first step in the process of addiction treatment. When the body becomes physically dependent on an addictive substance, it adapts so that the substance must be continuously consumed or else the body will go through withdrawals. As described in detail in Chapter Four, withdrawal symptoms vary depending on the class of substance used. For example, sedatives like alcohol and Valium can cause physical withdrawal symptoms that may include elevated blood pressure and heart rate, insomnia, nausea, hallucinations, and seizures. Sedatives may also cause emotional withdrawal symptoms like anxiety and depression. Detoxifying from sedatives presents a medical emergency and can potentially be fatal. On the other hand, detoxification from opiates like heroin or Oxycontin does not present the same level of risk. However, the physical and emotional grief that defines opiate withdrawal is so wretched that people often wish they were dead.

We will often employ sedatives like Librium and phenobarbital in order to safely guide patients through early withdrawal from alcohol and sedatives, so as to prevent a seizure or worse. To manage opiate withdrawal, physicians use agents like methadone, buprenorphine, and clonidine. Since detoxification is generally a medically managed process, physicians and nurses take leading roles during detoxification. Usually, the therapist's role during this first phase of acute withdrawal is of limited value, for many reasons. While it is important to begin stressing the importance of lifestyle changes, the brain in this phase of recovery is not in any shape to accept and process much more than concrete guidance.

While detoxification is often the best first step toward recovery, it must be followed by behaviorally based therapy. Too many patients and their families make the mistake of believing that detoxification alone is all that is necessary, but the truth is that the chances of relapse following a detoxification-only course of treatment are astronomically high. In fact, detoxification is comparatively easy—getting abstinent is much simpler than staying abstinent. Anyone can quit a thousand times. Staying stopped is the key, and that is not addressed by detoxification. As the National Institute on Drug Abuse (NIDA) clearly states:

> *Medications offer help in suppressing withdrawal symptoms during detoxification. However, medically assisted detoxification is not in itself "treatment"—it is only the first step in the treatment process. Patients who go through medically assisted withdrawal but do not receive any further treatment show drug abuse patterns similar to those who were never treated.*[145]

Psychosocial Treatment Options

Psychosocial treatments educate and empower addicts to make the changes necessary for recovery. Through a variety of modalities, psychosocial treatments increase healthy coping and life skills, assist in the identification and treatment of underlying issues, and help patients remain engaged in the treatment process. Whether or not detoxification services are needed, psychosocial treatments are the means to establish and continue recovery. Different treatment settings are available to address individual needs and differences. Some patients require intensive inpatient treatment in a residential treatment program for one, three, or nine months. Others are more appropriately served with outpatient treatment only. There are some addicts who find and stay in recovery by walking directly into twelve-step meetings, and others who do so through their religious institutions. The majority of addicts, however, are best served by a combination of the services available.

Residential Treatment

Residential treatment programs are very effective treatment options that are conducted in a variety of settings. Some are freestanding facilities in beautiful venues, others are basic in their facilities and environment, and some occupy a wing of a hospital. Intensive residential treatment programs offer care twenty-four hours a day, seven days a week. They provide room and board and allow the addict to intimately focus on him- or herself. In order to provide the highest level of intensity, residential treatments separate addicts from their usual day-to-day environment, free of the daily stressors as well as from the easy accessibility of drugs in their lives.

An important facet of residential treatment consists of peer interactions. That is, other residents and the community in general can be effective catalysts for change. An addict may be reluctant to hear from the staff or may have his or her defenses up against them, but when a fellow patient shares his or her own story or provides feedback, it tends to be a powerful influence that helps to connect residents and motivate them. The professional staff, some of whom may also be in recovery, provide education on the disease of addiction and its range of manifestations and effects, and conduct individual, group, and perhaps family therapy. In residential facilities that follow the Minnesota Model of addiction treatment, the disease of addiction is understood as a chronic, potentially fatal relapsing disorder, and treatment is focused on the whole person.

While family and social involvement can be crucial, the intensive therapy consists of a full schedule aimed at providing as much time for emotional, psychological, and spiritual work as possible in a short period of time. Residential treatment may be "away" from the patient's daily stressors, but it is far from a vacation. If engaged, patients work hard at establishing a foundation to jump-start new lives. They address tough emotional issues and learn entirely new ways of coping with the world around them. I'm concerned that some treatment centers concentrate too much on leisure activities and material amenities and not enough on biopsychosocial-spiritual programming. The days spent in treatment should feel like "work," because the type of change we are aiming for in early recovery requires attention and action; sitting back and passively spectating will not facilitate recovery.

The treatment plans are geared toward developing the addict's coping skill set, replacing substance use as the patient's primary coping mechanism with a variety of healthy options to address his or her particular social, mental, emotional, and spiritual challenges. This process includes exploring thought patterns so that addicts can become aware of their distorted, unhealthy beliefs and how these influence their patterns of behavior. Often, unresolved grief, anxiety, depression, personality disorders, and other illnesses, including medical conditions, are identified and either treated concurrently or referred out for continuing treatment. Residential treatment allows the addict to build a strong foundation of recovery that can be used as a springboard for his or her journey.

After residential treatment, patients are often "stepped down" to a lower level of care that could involve less-intensive residential care or outpatient services. A less-intensive residential level of care is known as a therapeutic community—a structured program in which patients remain at a residence, typically for extended periods of time that could last as long as two years. Therapeutic communities are designed to facilitate the resocialization of the patient to a drug-free and healthy lifestyle. Often addicts who find themselves in therapeutic communities have more serious addiction, social, and legal problems that require extended courses of treatment. There are also specialized therapeutic communities tailored for specific subgroups like pregnant women, mothers with children, professionals, or those on parole.

Partial Hospitalization/Day Treatment

Partial hospitalization, also known as day treatment, is essentially residential treatment without boarding. Patients participate in a highly structured daily program similar to that in residential treatment while they continue to live in the community, whether in their own homes or in transitional housing in the form of sober living/recovery homes. This level of care is a great stepping-stone down from intensive residential treatment to less-structured outpatient services.

Outpatient Treatment

Outpatient treatments are essentially composed of the same elements as residential treatment, but are scaled down in terms of the number of sessions and amount of time, and patients do not live where the treatment takes place. Patients participating in outpatient treatments attend sessions a few times a week rather than daily, with sessions that last a few hours rather than all day. Typically, an outpatient program will offer treatment in a clinical setting three days a week for three hours at a time. Outpatient treatment can be more intensive or less intensive. *Intensive outpatient treatment* consists of attending sessions three to five times per week for a total of nine to twenty hours, whereas *nonintensive outpatient treatment* usually involves one to three sessions per week for a total of one to six or so hours.

Patients are given the opportunity to identify their problematic behaviors and faulty thought processes in order to develop a healthier set of coping skills, just like they would be in residential treatment. Outpatient services are an option for initial treatment, especially for those who do not have severe manifestations of the disease, who have mitigating circumstances that prevent inpatient treatment, or who have healthy, well-developed social support systems. Outpatient treatment also costs much less than residential treatment and so may be the only affordable option for some. Nonetheless, outpatient treatment can be effective as well.

In addition to being a viable primary level of treatment, as I mentioned, outpatient programs serve as an essential "step-down" level of care. For those who have completed a higher level of care, the opportunity to explore and practice coping with daily stressors while living in one's own community is a key benefit to continuing treatment as an outpatient. Recall that length of engagement in treatment directly and positively affects outcomes. Instead of discharging some patients directly home without any follow-up professional care, it is often recommended that they continue their treatment in this less structured setting. It is quite often too much of a shock to the system when transferring from the safety of an intensive residential program to the hustle and bustle of the outside world. Outpatient treatment can serve as an effective bridge, allowing newly recovering individuals to return to their homes, families, and jobs while continuing in formalized group settings and receiving the benefits of professional counseling and peer support.

Aftercare

Obviously, following any particular treatment episode, there are no guarantees of success. As addiction is a relapsing disease, there is always a risk that even effectively treated people will face significant challenges that have the potential to lead to a relapse. The first several months after structured treatment are the riskiest. Aftercare, as the name suggests, is professionally provided follow-up treatment subsequent to primary inpatient/residential and/or outpatient addiction treatment. Aftercare can last anywhere from six months to two years, and usually takes the form of a combination of group and individual therapy, but sometimes only group. Aftercare helps to extend the influence and efficacy of primary treatment, reinforcing new learning and skills as these become increasingly integrated into the recovering person's daily life.

Aftercare services are available through treatment centers as well as independent companies. Other aftercare options use the advantages of information technology. There are social media recovery Web sites with programs that help monitor emotional changes and craving levels; the sites then convey that information (with the individual's informed consent) through cyberspace to the addict's support group. In the future it is likely that teleconferencing and videoconferencing will become more commonly available aftercare resources.

Minnesota Model

The Minnesota Model is an abstinence-based treatment model for addiction that was developed by the nonprofit Hazelden Foundation (now the Hazelden Betty Ford Foundation) in the mid-twentieth century. It involves group and individual counseling, infused strongly with twelve-step participation and principles. The Minnesota Model of addiction treatment is the most widely used treatment modality worldwide. Its core tenet is that addiction is a primary, chronic, and progressive disease and that permanent abstinence is possible:

> It is primary because it is an entity in itself and not caused by other factors, such as intra-psychic conflict. It is chronic because a client cannot return to "normal" drinking once an addiction is established. It is progressive because symptoms and consequences continue to occur with increasing severity as use continues.[146]

Although shaped by the staff and history of each different facility, treatment for addiction has been fairly similar at many residential rehabilitation programs across the United States because the general consensus of what works best for the disease of addiction is based on the overall scheme of the Minnesota Model. At most treatment centers in the United States, professionals assess each patient thoroughly in the first few days of treatment. The substance and/or process addiction history are only a piece of the puzzle. Remember, it is more important to know what sort of patient has the disease than what sort of disease the patient has. Hence, the staff explores the various aspects of each patient's biopsychosocial functioning to gain a thorough and holistic appreciation of whom they are trying to serve. The staff then formulates an individual treatment plan based on the patient's identified needs and goals along physical, spiritual, emotional, relational, developmental, and familial dimensions.

The primary goal is complete abstinence from all mind-altering chemicals. The Minnesota Model relies heavily on the Twelve Steps of recovery and employs individual and group therapeutics, education for the client and the family, and samples of various other behavioral treatments, all of which serve to stimulate behavioral changes and the development of healthy coping skills. After completing treatment, addicts are encouraged to continue their recovery program within the fellowship of the twelve-step group(s) applicable to their particular manifestation of addiction.

Matrix Model

The Matrix Model is an evidence-based group of outpatient treatment protocols that were developed in California in the 1980s. Originally developed for amphetamine addiction, the program has been expanded to address other drugs of abuse as well. Its success has been recognized by several leading national organizations, like the National Institute on Drug Abuse (NIDA). The Matrix Model draws heavily upon published literature pertaining to the areas of relapse prevention, family and group therapies, drug education, self-help participation, and drug abuse monitoring. Treatment materials are contained in detailed manuals and include worksheets for individual sessions, family educational groups, early recovery skills groups, relapse-prevention groups, conjoint sessions, urinalysis, twelve-step programs, relapse analysis, and social support groups. The fact that Matrix Model materials have been structured into systematic treatment protocols with instructions for use has facilitated the dissemination and replication of this approach.

Brief Interventions

Psychosocial treatments come in all shapes and sizes. One effective way to decrease problem drinking or other drug use in an individual considered to be at risk is referred to as "brief interventions." Just as the name suggests, it is composed of short counseling sessions that may be fifteen minutes in duration. In that time, the clinician's goal is to motivate people to recognize their own problematic substance use so that they become willing to change. Brief interventions are not meant for the individual who has gone so far down the path of active addiction that even a preschooler could recognize his or her need for intensive treatment or detoxification services. Instead, through the use of screening tools that can be applied during a brief interview, a clinician will identify the level of risk and work to facilitate increased self-awareness and self-motivation. Brief interventions are not confrontational, either. Rather, they are empathetic and guiding.

Studies have demonstrated that brief interventions are effective. Not only does substance use decrease, but so do other negative consequences of addiction. For example, we know that there is a group of individuals who repeatedly experience traumatic events that require emergency room visits when they are under the influence of mind-altering substances. When brief interventions are performed on such individuals before they are discharged from the ER, they are less likely to show up there again. Clinicians are also encouraged to recommend that identified high-risk individuals receive literature on twelve-step programs and support groups like Alcoholics Anonymous, Narcotics Anonymous, Celebrate Recovery, and others.

General Psychotherapy

One of the treatment modalities with the greatest diversity in terms of structure, approach, and intensity is general psychotherapy, known informally as "talk therapy." Psychotherapy can take the form of individual, group, or family therapy, and can include a wide variety of styles and orientations, including but not limited to cognitive-behavioral, supportive, psychoanalytic, solution-focused, grief, trauma, and spiritual. This wealth of diversity is extremely important since no single therapy approach is appropriate for every patient. Matching appropriate therapeutic techniques to patients' identified needs can best empower them to achieve their goals. Therefore, when choosing a therapist, it is advisable to select one who applies a wide array of tools from which to draw. A valuable question to ask any potential therapist is "What style(s) do use use with your clients?"

However, the particular model of therapy is not as crucial as the therapist himself or herself. That is, a trusting relationship with the therapist is paramount to success, while the style of therapy is not. In effect, whether it's family systems, grief, trauma, solution-focused, psychodynamic, dialectical-behavioral, or cognitive behavioral therapy, the model is only as effective as the therapeutic alliance between the patient and the therapist. Note that therapy in general is confidential—with a few exceptions directly related to safety considerations. This fact enables trust and provides a safe environment in which to dig deep.

Individual therapy usually occurs in a clinician's office, and, as its name suggests, is conducted one-on-one. As such, it is a patient-centered process with a high degree of individual attention. In my field, this type of therapy traditionally has focused on the addict's life in general, with a strong focus on the negative consequences of substance use and the inadequacy of coping skills in dealing with psychosocial stressors. The goals should be to decrease or stop use, accept referral to the level of treatment appropriate for the patient's disease state, and address some of the underlying issues.

Since addiction is a family disease, familial involvement is a vital factor in the recovery and healing process. As a result, treatment programs, especially at inpatient treatment centers, provide family education and various degrees of participation. In formal family therapy, though, the roles and interplay of everyone in the family system are explored in greater detail within the context of the addiction and other identified problems. Family therapy not only can help decrease alcohol and other drug use, it also often motivates healthy change in other areas for the family as a whole and for its individual members, and can assist in keeping the addict engaged in treatment.

Rarely is one person in a family system the only individual in need of help. Often, it is determined that other people significant in the life of the addict require therapy as well. Because those who live with addicts may become physically, emotionally, and spiritually sick as well, family programming helps to identify and refer those family members greatly affected by addiction to therapists who can help them work on themselves. Often through this process, others in the addict's family with addictions of their own are identified and referred for appropriate treatment.

Cognitive Behavioral Therapy

Cognitive behavioral therapy (CBT) is the most widely studied and applied therapeutic approach, which is effective for a variety of problems. CBT is a combination of therapeutic techniques that focus on the structure and patterns of thoughts and the relationship between thoughts and behavior. CBT emphasizes how maladaptive thoughts can contribute to both emotional distress and behavioral problems. In other words, according to CBT, feelings and behaviors are caused by a person's thoughts.

CBT addresses the thought process of clients in connection with their reactions to outside stimuli, ultimately teaching them that even though they may not be able to change their circumstances, they can change how they think about, interpret, and relate to them. By doing so, we can change how we feel and act. Perhaps my friend Chris Major put it best when he said, "If you want something to change . . . change the way you look at it." An example of this process would be to observe the difference in your mood when you are reactive compared to when you are responsive.

Imagine you receive news that your house was robbed. If you immediately went to a place of assuming the absolute worst, you would feel very distraught, violated, and angry, and you might act out on your anger, causing further turmoil and suffering. Now imagine that when you hear the news that your house was robbed, you think to yourself, "What can I really do about it right now? I have no way of knowing how serious it is until I see it for myself." How might that difference in thinking change the way you feel about the event and how you act? Chances are you will still feel violated because theft is a violation, but if you allow time to explore the mental landscape of possibilities, you will not act out in destructive ways that you will later regret.

CBT teaches people to explore and expand their options, and weigh their responses and behaviors first before reacting on impulse. There is good research-based evidence that CBT is effective for a wide variety of mental health issues like addiction, depression, and anxiety. CBT can be used in individual counseling, group settings, and self-help manuals. Focusing on the present, CBT distinguishes itself from other psychosocial treatments by not exploring the past.

In the treatment for addiction, the goal of cognitive behavioral therapy is to teach people how their thought patterns are connected to their use of alcohol or other drugs, and to make adjustments in their thinking that support recovery rather than active addiction. CBT also helps addicts to recognize situations in which they are most likely to use substances and teaches them how to modify their thinking so they may cope with these situations, as well as other challenging circumstances, in healthier ways. In other words, CBT enables addicts to identify, understand, and cope with the situations that lead them to substance use and, when applicable, a relapse. The insight gained through this awareness builds the resilience necessary to navigate through life on life's terms.

Motivational Interviewing

Motivational Interviewing (MI) is a directive, patient-centered therapy style that engages patients in developing the internal motivation to change. MI is a nonconfrontational and nonjudgmental approach based on the tenet that only internally directed change elicits any meaningful healing. MI is a psychosocial treatment style that can be most effective and appropriate when patients exhibit little or no motivation to change.

In MI, therapists are encouraged to provide empathetic feedback based on their understanding of patients' beliefs. The strategy serves to identify and expose differences between patients' values and their actions. As the saying goes, "The road to hell is paved with good intentions." Often when patients' actual level of substance use, along with their using-related behaviors and the consequences, are compared to their desire for meaningful personal integrity, the discrepancy between their choices/actions and their values becomes apparent, and sometimes painfully obvious. The patient can then be guided from a position of refusal to change to one of reluctance or ambivalence, and subsequently from there to a position of readiness to change.

Instead of confrontation, therapists utilizing MI accept the degree of resistance present at the time and *meet the client "wherever they are"* psychologically—even any rational person would accept that change is not only desirable, but absolutely necessary. Meeting someone where they are in this sense isn't a permissive, cavalier approach whereby unhealthy behaviors and attitudes are encouraged. Instead, it is an empathetic approach that engenders trust. Ultimately, MI's goal is to enhance self-efficacy through empathy, trust, and language to bring about change that comes from within the patient. Within the context of a comprehensive recovery plan, MI has been demonstrated to be effective for addiction treatment.

Contingency Management

Contingency management is a treatment modality that utilizes concrete positive reinforcements as the means to change behaviors and enhance recovery. Contingency management is akin to using a carrot on the end of a string to drive behavior. It can also be an effective tool if incorporated within the framework of a comprehensive treatment plan. An interesting but potentially expensive option, contingency management offers addicts actual rewards for staying abstinent. Often gift cards, groceries, household items, vouchers, or even amounts of money are provided as incentives for maintaining abstinence as measured by negative drug screens. Contingency management's effectiveness is highest among those who have failed repeatedly when treated under the traditional methods alone.

Aversion Therapy

Aversion therapy is a form of behavior therapy in which a punitive (aversive) stimulus is coupled with an undesirable behavior in order to eliminate or reduce that behavior. This option is used primarily on undesirable behaviors that have been resistant to other, more conventional forms of therapy, and is guided by the principle that unwanted behaviors can be unlearned.

Although aversion therapy has been used since 1932, more recently its use has been rare. It has demonstrated some effectiveness, but in general has fallen out of favor, perhaps due to some of its especially controversial applications, such as using electric shocks to treat "problems" like homosexuality or forcing people with obsessive-compulsive disorder to handle feces. Aversion therapy in the treatment of addiction involves inducing nausea and vomiting with alcohol and other drugs. The pairing teaches the brain to create associations between these two events, which are reinforced with experience over time. While it may be hard to imagine voluntarily subjecting oneself to ten days of "vomiting treatments," interestingly, treatment dropout rates for that exact application are not higher than for other forms of addiction treatment. At least it is fecal-matter-free.

Seriously, though, aversion therapy in addiction treatment is more comprehensive than merely inducing vomiting. Programs utilizing this technique have incorporated SMART Recovery and often seek to address certain underlying issues. Some alcoholics whose treatment included aversion therapy have claimed that years later they could not even walk past a liquor store without feeling nauseous.

Aversion therapy can have multiple physical contraindications. Folks with underlying heart disease, hypertension, or certain gastrointestinal disorders may be excluded. Aversion therapy does not have to be as dramatic as using electric shock or inducing vomiting. A more benign example is placing a bitter-tasting compound on fingernails so they are not chewed or bitten.

Twelve-Step Programs

Most people would agree that anything that can foster connection and brotherhood among disparate religious and political affiliations, noncompetitive spirituality, and a deep sense of caring and love, and do so without leadership, is a remarkable resource. Twelve-step fellowships do all of the above. What are twelve-step fellowships? They are loosely organized groups of similarly affected individuals (people struggling with and working to recover from all manifestations of addiction: alcohol, other drugs, food, sex, gambling, etc.), engaged in a community of mutual support based on guiding principles that outline an action-based course for recovery. Simply stated, these are mutual-aid programs for recovery from addictive substances and behaviors.

The Twelve Steps form the basis for a worldwide culture movement that began with Alcoholics Anonymous, and has grown to encompass nearly every type of problematic drug-related and other addictive behavior. These have historically been described as self-help programs, but are more accurately characterized as mutual-help programs. The "anonymous" in the names of most twelve-step programs follows from the spiritual principles of humility and anonymity, and refers to their members' use of first names only and not identifying themselves as members of a specific twelve-step fellowship in the press, on radio, or in film. This anonymity also serves to protect the individual and the fellowship from the social stigma still so broadly associated with addiction.

Alcoholics Anonymous (AA), the first twelve-step fellowship program, was founded by Bill Wilson and Dr. Robert Smith (also known as Dr. Bob) in Akron, Ohio, in 1935. The main text of AA, known as the Big Book, has sold thirty million copies since it was first published in 1939. Many other twelve-step programs, each with a somewhat different focus, have evolved subsequently, starting with Narcotics Anonymous (NA) in 1953. Twelve-step programs have been so successful and influential that in 1999, *Time* magazine named Wilson one of the top twenty of the "*Time* 100 Persons of the Century: Heroes and Icons" who exemplified "courage, selflessness, exuberance, superhuman ability, and amazing grace."[147]

By presenting alcoholism as a disease, Alcoholics Anonymous helped create the foundation for the biopsychosocial-spiritual disease model of addiction. AA, NA, and other twelve-step programs are based on the philosophy that one person with the disease can most effectively help another person who struggles with it, and that the programs grow through "attraction rather than promotion." They have intentionally avoided any connection with medical, psychotherapeutic, or other forms of professional treatment, or with other organizations, religious belief systems (twelve-step programs are spiritual, not religious), or social or political movements.

AA was an unlikely candidate as a vehicle of major change. It began as a group of garden-variety "drunks" who figured out they could help one another more effectively than could any of the other options available. Those who have never been exposed to twelve-step programs are often surprised to find that the meetings are full of hope, inspiration, wit, and spirituality, especially when they initially misunderstand the process of twelve-step recovery groups to be a bunch of "addicts who are complaining about not using." Nothing could be further from the truth. In spite of the deadly seriousness of recovery from active addiction, meetings are often imbued with gratitude and a sense of joy, and are sometimes so full of laughter that people who are new might wonder if they've walked into the wrong room.

There is something transformative and immeasurable that happens in this environment. The immeasurable aspect is due to the fact that we know twelve-step fellowships work, but we have not been able to discover precisely *how* they work. Positive psychology teaches us that personal transformations are more likely to happen among people with social contact and deep relationships. These meaningful social experiences are both promoted and facilitated by twelve-step program involvement, albeit informally.

These groups can take on a sacred status, as spirituality and virtue-rich living are encouraged and embedded throughout the Twelve Steps. I have heard twelve-step programs described as "a school for living," and to be "for people who have been to hell and do not ever want to return." I continue to find it fascinating that many of the same virtues extolled by various religions, Socrates, Plato, and others are integrated into the Twelve Steps as principles.

These principles of the Twelve Steps can be understood in different ways. As in life, they are open to perspective and interpretation—as variable as the individuals experiencing them. Since the journey of healing and recovery is a continuous process, the steps and their principles can embody different levels of meaning as time marches on, making them both constant and fluid. As is the case in life, growth continues and more insight is revealed throughout time as the process of recovery unfolds.

The following section details the fundamental principles embedded in each of the Twelve Steps. While the principles are applicable to the somewhat different versions of the Twelve Steps across all twelve-step programs, the version of the steps used below is the original—that of Alcoholics Anonymous.

Principle 1. Honesty

Step One: *We admitted we were powerless over alcohol—that our lives had become unmanageable.*

The working principle at the heart of Step One is honesty. Denial is one of those mechanisms at play when we are unaware of the processes that are actually helping the disease to flourish. Honesty here can be defined as embracing the truth—that is, shedding some light on the reality of our plight facilitates our escape from self-deception. Quite simply, if someone is unable to get honest about the extent of the problem, he or she will not succeed. Only after denial is set aside can healing and recovery be initiated by taking the first step and admitting, "I can't control or solve this thing."

Regardless of whether it takes weeks, months, or years, when the addict loses control over the use of alcohol or any other mind-altering substance, what started out as the servant becomes the master. In order for someone to continue down the road of addiction, honesty is one of the first things to be sacrificed. This is why Step One comes first. Recall that because addiction hijacks the brain, the disease makes decisions in order for the person to continue to use and avoid withdrawal. So dishonesty to oneself and others, as well as minimizing negative using patterns to conceal them, become means to an end and part of the addict's lifestyle.

Because addiction is a family disease, entire family systems get caught up in the lies. The family can become totally controlled by diseased thinking. Although the illusion of control may continue, their lives become unmanageable because alcohol and/or drugs are really in control, in ways that are cunning, baffling, and powerful. But recovery for the entire family can begin when someone finally breaks the cycle of denial. That first step begins with admitting powerlessness—finally becoming honest about the situation.

Principle 2. Hope

Step Two: *Came to believe that a Power greater than ourselves could restore us to sanity.*

After admitting to themselves that they cannot control or stop their use of mind-altering substances or manage their own affairs, how do addicts move forward? Hope that success is possible provides fuel to continue and fully engage in recovery. If the disease of addiction were not greater than the addicts themselves, they would be able to stop on their own. Some get caught on the barbs of this step. Just what is a "power greater than oneself," anyway? In short, even atheists and agnostics can appreciate that if they cannot stop on their own, something other than themselves may be able to help them. Since they have failed on their own, recruiting some help does not seem like such a stretch. In the Big Book (formally titled *Alcoholics Anonymous*), there is even a chapter that recommends putting off the inner debate about this power greater than oneself in order to glean the benefits inherent in the program as a whole. Reaching a state of hope that things can improve is not a finish line; Step Two is instead another springboard.

The reference to a power greater than ourselves can have a religious feel to it. But again, if one approaches the steps as a spiritual code instead of religious doctrine, the idea of a power greater than oneself becomes easier to accept. There are those who have faith and are "good with God," and they are encouraged to continue with their beliefs. Again, this is not a disease caused by a lack of faith. Twelve-step programs are not cults, and everyone is not only free, but encouraged, to find a power greater than themselves—a higher power—that works for them. New Age mysticism is absent, and there are also no specific doctrines to follow. Members merely accept their own understanding of something greater than themselves. They are not obligated to recognize anyone else's view of God.

The second half of this step may also cause some concern because of the word *insanity*. In this context, it is not used as a judgment. Insanity can be defined as continuing to do the same thing and expecting a different outcome. What could better explain the actions of someone trapped in the cycle of addiction? That can be a type of insanity. As the Big Book states, "We unsuccessfully yet repeatedly try to stop or control our drinking using the same tools we had that led to the problem. Since you can't fix what's broken with what's broken, finding something outside of ourselves and our best way of thinking helps us to find the way out."

Principle 3. Faith

Step Three: *Made a decision to turn our will and our lives over to the care of God as we understood Him.*

While this principle is critical, its undertones of religiosity can make it difficult for some people. However, the principle of faith rests on making a commitment to take action. Things that have gotten out of hand have a chance to become orderly, but it takes an act of faith. That faith involves trusting that others can lead the way by healthy example, and that by incorporating the recovery work done thus far, progress will continue.

What I say to those who will not or cannot yet believe in a higher power or a God of their own understanding is: "Good." The Twelve Steps are not religious, and they have been proven to work for people regardless of their particular belief systems and whether or not those belief systems include religion or a concept of God. The trick is to relinquish the "self-will run riot," the need to try to control life. Remember, addicts have too much willpower. After all, it takes discipline and diligence to continue using while your world falls apart due to your active addiction. It takes an iron-willed determination to keep using when the negative consequences mount and there are numerous signs to stop. All I ask of skeptical newcomers is that they make a commitment to improve themselves. Since the addict's will alone did not have such outstanding results, encouraging people to try faith in this and other suggestions is an easy sell.

A fascinating evolution and departure from earlier recovery movements can be seen here. The founders of AA decided to make room for all belief systems, faiths, and doubts by defining a relationship with a higher power or God of *one's own* understanding. Through this step, spirituality can start to work even in the most reluctant of addicts, and can be effective in those whose conception of God may be a fellowship or science or something completely different. People ignite the flames that help them grow throughout their lives in recovery by taking this step. The decision to forgo relying on one's will is not easy for anyone, and particularly for a group with a disease that focuses all of its resources and energies on the self. Yet, instead of being a relinquishment of power, the turning over of one's will is actually empowering.

Doing this step can be compared to two people on two different logs who hold onto toy steering wheels while floating down a turbulent river. Before taking this step we are trying like mad to steer the log. After taking the step, we sit back and enjoy the ride. Same river, same log . . . no fight, no struggle. A good piece of wisdom I was told is: "Allow yourself to take a backseat and be led, because you are not in control anyway."

Principle 4. Courage

Step Four: *Made a searching and fearless moral inventory of ourselves.*

Many take the first three steps and balk at Step Four. It can be scary and painful, but that is why it requires the virtue of courage. Making an honest assessment of how our behavior has done harm—to others and to ourselves—asks us to boldly look in the mirror of self-reflection. As opposed to the three previous, more contemplative steps, this step is the first true action step. Step Four serves as a foundation for one of the most important platforms of growth—in-depth self-examination. The only person an addict can change is him- or herself, and addicts begin the process of taking major responsibility for themselves by taking their own moral inventory. Bravery is needed in order to look fearlessly at oneself and become willing to take responsibility for those actions and the character defects that are found through this process. This step can also help stop the process of victimization.

Through Step Four, people examine exactly how their own behavior affected not only themselves, but also those around them. But this step is not about inducing or reinforcing shame and guilt. Assets as well as shortcomings are highlighted. There is also a strong emphasis on the humanity of the person engaging in this self-inventory. That is, no one is perfect; the best anyone will ever be is a human being. The truth about oneself is exposed in this step.

Principle 5. Integrity

Step Five: *Admitted to God, to ourselves, and to another human being the exact nature of our wrongs.*

After taking a thorough moral inventory, bringing the information it provides into the light of self-awareness produces a new form of integrity. It involves being called upon to profess ownership of one's assets and shortcomings—the good, the bad, and the ugly. This can be difficult for many people; it requires humility and courage to be thoroughly honest with another person about one's past. Albeit demanding, this step also is a vital platform for personal growth.

There is a valuable saying that epitomizes what this step is all about: "We are only as sick as our secrets." The disease of addiction causes good people to do bad things. Many of those bad things induce guilt and shame, and are kept hidden as secrets, sometimes for many years. Keeping those secrets creates its own form of stress and pain. Although it can be very painful to put this tainted past down on paper and share it with another person, liberation and healing come from the experience of eliminating such secrets and accepting—precisely as they are—one's past actions, one's "character defects," and, ultimately, oneself. Step Five acts as the catalyst to move forward to grow spiritually through the admission of and departure from the burdens of the past.

Principle 6. Willingness

Step Six: *Were entirely ready to have God remove all these defects of character.*

The virtue of willingness is necessary for substantial life changes to be implemented. Steps Four and Five exposed the character defects, the aspects of the addict's personality that contributed directly to the harm they caused to themselves and others. Subsequently, the readiness to relinquish those defects of character and the old behaviors they fueled must be evoked to move on, and the willingness to move on again relies on a power greater than oneself.

Where Step Six is both crucial and difficult is that twelve-step recovery requires some serious soul-searching. Character defects may be extremely difficult to relinquish, because many of them have served as coping skills for a very long time. "Am I really entirely prepared to expunge myself of my faults?" Even if these faults are self-destructive, some of them may be what we rely upon to handle stress, resentment, success, loneliness, and boredom. This challenge is no small reason why a higher power is called upon by many for strength. Moreover, had the addict been able to remove his or her character defects alone, without help, chances are he or she would have already done so.

Principle 7. Humility

Step Seven: *Humbly asked Him to remove our shortcomings.*

Willpower cannot cure any disease, and certainly not the disease of addiction. In fact, relying on willpower and acting on self-will were part of the problem. In this step, people ask for help from a power greater than themselves to amend their defects of character, their shortcomings. This is an action step that calls for the virtue of humility because, in asking for help, there is an acceptance of one's limitations and an acknowledgment that reliance on and trust in a greater power is necessary. After Steps Four, Five, and Six, where a moral inventory was taken, faults were uncovered and admitted, and the willingness to have them removed was fostered, Step Seven is the culmination wherein the addict asks for help in becoming a better person through the removal of those character defects.

Principle 8. Reflection

Step Eight: *Made a list of all persons we had harmed, and became willing to make amends to them all.*

This step has two important elements. In order to take responsibility for their actions and grow spiritually, addicts make a list and again become willing to make amends. Making this list is another level of taking responsibility for past actions. Reflection is the virtue at play here because it is only through somber (and sober) consideration that past obstacles can be removed. The saying is that we "become ready to sweep our side of the street clean." The list of people who have been harmed by one's actions can be difficult to make. The willingness to then take action on it by making amends is even harder. There is no quick fix, and there are certainly no guarantees that any particular outcome will transpire. Some past transgressions may not be forgiven by others or otherwise quickly "healed." This step is taken as further movement toward healing oneself by doing what is within our power to make sure that "our side of the street" is as clean as it can be.

Principle 9. Forgiveness

Step Nine: *Made direct amends to such people wherever possible, except when to do so would injure them or others.*

This is the step perhaps most often associated with the Twelve Steps in popular media. Forgiveness is an exalted virtue for sure, but in working Step Nine and doing everything possible to make amends, there are no promises that the addict will be forgiven for his or her past transgressions. Prior to making amends to those who have been harmed, the addict may discover some self-forgiveness. In order to believe that he or she is even worthy of forgiveness, an addict learns that addiction is a disease, and that they did the best they could under the circumstances of their substance-induced slavery. Asking forgiveness then becomes an act of compassion that the addict extends to him- or herself.

There are never any guarantees that forgiveness will be granted by those the addict has harmed, but the point of this step is not at all about receiving forgiveness. It is about accepting responsibility and changing behavior. Making amends entails more than saying, "I am sorry." Those words are often discouraged, as most addicts have uttered them so often that they have lost their meaning. No, making amends is an action step, because it also entails changing one's behavior. Amends are about making reparations and restitution. Step Nine seeks to protect the well-being of both the addict and others to whom amends are owed. Sometimes attempting to make amends even brings the potential do to more harm than good. This is an issue that requires careful consideration by the addict in consultation with his or her twelve-step sponsor—a recovering addict who serves as a mentor or guide. The potential reward for the addict does not outweigh the need to do no more harm.

Principle 10. Acceptance

Step Ten: *Continued to take personal inventory, and when we were wrong, promptly admitted it.*

This is the first of what are commonly known as the three maintenance steps: Ten, Eleven, and Twelve. These are also growth steps, because recovery is a journey and not a destination. In recovery, addicts continue to improve and evolve. The journey, which begins with abstinence, is all about progress, not perfection. Addicts accept that the best we will ever be is human, and humans are imperfectly perfect. As such, we will continue to make mistakes.

The virtue of acceptance is called upon for us to realize our own limitations. These limitations must be addressed through an ongoing program of spiritual progress. Best done on a daily basis, Step Ten allows addicts to quickly own up to their mistakes and amend any wrongs done. Again, this is all about one's own behavior, and Step Ten helps addicts to keep their side of the street clean in an ongoing way. In addition to helping addicts to accept that they are human, this step can help them to extend the same acceptance to others. That is, the more they appreciate their own humanity, the less likely they are to judge others and the more tolerant and compassionate they are likely to be. This approach helps make life a little easier for both the addict and those he or she comes in contact with.

Principle 11. Spirituality

Step Eleven: *Sought through prayer and meditation to improve our conscious contact with God as we understood Him, praying only for knowledge of His will for us and the power to carry that out.*

By the time someone has moved through the steps, the concept of God or a higher power has been visited enough to consider Step Eleven without much conflict. A saying relevant to this step is that "while prayer is talking to God, meditation is listening to God." Regardless of one's beliefs on the subject, this step evokes the virtue of spirituality directly. Spiritual practices are among the most discussed of all human endeavors because they are so important. Through an unseen and unknown source, an enormous bounty can emerge: it is through prayer and meditation that addicts endeavor to align their consciousness with that source to achieve progress in their journey of recovery and in their lives.

Step Eleven involves more than merely meditating and praying. It reminds addicts to align themselves with something greater in order to carry out actions according to the greater good. Addicts are known to be sensitive and self-absorbed. Step Eleven can serve as yet another catalyst to help keep them distanced from the ill-advised belief that they are the center of the universe. This is an especially powerful step because here, addicts can become more aware of their purpose in life and find deeper meaning and greater happiness in their lives.

Principle 12. Service

Step Twelve: *Having had a spiritual awakening as the result of these steps, we tried to carry this message to alcoholics, and to practice these principles in all our affairs.*

Step Twelve is the culmination of the spiritual principles embodied in each of the preceding steps. The virtue in Step Twelve is service. This is exemplified in the paradoxical but common twelve-step phrase, "You cannot keep what you do not give away." At one point in his active addiction, the founder of Alcoholics Anonymous was intervened upon by another drunk in service to help him achieve sobriety. Through service work, addicts carry the message of recovery to other addicts who still suffer. When one addict shares his or her own experience, strength, and hope, all parties benefit. That is, service is a two-way street. The one who shares and the one who receives both benefit from this principle when the message of recovery is carried.

Service work allows the solution found in the twelve-step programs to continue—from one addict to another, from one generation to the next. Without service, there would be an enormous vacuum. Those who give share the solution and help it to flourish while they themselves reap the rewards of engaging in the virtues of giving. This step is not limited to merely helping other addicts; a broader meaning is painted with those words. In order to make the most of this step, addicts are encouraged to apply their newfound life skills to all facets of their lives.

The Development of the Twelve Steps

In hindsight, the likelihood of an alcoholic salesman partnering with a physician also addicted to alcohol to form the most successful and effective self-help movement in history was minute. Bill Wilson and Dr. Bob were probably as surprised at the success of Alcoholics Anonymous as Jack was when he saw the magic beanstalk. Instead of magic, Bill Wilson credited three major influences for the inspiration to develop AA: the Oxford Group, Dr. William Silkworth, and William James.

The Oxford Group was an evangelical movement in the 1920s that emphasized one-on-one personal work among its members. Bill credits this for the last step. Dr. Frank Buchman, who was a Lutheran minister, led the Oxford Group movement. Like modern-day fellowships, they had a set of guiding principles such as love, purity, honesty, and selflessness. Moreover, they practiced a type of absolution through confession, which inspired Steps Eight and Nine. According to Bill Wilson, they also believed deeply in their "quiet time," a period of meditation practiced by groups and individuals alike in which the guidance of God was sought for every detail of living, great or small. This influence can be seen in Step Eleven.

One of the most common criticisms I hear about twelve-step programs involves difficulty with the notion of God. As noted above, it's important to understand that twelve-step programs encourage each and every member to find a power greater than themselves—a higher power—that works for them. Everyone is free to define what it is for him- or herself. That may involve a particular conception of God and a specific formal religious belief system, or it may have absolutely nothing to do with any particular conception of God or formal religious belief system.

As a matter of fact, Ebbie, who was one of the first three members of AA and the one who intervened on Bill Wilson, achieved sobriety through the Oxford

Group even though he did not believe in God. Agnostics and atheists in the burgeoning ranks of AA convinced Bill Wilson to include verbiage allowing for the understanding of a "higher power" instead of a God. To me, this signifies an open door for a variety of beliefs and avoids the potential for twelve-step fellowships to be pigeonholed as religious or cultish.

During one of his numerous inpatient treatments while still drinking, Bill Wilson was admitted to the Charles B. Towns Hospital in New York City under the care of Dr. William Silkworth. Dr. Silkworth recognized even then that alcoholism was a disease that included a physical and a spiritual component. The physical part, he explained, is characterized by craving and the spiritual component is characterized by a mental obsession about drinking. What we have now learned through science, Dr. Silkworth knew even then. To me that is amazing, because so little was known at that time about the science of addiction. Dr. Silkworth knew that alcohol, when introduced into the body of an alcoholic, creates the phenomenon of craving, where larger amounts are uncontrollably sought. Today we call this "priming." Addicts cannot predict or control their intake of substances or their behavior for long after they have that first drink, pill, puff, or injection. For nonaddicts, that first use creates a state of happiness and satiety. For an addict, it may satisfy briefly, but it quickly creates a state of anxiety that only MORE can fix, and the fulfillment that "fix" provides is fleeting. Dr. Silkworth also appreciated the amazing dynamics of one alcoholic helping another and assisted in Ebbie's intervention on Bill W three days after his admission on December 14, 1934.

The third influence in the development of AA was William James. He was arguably one of the most influential psychologists in modern times, and is sometimes referred to as the "father of modern psychology." He was the brother of novelist Henry James and of diarist Alice James. A student of many subjects, he received his medical degree but never practiced medicine. James worked throughout his entire academic career at Harvard. He was drawn to psychology and philosophy more than to medicine, and reported that the first lecture he ever heard on psychology was the one he gave. One of his most influential teachings touched Bill W in a profound way. Specifically, William James believed that even the most hopeless people could transform their lives entirely through either rapid or gradual spiritual experiences.

When Bill Wilson finally had a spiritual awakening and achieved sobriety, he eagerly joined with the Oxford Group but found that his concentration solely on helping alcoholics was not welcomed unconditionally. Moreover, his ambition to make the whole world sober was greeted with equal condescension. Yet he continued to persevere. He would actually go around Brooklyn and bring drunks back to his home. He attempted to speak of his spiritual experience and pleaded with others to join him, but until he was on a business trip in Akron by himself and close to a drink, he made no progress. For a short while, the only recovering people in his life were he and his mentor, Ebbie. Although despondent over his initial lack of success in helping other alcoholics, he did not quit trying.

After some guidance from Dr. Silkworth, Bill decided to tone down his preaching when he encountered Dr. Bob Smith in Akron, Ohio, on June 10, 1935. Dr. Bob reported later that he recognized in Bill the same issues he had been dealing with for his whole drinking career. In essence, it was one drunk speaking to another drunk that catalyzed the explosion that was to develop into the most successful self-help group in history. Over the next three years the approach that Bill W and Dr. Bob began to put together increasingly departed from the Oxford Group and its four pillars of love, purity, honesty, and selflessness. Through individual successes, this initiative and its ideas, along with the number of participants, began to grow. What evolved into the Twelve Steps initially consisted of six principles that formed the backbone of the program to come:

1. We admitted that we were powerless over alcohol.

2. We got honest with ourselves.

3. We got honest with another person, in confidence.

4. We made amends for harms done to others.

5. We worked with other alcoholics without demand for prestige or money.

6. We prayed to God to help us to do these things as best we could.

The Twelve Steps of AA were formally established in 1939. A vocal agnostic and atheistic group of alcoholics influenced Bill to use "higher power" instead of "God" in some of the wording in order to make it more inclusive and broaden the program's atmosphere of acceptance. Even in the very early stages of the program, there were concerns about the possibility that monotheistic or religious-sounding language could be experienced as off-putting to some and less welcoming in general. Later the Twelve Steps would be welcomed not only by a wide range of religious denominations, but also by the medical and psychotherapeutic communities.

The Twelve Steps provide an approach to recovery and a philosophy of life based on deep-seated spiritual principles. Twelve-step programs have been proven to work for millions of addicts, but it is important to be aware that there are other self-help and support programs available to those with addictions. There is no single treatment or self-help approach that is 100 percent successful for everyone. When exploring recovery-related resources, the key is finding the right fit for the individual addict.

As mentioned above, the Twelve Steps and the Twelve Traditions originally set forth by AA have been adapted to address many other addictions and compulsions. It is estimated that more than forty self-help organizations—known as fellowships—with a worldwide membership of many millions currently employ the twelve-step principles of recovery. Narcotics Anonymous was created by those who identified with addiction to mind- and mood-altering substances other than just alcohol. Cocaine Anonymous, Crystal Meth Anonymous, and Marijuana Anonymous (among others) focus on specific substances.

Behavioral forms of addiction inspired the development of fellowships such as Overeaters Anonymous, Sex Addicts Anonymous, and Gamblers Anonymous. Lois Wilson, Bill's wife, founded Al-Anon for families and friends of the person with addiction. A maladaptive set of behaviors commonly exists among the families and friends of addicts that actually perpetuates the addiction cycle. These behaviors are collectively known as "enabling" and often reflect codependence, which will be discussed in the chapter on intervention. Nar-Anon is a similar fellowship that focuses on recovery for significant others of those with addiction. These fellowships can be invaluable resources for the social and family network of addicts—providing opportunities for identification and mutual support that facilitate growth, health, healing, and spiritual development—whether or not the addict him- or herself is in recovery.

Celebrate Recovery

There is a growing resource for those who wish to utilize a church for an organized community of recovery, known as Celebrate Recovery. I tell my patients that although stringent outcome evaluation measures and scientific results are lacking, twelve-step programs are generally considered to be the most effective tools for recovery. However, there is no single approach that works for everyone. I honor those with faith and who choose faith-based recovery programs. Celebrate Recovery is based on the Bible and emphasizes a Christian spiritual commitment to Jesus Christ. Celebrate Recovery also addresses all types of hurts, hang-ups, and habits. Thus, for those who grew up with an addicted parent and who are themselves addicted to drugs, food, or sex, if Celebrate Recovery is the right fit for them, they can potentially get the recovery they need under one roof.

SMART Recovery

SMART (Self-Management and Recovery Training) recovery is a self-help approach to addiction recovery based on the work of Albert Ellis, PhD, a psychologist who developed rational emotive behavior therapy (REBT). SMART uses the methods of REBT and cognitive behavioral therapy to focus specifically on the mental aspects of addiction. The emphasis is on identifying and trying to correct the faulty patterns of thinking and the distorted and irrational beliefs that contribute to the addictive process. SMART takes the approach that rational thinking leads to healthy decision making and improved behavior, and is the key to recovery.

SMART is a volunteer-run nonprofit organization dedicated to providing free local and online self-help meetings and information to help people seeking independence from harmful addictive behaviors. SMART meetings are led by professional and lay facilitators supported by a local professional advisor and a national board of addiction specialists who offer ongoing facilitator training.[148]

Chapter 9:

New and Existing Medical Treatments

Professionally facilitated therapeutic interventions and recovery self-help fellowships are especially effective tools for addressing the behavioral components of addiction. They specifically address the psychosocial aspects of the disease. This chapter is dedicated to the medications available today that target the biologic aspects of addiction and complement the other therapeutic treatments, including medication management.

Medications for the Treatment of Alcohol Addiction

As described previously, alcohol is a mind-altering sedative drug that affects multiple brain chemistry systems that include dopamine, serotonin, endorphins, NMDA, and GABA. There is one Food and Drug Administration (FDA)-approved medication that specifically targets cravings for alcohol: Campral. Also, there is an FDA-approved medication that discourages use by making someone very ill when he or she drinks alcohol: Antabuse. The FDA has approved a third medication that discourages drinking and may decrease the amount consumed when alcohol is used, and it comes in two forms, as a pill and an injection—Revia and Vivitrol, respectively.

Campral (Acamprosate)

Campral is a medication used to treat alcohol addiction (alcoholism). The mechanism of action of acamprosate in the maintenance of alcohol abstinence is not completely understood. It is thought to work by restoring the balance of neurotransmitters in patients who have used large amounts of alcohol. Like every other pharmacological agent, Campral is most effective when used in combination with a comprehensive treatment program that includes psychosocial support.

Chronic alcohol use disrupts the natural balance, or homeostasis, in our nervous system. Alcohol affects several neurotransmitter systems, but chronic use has a rather significant effect in altering the normal balance between neuronal excitation (glutamate) and inhibition (GABA). Research suggests that Campral works on the glutamate and GABA neurotransmitter systems and restores a more natural balance between them. Research has also demonstrated that Campral decreases alcohol use in alcohol-dependent animals.[149] Campral has little other effect in the central nervous system, indicating that its effects are targeted to alcohol-related impairments. That is, there is no sedation, depression, tolerance, withdrawal, or other appreciable effect on the central nervous system.

Campral has an FDA indication for the maintenance of abstinence from alcohol in patients with alcohol dependence who are abstinent at the beginning of treatment. Campral was also studied in people who were addicted to alcohol with histories of abuse of multiple substances, and in those who had not undergone detoxification and were not required to be abstinent at baseline. Since the results of the study involving those who were not abstinent before starting Campral failed to show that it was superior to a placebo, the FDA indication is limited specifically to those who are already practicing abstinence at the start of treatment.

How do we know that it works? There have been no less than four double-blind, placebo-controlled (the gold standard of research) studies using Campral with a total of nearly 1,000 alcoholics. The studies varied from ninety days to a year in length, and participants were abstinent prior to the initiation of the studies. Campral or placebo pills were given in conjunction with psychosocial treatment. In these studies, Campral proved to be clinically better than placebo in maintaining abstinence from alcohol.[150,151,152,153]

Unlike with Antabuse (discussed below), using alcohol while taking Campral does not have adverse effects. In fact, since it is quite safe, I use it whenever possible as part of a comprehensive treatment program with someone who is still drinking but who is motivated to stop. Campral is not a detoxification medication, and it does not eliminate or diminish withdrawal symptoms. There are, however, contraindications to Campral for those who have exhibited previous hypersensitivity or allergy to it, and for those with severe kidney disease.

Topamax (Topiramate)

Topamax is a medication that has been used primarily for seizures and headaches. It is a seizure medication, also known as an anticonvulsant, used to prevent seizures in adults and children who are at least two years old. In addition, Topamax is used to prevent migraine headaches. While it will not alleviate a headache once it has already started, it is used to prevent migraines and reduce the number of attacks. Topamax causes changes in the GABA and glutamate systems that, in turn, also inhibit dopamine and affect the serotonin systems.

Recent studies indicate that Topamax may also be useful as an anticraving medication for alcohol addiction.[154] In one study, 371 alcoholics who took Topamax exhibited a higher abstinence rate for twenty-eight consecutive days than did those who took a placebo.[155] Interestingly, even the placebo group showed some improvement in abstinent days, due to the fact that they received counseling. The same study showed that Topamax significantly decreased obsessional thoughts and compulsions related to drinking, decreased heavy drinking days, and promoted abstinence. The use of Topamax was also associated with the extra benefits of decreased blood pressure, decreased weight, decreased plasma cholesterol levels, and increased quality of general activities, leisure activities, and chores.

Topamax is promising in light of its ability to reduce cravings and relapses while tempering withdrawal symptoms. Physicians often use anticonvulsants like Topamax for alcohol detoxification to help minimize some withdrawal symptoms and stabilize moods. In effect, this is one particularly valuable medicine that can be used to intervene at a point of maximum crisis, when the alcoholic is still drinking.

However, Topamax is currently approved by the FDA only for use in seizure disorders and migraine headaches. When a medication is used for a condition other than those that are FDA approved, we refer to that use as "off-label." Many physicians make use of off-label medications because they are often effective in ways that have not been formally studied and approved for use by the FDA.

Topamax is *not* a magic bullet or without its share of serious side effects. In fact, side effects may preclude its widespread use. These side effects are significant and include increased body temperature, dry mouth, increased thirst, sudden vision loss, confusion, pain around or behind the eyes, drowsiness, decreased sweating, nausea, vomiting, muscular problems, increased urination, fast heart rate, fainting, memory problems and slowed thinking, trouble concentrating, problems with speech or balance, numbness or tingling, anorexia, dizziness, headache, weight loss, and insomnia.

Lioresal (Baclofen)

Baclofen, a muscle relaxant, is used primarily to treat muscle spasms. It works as a GABA receptor agonist. Remember that GABA is a neurotransmitter that is the predominant inhibitory neurotransmitter in the brain. So, GABA can be said to be the central nervous system's "brakes," and, as an agonist, baclofen does essentially the same thing. That is, it slows down the muscle twitching associated with cramps and so can be used as a muscle relaxant. While it has an indication for use in muscle spasticity, it is also used off-label in other medical conditions like hiccups, tardive dyskinesia, trigeminal neuralgia, and now in addiction.

Baclofen has demonstrated that it can reduce alcohol use in alcohol-preferring rats as well as reducing both alcohol use and cravings in an open study in humans. A placebo study demonstrated that more people were totally abstinent from alcohol and had more total days of abstinence with baclofen compared to the placebo group. Moreover, there was a decrease in the obsessive and compulsive components of craving in the baclofen group compared to the placebo group, and when alcohol was used, intake was reduced in the baclofen group. Further, there was a beneficial decrease in anxiety among those in the baclofen group compared to the placebo group.[156] The study sample was not enormous, but the results were promising and no one dropped out due to side effects. In addition, baclofen has a very low abuse potential. Baclofen's side effects include nausea, vertigo, transient sleepiness, and abdominal pain.

Baclofen has additional properties worth considering. Its GABA agonist properties may make it valuable in treating withdrawal symptoms by toning down the hyperexcitability seen in withdrawal from alcohol and opiates. Baclofen was also studied in treating cocaine dependence; when used in conjunction with counseling, baclofen significantly reduced cocaine use in recovering addicts compared to placebo coupled with counseling. Baclofen also is safe to use with and improves the clinical state in patients with alcoholic hepatitis.[157]

It is worth mentioning that baclofen received a lot of attention from Olivier Ameisen, a French cardiologist, who believes that baclofen is not just a treatment for addictive drinking but a miracle cure. He reports that after he took large amounts of the medication, he was cured of his own alcoholism.[158] I have not seen anything like the results he claims, but unfortunately I have encountered numerous patients who try baclofen hoping for the same incredible results, only to fail. Baclofen was also recently used in a pilot study for helping alcoholics who smoke to stop both. The results demonstrated that percent days of co-occurring use and alcohol and tobacco declined more for the placebo group than for those who received baclofen.[159]

Zofran (Ondansetron)

Zofran is a medication that is used to treat nausea. It is fairly strong and is most often used to treat the nausea and vomiting that can be caused by chemotherapy cancer treatments. It is currently being considered for FDA approval for early-onset alcoholism. Early-onset alcoholism refers to those cases that develop before the age of twenty-five. An eleven-week study demonstrated that its use decreased drinking and improved abstinence by nearly 40 percent in early-onset alcoholics.[160]

Antabuse (Disulfuram)

Antabuse has been on the market since the 1940s and was the first medication ever to be granted FDA approval for use in the field of addiction treatment. It is indicated for the treatment of alcohol addiction, acting as a powerful physical and psychological disincentive for someone trying to stop using alcohol. Antabuse does not reduce the person's craving for alcohol, nor does it treat alcohol withdrawal symptoms. It works as a negative reinforcer by causing a set of wretched consequences if someone drinks while taking the medication. Antabuse causes the buildup of toxic by-products when alcohol is consumed.

In our bodies, alcohol is metabolized into acetaldehyde, a toxic material that causes unpleasant symptoms, which is in turn metabolized into acetic acid, a harmless by-product. Antabuse blocks the body's ability to break down the acetaldehyde into acetic acid. Therefore, Antabuse causes the concentration of acetaldehyde occurring in the blood to be five to ten times higher than that found during the normal metabolism of the same amount of alcohol. Antabuse does not affect the rate at which alcohol is eliminated from the body; it works only by stopping the final part of the metabolic process. As it does so, there is an enormous buildup of acetaldehyde in the blood that causes the person to get acutely and violently ill.

The physical illness caused by the combination of alcohol and Antabuse results in what is known as the "disulfuram reaction." It is characterized by headache, flushing, sweating, shortness of breath, anxiety, nausea and vomiting, chest pain and heart palpitations, vertigo, low blood pressure, loss of consciousness, weakness, blurred vision, and confusion. In severe cases, it may even cause heart attacks, heart failure, seizures, breathing cessation, or death. Antabuse can also be toxic to the liver. Since alcoholics often have liver damage to begin with, it is imperative that blood levels of liver functions be checked frequently. The medication should only be given to those with a full understanding of the consequences inherent in this treatment.

Anatabuse's effectiveness is entirely predicated on compliance. Addicts are far from dumb, so those who take Antabuse yet wish to drink alcohol usually simply stop taking the medication or drink anyway. Only those who are extremely motivated and whose compliance can be assured are considered candidates for this medication. For this reason, Antabuse has generally fallen out of favor in the United States. In contrast, it is more widely used in Europe, where long-term research has demonstrated an abstinence rate as high as 50 percent in some studies.[161] In any case, when Antabuse is used, it must be combined with adequate psychosocial therapy. If not, the likelihood that it will have any significant effect in terms of abstinence and recovery is minimal at best.

Revia and Vivitrol (Naltrexone)

Naltrexone is a medication that blocks opiate receptors. It comes in two forms, an oral form (pill) and an injectable form. The oral form is used daily, and is known as Revia. Revia is indicated in the treatment of alcoholism and opioid addiction and to block the effects of street drugs and medications in the opiate/opioid family. The injectable form comes in a monthly depot formulation (that is, a sustained-action drug formulation that allows slow release and gradual absorption), known as Vivitrol, which is injected into a muscle once a month. Vivitrol is indicated for the treatment of alcohol addiction in patients who are able to abstain from alcohol prior to treatment. Vivitrol is also indicated in opioid dependence for the prevention of relapse following opioid detoxification. The monthly preparation of naltrexone has the advantages of increased compliance and a more favorable side-effect profile compared to the oral form.

In case of a life-threatening overdose of opiates like heroin or painkillers, naltrexone will reverse the effects of the opiates and can help to save a life. It works by binding very tightly to the opiate receptors in the body. It binds so tightly, in fact, that it displaces any other opiates from working and so reverses the effects of too much opiate in the bloodstream that could stop one's breathing. It effectively overrides the acute effects of opiates.

When one drinks or uses other drugs, there is a release of the rewarding natural opiate neurotransmitters known as endorphins. This also happens when one merely thinks about drinking or using other drugs. Naltrexone blocks this initial anticipatory euphoria and dampens the actual initial physiologic high, or "buzz," from the use of alcohol or opioids. Since naltrexone blocks the pleasurable feelings associated with alcohol and narcotic use, its primary application in addiction medicine is to thwart the positive reinforcing effects of using these substances. If using is less pleasurable, people have less incentive to use and more opportunity to consider the benefits of abstinence and recovery.

An interesting new set of off-label applications that naltrexone is being used for is in treating the behavioral manifestations of addiction, such as gambling, shopping, and sex. As an agent that blocks the euphoria associated with the anticipation of reward, naltrexone can potentially have a big impact in these other arenas of addiction medicine.

Research has demonstrated that naltrexone decreases alcohol intake (especially when there is a strong family history of alcoholism), decreases alcohol craving, increases the time to take a first drink, and results in fewer overall drinking days and fewer heavy drinking days.[162] The positive outcomes were maximized by applying community-based support and utilizing appropriate psychosocial support with the naltrexone. Naltrexone has not been shown to provide much therapeutic benefit to patients except as part of a more comprehensive plan of management for the addiction.

Unlike Antabuse, naltrexone does not induce a state of physical illness if one drinks alcohol while taking it. However, if one takes naltrexone while there are opiates already "on board," the user can be thrown into a rather unpleasant state of withdrawal. It is recommended that someone be free from narcotics for at least ten days before starting naltrexone to reduce opiate use. In fact, when physicians have any doubt as to whether their patients have taken any opiates, it is recommended that they give the patient a small test dose of naloxone (see below) to ensure a horrible withdrawal state will not follow administration of naltrexone. On the other hand, if the naltrexone is used first and is in the bloodstream first, then the subsequent use of most narcotics will have little effect.

Naltrexone has some possible side effects. The most common ones include nausea, dysphoria, headache, tension, insomnia, drowsiness, dizziness, constipation, and anxiety. Naltrexone can cause liver disease and is contraindicated for use in patients with liver failure or acute hepatitis. Because naltrexone blocks opioid receptors, it can also theoretically block the body's natural endorphins, leading to a general sense of malaise or dysphoria and a lower sense of reward experienced with routine pleasurable activities.

The injectable monthly form of naltrexone, Vivitrol, carries its own unique risk profile. Vivitrol may cause injury at the site of the injection, including pain, itching, redness, tenderness, swelling, or bruising. In some cases, the injection site reaction may be very severe, requiring medical intervention.

Narcan (Naloxone)

Naloxone is a full opioid blocker or antagonist. It not only blocks the effects of opioids, it counteracts them. As a result, naloxone can actually reverse an opioid overdose and revive someone who was unresponsive. Narcan is administered by intramuscular injection via an injector pen into the muscle of the arm, thigh, or buttocks, or through a nasal spray. It generally works within about five minutes. Repeated doses may be necessary if a person is still showing signs of overdose even after the first dose. With the dramatic rise in opioid/opiate overdoses and overdose deaths stemming from the opioid epidemic, first responders—police, firefighters, and paramedics—in an increasing number of states, counties, and cities are authorized to carry Narcan in order to revive people who are unconscious due to overdose. This allows these prehospital first-line personnel to intervene quickly because every second counts when an overdose has stopped breathing, and the brain, heart, and other vital organs are deprived of life-sustaining oxygen.

COMBINE Study

There has naturally been some curiosity surrounding the efficacy of combining some of the medications and behavioral components to treat alcohol addiction. Antabuse, naltrexone, and Campral can theoretically be given together to reduce the risk of relapse because they have different mechanisms of action. Further, they do not cause negative drug-to-drug interactions among themselves. The COMBINE study explored how the use of behavioral therapy and medication combinations—specifically, naltrexone and Campral—would affect the outcomes of treatment. Recall that naltrexone blocks the rewarding effects of anticipating and receiving rewards while Campral blocks cravings through a different system.

Eight groups of patients received medical management with sixteen weeks of either naltrexone or Campral, both naltrexone and Campral, and/or a placebo, and with or without a combined behavioral intervention (CBI). A ninth group received combined behavioral therapies only (no medications). Patients were studied for up to one year after treatment. The study's conclusions were that patients who received naltrexone, CBI, or both fared better on drinking outcomes. In contrast, those receiving Campral showed no evidence of improved outcomes—with or without CBI. No combination of medications and psychosocial interventions produced greater improvement than naltrexone or CBI alone. Moreover, placebo pills and meeting with a healthcare professional had a positive effect above that of CBI during treatment. Finally, the study's authors concluded that naltrexone with medical management could be delivered in healthcare settings, thus serving alcohol-dependent patients who might otherwise not receive treatment.[163]

The results were interesting and surprising for some. The patients who received a placebo and met with a healthcare professional did well. Not surprisingly to me, there was a sizable placebo effect. That is, when addicts see a healthcare professional, receive a treatment—even one that is inert, as is the case with a placebo—and get repeated advice to attend twelve-step programs, they do better. The study revealed that when a comprehensive treatment program is applied, outcomes improve.

This result demonstrates why combining psychosocial treatment with pharmacologic therapy is so vital. My patients will fail if they only receive a pill. And yet, the opposite is also true for some. There are those who need medical management assistance above and beyond psychosocial treatment alone. Remember that psychosocial therapy has its own benefits, including addressing the range of problem areas that may not be targeted by medication alone, providing a safe environment in which long-term issues can be explored with the proper attention over time and improving medication compliance.

Medication management, including use of fast-acting agents able to quickly target symptoms and provide immediate relief, can often enhance treatment retention and assist with acute and postacute withdrawal symptoms. The bottom-line result of this research is that when properly combined, psychosocial therapy and medication management complement each other and have synergistic effects that boost treatment outcomes.

Medications for Opiate/Opioid Addiction

The term *maintenance,* as in methadone maintenance, refers to keeping addicts on a substitute pharmacological agent as an alternative to active addiction, to stave off the often-horrific withdrawal symptoms, eliminate or greatly reduce cravings, eliminate the need to engage in criminal or other high-risk activities to get street drugs, and facilitate engagement in a fuller range of life activities than otherwise would be possible. Maintenance, now referred to as medication-assisted treatment or MAT, is a remedial but not curative treatment. Maintenance therapy was primarily utilized in the past to place heroin addicts on methadone. Today, newer agents, primarily formulations of buprenorphine, have expanded this option to opiate addicts who use heroin or prescription opioid painkillers of any kind.

The principle behind maintenance is *harm reduction.* Opioid maintenance, sometimes referred to as opioid substitution, is a medically managed, physician-supervised protocol designed to reduce involvement in high-risk activities and decrease serious adverse consequences for both the individual and the community. Its goal is to enable addicts to function at a higher level more quickly. The use of maintenance medications is pragmatic—it recognizes that not all addicts are ready for ongoing abstinence.

One advantage of opioid maintenance/substitution medications lies in their ability to significantly reduce the harm intrinsic to active addiction, including the temptation to relapse. These medications are no panacea: depending upon the dosage, some people get high from them, and they also create physical dependence, so withdrawals ensue if the medication is discontinued. As a result, this approach is controversial not only among addiction professionals, but also within the recovery community and the general population.

In spite of the recent emergence of the concept of *medication-assisted recovery,* there are a great many people who do not consider maintenance to be a valid recovery option because it is not abstinence based. However, it can be valuable and effective. Patients managed in this way are involved in some form of addiction treatment. Though perhaps less than ideal for some addicts, medication-assisted treatment is, at least initially, a more realistic and practical approach that has become increasingly necessary and prevalent in the face of the havoc wreaked by the opioid epidemic over the last fifteen years.

According to a morbidity and mortality report by the the Centers for Disease Control and Prevention (CDC), from 1999 to 2014 drug overdose deaths in the US nearly tripled, and among 47,055 drug overdose deaths that occurred in the US in 2014, 28,647 (60.9 percent) involved an opioid. Moreover, the CDC reported that in 2015, there were over 52,000 overdose deaths,[164] an increase of 11 percent over the previous calendar year. Heroin alone accounted for 21 percent of those deaths. I cannot express how shocked I continue to be at the ever-increasing number of young heroin addicts I treat in rehab facilities. Since the first edition of *When the Servant Becomes the Master,* pills have become somewhat harder to find, and heroin simply became a more easily accessible and cheaper alternative.

In any case, the debate looms large among addiction professionals and in recovery communities throughout the world. The key for each individual is to find the best treatment consistent with his or her values, needs, and goals via the safest and most pragmatic means available.

Harm reduction is the term used for the application of therapy to those who are currently unable or unwilling to achieve total abstinence. As much as

I would like to believe that all addicts can achieve total abstinence from their first exposure to recovery, over the course of my personal and professional experience I have gained a deep appreciation for individual differences within the process of recovery and the diversity of recovery tools available. In my practice of addiction medicine, my goal continues to be abstinence. Yet today I am able to view the harm-reduction approach with an open mind, because there are those who can benefit from this style of treatment. In addition, society as a whole benefits through decreases in crime, decreases in the transmission of infectious diseases, decreases in healthcare costs, and increases in productivity.

Harm reduction is not limited to medications. It may also include needle exchanges, safe physical spaces for addicts to openly use drugs, addiction education for both the addicts and the community, social policy initiatives, and law-enforcement cooperation. If the thought of handing out needles or allowing safe havens for drug use turns your stomach, at one time I had that exact response, and it is understandable. While harm-reduction policy does not try to minimize or ignore the very real dangers associated with addiction, it offers a practical and incremental approach to a massive public health problem. It can also be used in concert with other treatment approaches to assist those addicts who are not yet ready for total abstinence, and can be utilized for both illicit and legal drugs like alcohol and tobacco. It can be an effective tool in empowering addicts to reduce the risks of harm at the personal and societal levels as they work toward a more complete program of recovery. Education and appropriate psychosocial treatment referrals are a must, as is cooperation among the social, medical, spiritual, behavioral health, and legal communities.

My commitment to abstinence as the ultimate goal of addiction treatment and recovery is unwavering. Nonetheless, harm reduction plays an important role, effectively extending the reach of care to a greater number of people struggling with addiction.

Methadone

Methadone was the first medication sanctioned for opiate addiction and is most recognized for treating heroin addicts. Only physicians and clinics that are specially licensed can dispense methadone. It is a powerful opioid, a potent full agonist (it exerts its effects fully at the opiate receptor) narcotic used in opioid maintenance/substitution. Due to its strength and its long duration of action, methadone is also used for the treatment of severe pain. Unfortunately, a recent surge in its use as a painkiller has been accompanied by an increase in overdose deaths. Maintaining opiate addicts on methadone within the context of a proper comprehensive treatment regimen is known as methadone maintenance treatment (MMT).

Addicts who enroll in MMT do ultimately become physically dependent on methadone. The advantage, however, is that they are liberated from the drama and trauma of the street-oriented addiction lifestyle. Because it binds directly to the same receptors as other narcotics, methadone can eliminate or minimize an addict's withdrawal symptoms, and, if continued, can block the euphoric effects of other opiates so that the addict will be less inclined to use other street or prescription drugs. It is also longer acting, resulting in less of a high and aiding in maintaining patients on stable daily dosing. The dispensation of methadone is supposed to be tightly controlled to decrease the chance that it will be diverted and sold on the streets. Unfortunately, methadone is frequently diverted to the streets and abused. Moreover, it may cause the user to feel high, and for these reasons it is highly criticized in some addiction treatment and recovery circles.

Methadone has another significant drawback in that its discontinuation precipitates painful withdrawal symptoms. Withdrawal from such a potent and long-acting drug can be extremely severe and overwhelming—many addicts describe methadone withdrawal as much worse than withdrawal from heroin, and many addicts receiving MMT choose to stay on it longer than planned. Methadone has its proponents, and the numbers of addicts who are safely maintained on it justify its judicious use in certain populations.

MMT has been demonstrated through numerous research studies to be an effective tool in treating addicts and benefiting society. Addicts remain in treatment and away from nonprescribed drug use more often in MMT. As a result, they have fewer overdose deaths; less transmission of HIV, hepatitis, and other sexually transmitted diseases; and improved health. When opiate addicts are properly maintained on methadone, they can enjoy a respite from the cycle of addiction, perhaps for the first time in many years. Methadone maintenance facilitates a greater degree of self-care than would be otherwise possible. As a result of being free from the grip of the active disease state, addicts can address their biopsychosocial needs in therapy. They can also begin to attend recovery meetings and participate in recovery communities.

Buprenorphine and Buprenorphine/Naloxone Combinations— Suboxone, Subutex, Zubsolv, Bunavail, Buprenex, Butrans, Probuphine, Belbuca

Buprenorphine is a semisynthetic narcotic analgesic that was approved in 2002 by the US Food and Drug Administration for use in the United States as a medication for opioid addiction. Buprenorphine can also help manage moderate acute and chronic pain. Buprenorphine is a partial opioid agonist sold under the brand names Subutex, Probuphine, Buprenex, and Belbuca.

There are a number of medications that combine buprenorphine with naloxone, an opioid receptor blocker similar to naltrexone. The formulation of these combination meds applies a unique built-in safety feature designed to prevent misuse by those who may try to inject the drug. When injected, the naloxone counteracts the buprenorphine and throws the person into immediate withdrawal (now, that's a disincentive!).

But, when used as directed and allowed to be absorbed sublingually (under the tongue), the buprenorphine works while the naloxone does not get absorbed. Suboxone, Zubsolv, Bunavail, and Butrans contain buprenorphine plus naloxone.

Therapeutically, buprenorphine is used to eliminate or minimize withdrawal symptoms. Buprenorphine selectively and powerfully binds to opiate receptors in the body, eliminating craving and withdrawal and decreasing relapses. It may powerfully bind to receptors, but it only moderately activates them. As a result, it causes limited euphoria compared to other opiates/opioids, including methadone, but it works sufficiently to aid in the detoxification process, as well as maintain those engaged in treatment during the maintenance phase, if that option is chosen. Buprenorphine differs from methadone in that it is a partial agonist, whereas methadone is a full opioid agonist. While I continue to strive for and prefer the goal of abstinence for recovery, I cannot ignore or deny that both methadone and buprenorphine are underutilized evidence-based options for the treatment of opioid addiction.

Prior to its approval for use in the US, buprenorphine had been available for decades in other countries as a pain medication. Its FDA-approved application for use in addiction medicine application is sublingual (placed under the tongue and allowed to dissolve in the mouth) or implanted (Probuphine) and allowed to be delivered to the body over several months.

Buprenorphine's excellent safety profile is due to its "ceiling effect." That is, as a partial opioid agonist, the strength of its effect plateaus. After a certain dosage, taking more of the drug does not equate to feeling more of an effect. It has far less of an effect on sedation and on breathing and causes less respiratory depression than other opioids, and since buprenorphine causes less euphoria than other opiates, it has less potential to be abused. However, some people do use it to get high, and the medication is sometimes diverted, meaning it is used in ways other than intended such as being sold on the streets or shared, mostly to minimize withdrawal symptoms. Over the years, several of my patients have informed me that their drug dealers give out Suboxone to help their customers who are in withdrawal to get help in tempering the misery. It is important to stress that any prescription drug diversion is illegal, is dangerous, and should be avoided, no matter the means or the ends.

Buprenorphine's favorable profile also makes it an excellent and effective medical treatment option for detoxification from opiates or to maintain an opiate addict on therapy. As a partial agonist, it stimulates opioid receptors a bit, eliminating cravings, but buprenorphine has another unique and advantageous property in that it binds so tightly to opioid receptors that it prevents most other opiates or opioids from working if they are ingested. So, if an addict who may be taking Suboxone, Zubsolv, or Probuphine, to name a few, has a moment of weakness and takes another opiate, it will not have much of an effect, if it works at all. Most opiate addicts who do test these waters while on buprenorphine quickly recognize that it is basically a waste of time because there is little to no effect. In fact, buprenorphine binds so tightly that it should not be given to anyone who still has opiates circulating in his or her system because this will precipitate withdrawal by displacing the other opiates. It is for this reason that buprenorphine induction and maintenance should only be performed by specially trained and licensed physicians.

In clinical trials, when used in conjunction with psychosocial counseling, buprenorphine was shown to significantly increase treatment retention versus low-dose methadone, significantly increase opioid-negative urines versus placebo, and significantly decrease cravings for opiates versus placebo. However, buprenorphine was not as effective as methadone when higher doses were required. Despite their advantages, using either buprenorphine or methadone can cause extremely painful withdrawals when the time comes to stop either medication.

Buprenorphine is not a magic bullet. Alone, it accomplishes very little. Like all medical treatment options, it needs to be used within the context of a comprehensive treatment approach. It is also not without side effects. It has the potential to cause drowsiness and sedation, and, like all opioids, in large enough doses it has the potential to depress or even stop breathing and cause death. This is especially true and can be dangerous if it is mixed with alcohol or other drugs, especially sedative-hypnotics like Xanax, Valium, or Klonipin.

Naltrexone—Revia and Vivitrol

Naltrexone, the active ingredient in Vivitrol and Revia, was featured in the section above on medications for the treatment of alcohol addiction. Revia was approved by the FDA in 1984 to treat heroin addiction. Vivitrol was approved in 2010 to help prevent relapse in people who have completed opioid detoxification. Revia, a 50 mg pill taken daily, blocks the effects of opioids for twenty-four to thirty-six hours, while Vivitrol, a 380 mg once-monthly injection, blocks opioids for approximately thirty days. Vivitrol, then, provides a better and safer way to get the naltrexone into the system slowly over a thirty-day period. A literature review revealed that Vivitrol is well tolerated and more effective for relapse prevention than Revia, probably because it lasts so much longer—thirty days as opposed to one to two days.[165]

Again, as an opioid antagonist, naltrexone blocks opiate receptors so that other opiates will not have an effect if ingested. In other words, if someone who is taking naltrexone has a weak moment and relapses on pain pills or heroin, the drugs will be blocked from causing euphoria. Naltrexone yields no pleasurable effects, is not habit-forming, and does not cause any withdrawal symptoms when it is discontinued. However, there is always the risk that an addict will overdose by attempting to overcome the opioid blockade during treatment with naltrexone, or due to a lowered tolerance after treatment is stopped. Due to its blocking effects, some state medical boards require anesthesiologists diagnosed with addiction to use naltrexone, and many commercial airlines do the same thing for their pilots diagnosed with addiction.

Ultrarapid Opioid Detoxification

Another option that exists for opiate addiction is known as ultrarapid opioid detoxification, or rapid detox. It involves a more risky path through detoxification because it uses general anesthesia, rendering patients unconscious. The attractive benefit that makes it worth the risks and considerable costs for some people is that the use of general anesthesia enables them to avoid the conscious experiencing of withdrawal symptoms. In medical circles, rapid detox is quite controversial—the benefits are less than clear and the risks are uncertain. Currently, the only thing that is clear with regard to ultrarapid opioid detoxification is that further research is necessary in order to accurately determine both its merits and its potential pitfalls.

Medications for Stimulant Addiction Treatment

As described in Chapter Four, stimulants are the class of drugs that include cocaine, ecstasy, and amphetamines. There are no FDA-approved medications for stimulant addiction, and the major concerns during withdrawal are lethargy and depression. Usually stimulant addicts crash after a period of binge using, and sleep for several days. The detoxification period is rather short and is not life threatening. However, after detox, the cravings and other symptoms during postacute withdrawal can be especially intense for stimulant addicts.

Cocaine Vaccine

The cocaine vaccine was developed as a novel and creative approach to treating cocaine addiction. At the time of this writing it is not FDA approved, but research on it continues. Cocaine abusers experience significant cravings in early recovery, and the rapid and destructive downward spiral of cocaine (and methamphetamine) addiction is especially horrible. With the need to address this problem in mind, the Xenova Group developed a vaccine that showed promise in early studies. The cocaine vaccine was formulated by combining norcocaine with inactive cholera toxin. It was designed to eliminate the effects of cocaine and work in the same way as a regular vaccine. It stimulates the body's immune system to produce antibodies that attach to cocaine, prevent the drug from crossing into the brain, and destroy it before it reaches the brain. In preventing cocaine from reaching the target organ of addiction, the vaccine prevents any high or euphoric and rewarding effects of the drug from being experienced. It does not, however, dampen cravings.

The initial animal trials were promising, so human studies were initiated. A problem surfaced in that the vaccine works in only some of the cocaine addicts who were studied, and among those in whom it did work, only half remained cocaine-free half of the time. Overall, people did not produce enough antibodies to cocaine for the vaccine to be effective. In addition, some cocaine addicts in the studies were not ready to stop and so would take larger and larger amounts of cocaine in order to feel its effects. Because the vaccine prevented the euphoria from cocaine only up to a certain threshold, these addicts discovered that if they simply took more cocaine, they could override the blocking effects of the vaccine. Some would take as much as ten times the amount they used before receiving the vaccine. A considerable problem is that higher and higher doses of cocaine place an individual at risk for serious adverse health consequences, including overdose, seizure, and death.

Heroin Vaccine?

Recently, researchers in California have reportedly successfully tested a heroin vaccine on monkeys and have shown vaccines against fentanyl, oxycodone, and hydrocodone to be viable in rodents. Another research team in Maryland has reportedly successfully tested a heroin vaccine on rodents.[166] Vaccines are significantly different from medication-assisted treatment because, similar to flu vaccine, they spur the production of antibodies to ward off molecules of the targeted drug as if they were invaders. They are designed to prevent the drug's molecules from reaching the brain altogether, preventing any rewarding effects. As intriguing as the concept is, animal testing is a long way from demonstrating efficacy in humans. Furthermore, even with successful testing on humans and FDA approval, such vaccines would be effective only for those who are committed to recovery and wouldn't seek out other drugs. When and if opioid vaccines ever become available, they would be best utilized in combination with other available therapies.

Chantix (Varenicline)

Nicotine is a mind-altering drug that works in the mesolimbic dopamine system and is a highly addictive substance. The medical consequences of nicotine exposure are vast. Smoking is a risk factor for emphysema, bronchitis, and numerous cancers. In fact, tobacco use accounts for one-third of all cancers.[167] Lung cancer tops the list as the number-one killing cancer for both women and men.[168] Cigarette smoking is the most preventable cause of illness, death, and excess healthcare costs in the United States, accounting for 440,000 deaths annually and $157 billion in health-related costs.[169] It is difficult to accept that greed justifies the tobacco industry, when one considers the grave impact it has on lives and society.

In the face of such dire consequences, there is a recent and effective medication for nicotine addiction on the market that has received considerable media attention. Chantix is a selective partial acetylcholine nicotinic receptor agonist. That means it binds to the same receptors that nicotine binds to when someone puts that drug in his or her body. The highest concentrations of nicotine receptors in the body are in the mesolimbic dopamine system (the pleasure center).

By blocking the nicotine receptors, Chantix prevents nicotine from stimulating the central nervous system, which, in turn, prevents the shot of dopamine normally released by nicotine ingestion. Less dopamine release and less central nervous system stimulation in turn cause less of a rewarding effect from the nicotine, and the user is less inclined to use it again because the pleasure is lessened. Also, by filling the nicotine receptors, Chantix helps to dampen some of the withdrawal symptoms normally experienced when someone tries to quit smoking. Both effects help the nicotine addict quit with less discomfort.

Chantix is taken for a week before the actual quit date. Chantix will not prevent a smoker from lighting up, but it will help those who do quit. Chantix, like other addiction medications, is most effective if utilized with counseling. Research has demonstrated that its effectiveness is superior to that of both Zyban, the only other FDA-approved nicotine-cessation medication aid, and nicotine-replacement therapy using nicotine patches.[170] If there is no significant decrease in nicotine use after six to eight weeks, it is recommended that Chantix be discontinued. Common side effects include nausea, insomnia, headache, and weird dreams. There is also a black-box warning on the product due to an increased risk of suicidal thoughts or plans. It is best to address the use of this and all medications with your physician's oversight.

Summary

Therapeutic and medical management interventions are effective tools in treating addictions. The form and format of behavioral interventions are generally varied, and their effectiveness often depends upon the therapeutic bond and level of trust between the provider and the patient. We have come a long way since the middle and later part of the twentieth century, when we essentially had only one medicine for the treatment of addiction—Antabuse, which is specific to the treatment of alcohol addiction. Today, there are a number of other medications available that assist in the treatment of other forms of addiction, and more are in the pipeline of pharmaceutical research and development.

Currently, when we are able to treat an addict we can employ a host of biopsychosocial interventions that help to safely detoxify and guide the addict through the course of his or her treatment and into the journey of recovery. However, we do not always have immediate access to those addicts in need of treatment. Denial and delusional thinking are inherent aspects of the disease of addiction, and so we often encounter resistance from those who are in dire need of our help. The progressive nature of the disease and the pain it causes in everyone around it can be brutally frustrating, leaving family members feeling hopeless and helpless. When other avenues of help fail, there is a powerful and effective tool available to reach the addict and help to start the healing process for everyone who has been affected by the disease of addiction. This tool is known as an intervention, and we will explore that in the next chapter.

Chapter 10: Intervention

A ddiction is a chronic, progressive, relapsing, and potentially fatal disease. It most often requires an interruption of some sort—an intervention—to break the downward and destructive spiral in which the addict is caught. The disease of addiction is not curable and, when left alone, often progresses according to a tragic but predictable course. Negative consequences amass when active addiction continues unchecked.

The social, relational, emotional, spiritual, and physical arenas in the addict's life and in the lives of those with whom he or she has close ties suffer immensely. Drama and trauma become commonplace to everyone caught in addiction's web. The family and social circle also face physical, spiritual, and emotional pain. Family members and significant others commonly experience loneliness, hopelessness, isolation, anger, guilt, and grief. The toll addiction takes is intense and long: addiction is a process. It does not develop overnight.

Recovery is also a process, and it has a course—a long one, to be sure. What might at first seem counterintuitive is the reality (well-known to addiction-treatment professionals) that getting someone with an active addiction to a drug-free state is probably the easiest part of the recovery process. Merely detoxifying someone is not the goal, though in many cases it is the first course of action. After detoxification, the long road of recovery is just beginning, and it is full of change and challenge for everyone involved.

There is a saying: no one comes into treatment voluntarily. There is usually an intervention in some shape or some form of consequence that motivates and creates leverage, formally or informally, for the addict to enter treatment. The need for treatment is generally present long before treatment actually takes place. No one has ever hired me as an interventionist prematurely.

Would you be surprised to learn that the possibility of success is the same no matter what the leverage is? Perhaps counterintuitively, those who come into treatment because the law has intervened have the same chance of a successful recovery as those whose spouse threatens to leave, whose job is threatened, or who is sick and tired of being sick and tired. My intervention partner, Chris Davis, usually tells the families we work with, "They don't need to be willing; they just need to come in to treatment." Initial willingness alone is not an accurate predictor of success—consistency and engagement in the recovery process are. Those who are initially unwilling but are open and teachable are more likely to succeed than the willing who fall back into self-sufficiency and complacency.

When the addict comes into treatment, the family system enters treatment—directly or indirectly—as well. While a deeper exploration of the family dynamic and the intervention process is not addressed here, I will provide a brief overview. Simply put, the family system becomes dysfunctional over time due to the presence of addiction in one of its members. The change is usually gradual enough that the other members learn to adapt to their new roles without awareness of much, if any, change taking place. This adaptation is too slow to notice and helps to perpetuate the disease.

Spouses, children, and even extended friends and family do any number of things in an effort to "help" when troubles arise from the addiction. These efforts, intended to help, most often protect the addict from negative consequences of his or her disease. This protection arises out of a combination of love and self-interest, and is known as enabling because it allows or "enables" the active addiction to continue. Enabling typically has a negative connotation, but it is important to keep in mind that it takes place in the context of ignorance related to the disease, genuine caring about the addict and the integrity of the family, and the need to cope with a threatening and stressful situation. Indeed, I've stopped using the term entirely in favor of viewing the process simply as overuse of the character strength "love."

Over time, families and friends try almost anything to help the addict. Energy is invested in trying to control or "fix" him or her. Addiction cannot be cured, controlled, or fixed by these attempts, and a sense of learned helplessness develops. The failed attempts to make the situation better can be extremely frustrating and confusing. Anger builds. In turn, as an interventionist, the majority of time I spend with the addict's family and friends is used for the purpose of educating and coaching them on the concept of overuse of the character strength "love," and on how care for themselves and appropriate use of (tough) love can thwart the downward progression of addiction.

Interventions are emotionally challenging for everyone. The addict's support system often experiences the intervention process with a fair amount of trepidation, doubt, and anger. There is often a sense of betrayal and guilt. These are perfectly normal feelings, considering the difficult and naturally conflicted decisions that must be made. For these reasons, an intervention involves thorough attention to the drama and trauma the family and friends have endured.

A successful intervention teaches everyone involved how to remove themselves from participating in the disease process and move forward into the future with an enlightened perspective. The goal of an intervention is to start the journey of recovery for *both* the addict and the support system. A successful intervention is not necessarily determined by whether or not the addict goes into treatment, but rather by the extent to which those affected by a loved one's active addiction experience relief from their suffering as a result of taking appropriate care of their own needs—making changes in their thinking, the way they relate to their feelings, and how they act, particularly in response to the addict in their life.

As described earlier, denial is a form of delusion inherent in addiction. Denial is an illogical construct of the addiction cycle, providing a warped sense of order to the chaos of an addict's life. This is how, after a spousal argument over broken promises or frustration at continued using, denial fabricates the thought, "If you were married to this man/woman, you would drink, too. . . . Okay, so I'll have a drink!" Denial creates resentments and frustrates rational attempts at control or order. Denial is not limited to the addict; it can also infest the otherwise rational thinking of each person in the addict's support system.

Essentially, everyone affected by addiction falls victim to a variety of delusional belief systems and webs of subconscious lies that are fabricated to protect oneself, but which in the end serve to perpetuate the disease. A major reason why few people enter treatment completely voluntarily is that during active addiction—driven by the primitive midbrain, as described in Chapter Three, and propelled by the addiction cycle detailed in Chapter Five—the voluntary part of the addict's brain is not in control; the involuntary part of the brain is. The voluntary part of the brain is under the spell of denial.

Some addicts are intervened on by the legal system. A few addicts go into treatment and find recovery by asking for help themselves, so I don't mean to suggest that everyone in active addiction needs an intervention. A professional intervention is most beneficial and effective for those who are in denial and resistant to change. With the guidance of a professional, the spell of denial can be broken. An intervention that uses love, dignity, and respect can reach past the denial and anger to touch the authentic person and stop the downward progression for all those involved in an effective and healing way.

Interventions are often necessary, though. Usually, when I am called upon to lead an intervention, it is because there is a crisis or the family system has exhausted its set of solutions. Families are routinely traumatized as a result of experiencing their loved one's active addiction, often for years. There is a general sense of helplessness around the numerous previously failed attempts to cure or control the problem on their own. The dysfunction usually progresses for quite some time, because without professional guidance and counseling, most families are not equipped to identify and manage the disease of addiction.

Over the course of living with addiction, individual family members will attempt in vain to control or fix the situation. It is very easy for any one person to be manipulated or simply beaten down emotionally when attempting to intervene upon the addict on their own without the determined, united support of a group. Besides, it is irrational to try to reason with an illogical disease. A cohesive group, though, is difficult to influence; there is strength in numbers. Properly implemented, an intervention that facilitates group cohesiveness is most effective and avoids further trauma for the family and the addict.

One myth that must be corrected is that interventions do not work. There is a common false belief that addicts cannot get well unless they have hit bottom all by themselves and are willing to enter treatment on their own. In my own experience, I would not have survived much longer had I not been intervened upon. Countless others besides myself, including AA's founder, Bill Wilson, have also been successfully rescued through interventions. Sadly, however, many more have not been intervened upon before ending up in jail or dead. Interventions can stop the downward progression of this fatal disease by creating a loving "bottom" that is higher than what would be experienced by the addict if he or she were allowed to continue unimpeded.

People have the same chance of success through treatment of their addiction regardless of how they came into that treatment. It is in treatment that the unwilling discover a ray of willingness. I actually welcome encountering an addict's resistance, because I know it is only the subconscious remnants of the active disease that are attempting to thwart the recovery process. Many times addicts who are very resistant and unwilling to enter treatment actually make exceptional progress. It is also true that some enter treatment seemingly ready and willing, complete treatment successfully, and then quickly relapse. Any combination of events is possible, because there are no guarantees.

Another misconception is that interventions are aggressive and threatening. In contrast to this stereotyped image, it is love, compassion, and respect that are used. These are the key elements that help penetrate the addict's wall of defensiveness and denial. Anger and judgment on the part of those participating in an intervention merely reinforce the mental and emotional aspects of active addiction. This will be further discussed later in this chapter.

If there are no guarantees, the question arises as to what course of action should be taken when the active addiction needs to be addressed. Many times, not doing an intervention could be a grave mistake. Addiction is a fatal disease. Along the way there may be pit stops in jail or other institutions, but the disease is chronic, progressive, and fatal. Wait, and it may be too late. So, when there is a high degree of danger, urgency dictates that action should be taken immediately.

Even though it is impossible to see accidents coming, addiction is a severe, life-threatening condition. Therefore, treatment should not be delayed if the warning signs of addiction are present. When in doubt, it is best to err on the side of safety. While nothing can guarantee success—the addict may or may not enter or complete treatment, or he or she may relapse and end up institutionalized, incarcerated, or dead—when all is said and done, interventions arm the loved ones of addicts with a heroic and viable means to disrupt the downward progression. Half measures, including continuing attempts at controlling or fixing the addict, only perpetuate the disease and end up creating more pain and suffering for everyone.

The Intervention Process

An intervention can be defined as *any intentional course of action that introduces transformation into people's thoughts, behaviors, and feelings.* Interventions come in many shapes and sizes. When a concerned group meets in order to communicate their observations and concerns, an intervention happens. The group of concerned individuals is composed of friends, coworkers, and family members. There are several ways in which a group can conduct one of these meetings. A group may conduct an intervention without a trained professional, but it is not recommended. The group system engaged in the dysfunction caused by the addiction process is usually unable to recognize what a trained and objective third party can. Furthermore, skilled interventionists can facilitate the group's empathy and love to replace anger and judgment. Interventions that do not utilize an approach based on dignity and respect can cause more trauma and damage.

Today, there are several well-established intervention methods. The history of intervening on addiction can be traced back to an Episcopal priest and recovering alcoholic, Vernon Johnson. He was a passionate recovering alcoholic who wanted to prevent others from suffering the negative consequences he experienced as a result of the progression of his own addiction. He dedicated his life to recovery and is known as the father of the modern drug and alcohol intervention.

Vernon Johnson began refining his intervention technique, known today as the Johnson Method, in the 1960s with the members of his church. The Johnson Method involves a group that meets ahead of time, usually several times for discussion and preparation, and then surprises the addict with a meeting wherein they communicate their concerns, how they have personally been affected by the addiction, and the consequences they are willing to impose if the behavior of the addict does not change. His method continues to be the standard against which other models are measured. The success of his method has spawned myriad different techniques and applications over the last forty years. His method has been modified and expanded and sometimes even replaced by modern interventionists who have been able to fuse their unique strengths and areas of focus into hybrid and even unique models of intervention. Today it is common for interventions to be convened in connection with all forms of addiction: alcohol and other drugs, Internet/computer/gaming, sex and love, gambling, shopping, and eating.

On a Personal Note

I began my career as an interventionist after I entered recovery and began working in a treatment center. I entered treatment myself (in a different place than where I began working) only as a result of an intervention. I decided that entering treatment was easier than facing the consequences of not doing so—not uncommon for the person being intervened upon. I disagreed with the folks intervening on me and colorfully offered them options as to where they could go. My outsides were angry, but something incredible and entirely different happened deep within me. I can best explain it by saying that my addiction was protesting the intervention while my soul took a deep, long sigh and said, "What took you guys so long?" I will be forever grateful for having people who cared enough to act so bravely on my behalf.

I had attempted to stop on my own so many times that I was under the impression that it was not possible to stop. I had no intention of staying stopped, because at the time that meant a horrible life. Before I filled up my life with a program of recovery, being abstinent meant being dry, being without, which meant I would suffer horribly, with no end in sight. While it was true that my life was pitiful and unmanageable, I was under the warped impression that I was still receiving a benefit from using, and I was under the subconscious illusion that using meant survival.

However, soon after I was admitted into rehab, I became willing to at least try the solutions that were being offered, and I have not relapsed since. My life is unbelievably rich with relationships and joy, and the times that are difficult are managed effectively today with the tools I have been given. I am so very grateful to have been offered a second chance to do things right, so it has been easy to dedicate my life to helping others have the same opportunity. Indeed, interventions can be the most powerful and gratifying aspect of what I do. Witnessing the power of love, applied in the right amount, in catalyzing significant change is something that must be experienced in order to be appreciated. It is truly extraordinarily moving.

Prior to and shortly after getting sober, I was disillusioned with the professional life I had chosen. Wanting to be a true healer, in the sense that I wanted to really know my patients and intervene effectively in their lives to improve their well-being, I found that the unforgiving, harsh reality of practicing medicine left little, if any, time to approach my craft ideally. Had I not wanted to give back to the force that empowered my personal transformation, I would have quit medicine altogether. Thus, I became an interventionist and an addictionologist. I read all I could and attended conferences, discovering that I was pretty effective, and haven't felt like I have "worked" since. I love what I do, and would be doing the same thing even if I won the lottery.

Working in a rehab, I found that I was constantly intervening on addicts during the normal course of their treatment stay. Many folks get well quickly— too quickly, in fact. What is amazing is how swiftly many addicts want to leave treatment after a very short period of time. This rapid course is called "flight into health" and reflects an unrealistic and unhealthy mind-set. A good addiction professional will motivate continued engagement and participation in treatment through a variety of strategies. When all else fails, a potent method for helping the reluctant addict to stay engaged in treatment is to enlist the support of his or her family and social network. After I began conducting formal interventions, I discovered that there were many similarities between formal interventions designed to motivate addicts to enter treatment and informal interventions that were conducted on patients while they were still in rehab.

I also learned that although I was effective in leading interventions solo, I could offer an even higher level of service with the help of a partner. Chris Davis is a licensed chemical dependency counselor who has become one of my closest friends in addition to my intervention partner. Whenever possible,

I choose to do interventions with a partner, although those led by a single skilled professional can certainly be effective and successful. Overall, there are several techniques, strategies, hybrid models, and schools of thought that can be utilized during the course of an intervention.

No matter the technique, interventions have some basic properties. Friends and family of someone in trouble go through a process of preparation. They eventually address that person, the person's addiction, and his or her behavior. There is an initial interview and assessment with a professional interventionist, followed by a determination of whether or not to move forward. There is a decision on whom to include, as well as meetings to prepare for the actual intervention. Education on addiction and family dynamics is provided, and treatment options are covered. Strategies on the exact mechanics and care plan are also formulated, and there is a meeting with the addict wherein communications are delivered and exchanged.

Again, the type of effective communication required in an intervention is best formulated with the assistance of a trained professional. It is best for participants to focus the communication of their own experiences and feelings around events that have actually transpired. For example, expressing how it felt to witness and be subjected to the intoxicated ranting of a spouse is helpful. On the other hand, remarking that someone "acted like a fool" is not. When an addict hears judgments or anything that sounds like blaming, his or her defense system hooks onto those statements and uses them to generate reasons why everyone in the room is wrong and is "out to get" him or her.

When an addict hears critical comments, for example, related to him or her having been intoxicated at a family gathering and acting like a fool or disrespecting everyone, the natural tendency is to become defensive. The addict's defense system will pinpoint the one person he or she didn't disrespect, and the five minutes during which he or she was calm and collected, and will think, "*See? They're always picking on me!*" Surrounded by people like this, who wouldn't need to use drugs? Or, if an addict gets into a car wreck and his or her family mistakenly assumes it was due to impairment, the addict's defense system will spring into action: "See? They are making things up again; everything they say is biased." The person being intervened on then usually shuts down with defenses up, and the process has a low chance of success.

Focusing on observations while reducing opinions, assumptions, and judgments simplifies the process and minimizes distracting hooks that the addict will latch onto in ways that can escalate or deflect the issues at hand. Communication must be honest and will often include hard truths and difficult emotions. With assistance, though, the process can flow smoothly.

The classic intervention usually lasts less than forty-five minutes. The preparation time is longer, including multiple meetings with the support group occurring over several days to several weeks. In contrast, the Family Systems Model of intervening does not require as much preparation. Often with this model, the addict is even invited to the first meeting, and the process unfolds with participation from all members. Communication is not prepared, and the intervention day itself is therefore not a surprise like it is when the Johnson method is used. More intervention models exist and, though they are not covered here, can be excellent options. I prefer using a modified Johnson approach, but I have received training in other models.

Family Roles

As described earlier, a principal aspect of addiction as a family disease is that, over time, the family adapts to the presence of the disease by forming its own dysfunctional balance. The family grows accustomed to behaviors that are required to cope with the presence of active addiction. When family systems were studied, it became clear that certain well-defined universal roles begin to be adopted as a result of addiction in the family. These roles may be present in dysfunctional families without addiction, but are more pronounced and predictable in families with an addict. In such families, the disease of addiction takes center stage.

Families change to create a new balance in the face of the addiction's force. The addict essentially becomes the center of the universe because the drama and trauma inherent in the disease and the negative consequences brought about by active addiction demand lots of time and energy. This adaptation often occurs so slowly and gradually that even though family members may have perfected their respective roles, the changes have gone unnoticed.

The first role that forms is that of the *Caretaker,* or *Chief Enabler.* This family member (usually, but not always, the spouse or primary partner) works very hard to placate everyone else. He or she is concerned with avoiding harm and confrontation while trying to make everyone else in the family happy. The Chief Enabler's underlying motivations include feelings of fear, insecurity, and helplessness. He or she works hard to keep the problem in the shadows, avoid bringing the addiction to the forefront of the conversation, and maintain good appearances for the world to see. The Chief Enabler facilitates all the other roles.

The *Hero* is the family member who seems "perfect." By excelling at everything, the Hero makes the rest of the family system appear good and normal. His or her underlying motivations include feelings of fear, shame, and guilt. By ignoring the problem and reaching a venerable status, the Hero is the family system's "front" to the world. The Hero role is necessary in order to make the family and the other roles people play within it look respectable.

The *Mascot* is the family member who plays the role of court jester and provides comic relief. The Mascot's underlying motivations include feelings of shame, anger, and embarrassment. By creating a sense of levity through humor, the Mascot effectively deflects attention from the painful reality that the family is experiencing.

The *Lost Child* is the family member who sort of disappears into the woodwork. The Lost Child is rarely seen or heard and stays out of the way as much as possible. His or her underlying motivations include feelings of abandonment, anger, loneliness, and guilt. Often the Lost Child is shy and introverted, and may bond more easily with animals than people.

The *Scapegoat* is the family member who absorbs the brunt of the negative energy in the family system. His or her underlying motivations include feelings of anger, guilt, and shame. The Scapegoat will do whatever it takes to divert attention from the real cause of family strife by getting into trouble, rebelling, and acting out.

Often the healing process begins when there is a crisis or other strong enough instigating event that shakes the foundation of the family system, and the proverbial house of cards begins to tumble down. When this happens, the family's dynamics can be interrupted in the same manner as the addict's cycle of addiction. The role that each family member plays can be overcome with guidance and education. Before the addict gets into recovery, the rules of the family are governed by denial and avoidance; open and honest communication is also not encouraged. The recovery process for the family includes learning how to communicate openly and honestly, expressing emotions in significantly healthier ways. Making this change, though extremely positive, can be very difficult. As with any substantial change process, it is reasonable to anticipate that there will be many challenges for family members who, like the addict, are faced with a new way of life.

Strangely, even though recovery is the goal, the family system with an addict in recovery is vastly different from what the family members have been accustomed to, and so this change is often disruptive and frightening. Getting the addict well may have been the primary driving force and the single greatest wish for family members, but the transition to a life in recovery requires many adjustments. The family knew what to do when their loved one was ill, but they are not prepared for the changes that occur as they progressively become well. Recovery involves actions and major change. For example, the partner, father, mother, son, daughter, or friend who is gone "at those meetings" is doing what he or she needs to do for recovery, not abandoning his or her support system. But for many family members, it feels that way. As the family system adapts to a new and healthier "normal," there may be a grieving process to mourn the loss of the way of life the family members were used to. Even if it was fraught with upset, confusion, anxiety, anger, and fear, it was what they were used to, and they knew what to expect. When an active addict works a process of recovery—as positive as that is—the old balance is turned on its head. Participation in Al-Anon or Nar-Anon—twelve-step programs for the family members and significant others of addicts—can be extremely valuable in helping the loved ones of a recovering addict adapt to their new way of life. Other times, therapy is needed for individual family members or for the family as a whole to help them adjust successfully to the monumental changes in their lives.

Summary

A formal intervention can be the start of the path to health and wholeness for the entire family. The intervention professional will guide, counsel, and educate the family. Follow-up treatment will be recommended to assist in the long-term healing process. Interestingly, when I started performing interventions, I thought the only goal was to get the addict into treatment. Now at least 50 percent of my intention in every intervention I perform is to facilitate the education and rehabilitation process in the family system as a whole. If the family does not learn to recognize the roles they play and the dysfunction that has infected their own lives, merely getting the addict into a treatment center will do very little in the long run.

An intervention is an effective tool to start the process of freeing the addict and the affected family system from pain and suffering. The intervention is not the end of the process, but merely the beginning. When the addict goes into rehab, the recovery process is only beginning. In a vital way, all treatment is an intervention in the addiction cycle. Recovery is not a spectator sport; it demands action from all those affected. Family members are asked to participate in therapy, but they can often be reluctant to do so because of the misconception that the addict is the only one who needs help. How can family members expect the addict to be the only one in a dysfunctional system to get help? When the family understands that all members have contributed in some way to the problem, they can accept that a solution also requires everyone's involvement.

Chapter 11: Relapse Prevention

Defining Recovery and Relapse

Removing drugs and addictive behaviors from one's life does not cure addiction. Some of the dysfunctional changes caused by addiction either are permanent or take months or years to undo. Addicts will always be susceptible to a reactivation of the disease process because, as demonstrated by the research of Dr. Volkow at NIDA and others, addiction causes long-standing changes in the brain's mesolimbic dopamine system (MDS). Other, more global brain dysfunctions in the prefrontal cortex (PFC) and associated higher processing centers do resume normal functioning after years of recovery, though. The critical key to recovery, then, is time and, of course, preventing a relapse.

Relapse prevention is essentially the heart of what is taught to the newly recovering addict. What is *recovery* if not disease management? Staying sober/abstinent is equivalent to the diabetic's control of blood sugars or the asthma patient's breathing management strategies. Sobriety/abstinence is, of course, necessary, but it is only one part of the recovery process. Staying in recovery is the end result of managing the chronic disease of addiction and thwarting a decline in health. Without vigilance, relapse and a return to active addiction are just lying in wait, preparing to strike. Addiction does not spontaneously go away when an addict stops using, and, as noted previously, there is no cure. Because addiction is a chronic, relapsing disease, continuous measures must be consistently adopted to prevent reactivation of the disease. Relapse prevention is critical, because experiments have shown that extinguished behavior such as drug use can quickly return by exposure to a triggering event that restores the short-term connection involved in reward expectancy.[171]

Recovery is far from simple—it incorporates many elements, because it has to. The hijacked brain, impaired motivation and reward systems, and behavioral symptoms inherently necessitate a comprehensive approach. In order for addicts to make the transition from a life in the grip of active addiction to a free life in recovery, a number of steps must be taken. As described in detail in Chapter Three, neurotransmitter-mediated, subconsciously driven commands enslave the addict. Overriding this enslavement takes time and effort and is key to long-term recovery. Like Mark Twain suggested, an addict can "quit" a thousand times. Staying quit is the hard part. In treatment, I cannot merely say, "Don't use and don't act out." That is like saying, "Just say no." If that were enough, I would not have a job, this book would not be published, and addiction treatment centers would be unnecessary. Removing what began as the servant from the master's role takes time, consistent effort, and strategic planning.

I tell my patients that relapse is possible whether they have a day or a decade in recovery. No one is immune to relapse. It does not matter how much money or luck one has; relapse is possible. Relapse is part of the disease of addiction; it does not care how many therapy sessions you've had, how many vitamins you take, how often you exercise, or how many twelve-step meetings you've been to in the last month. Relapse is out there and in here. Preventing a relapse is not a passive process. It is an action that requires a life-revering amount of dedication. There is a saying in recovery that sums it up best: all an addict has to change is one thing: *everything*. That may sound like a tall order, and it is. But what a ride!

This chapter will include definitions of recovery and relapse followed by an overview of the major areas of life that must be addressed in a recovery plan: red flags, stress and other emotions, and cues. Focusing on relapse prevention is so vital because addiction is a primary, chronic, *relapsing* illness. An effective, albeit nonscientific, way to properly understand this concept is to think of relapse as a predator, waiting for the right moment to strike. It is a disease that causes dysfunction in the subconscious part of the brain. Thus, it is beneath the radar of consciousness and will. Since addiction does not care what someone wants, the disease can be thought of as having a mind of its own.

Addiction-induced MDS dysfunction commandeers the brain to act. It does not consult the thinking, logical, and ethical cerebral cortex in making decisions. This type of irrationality is colorfully explained by many addicts who claim that their addiction thinks it can kill them (the host) and keep on living. Funny, yes. Alarming, yes. Logical, no! The chronic nature of addiction cannot be stressed enough. As I have heard it said, "Just because you got the monkey off your back doesn't mean the circus has left town." To be successful, relapse prevention must be an ongoing, active, and comprehensive process.

What is a relapse? This is an important concept that took me a couple of years to fully appreciate. I used to view any use of alcohol or other mind-altering substance or resumption of addictive behaviors as a relapse. I now understand, though, that relapse can only occur once recovery has been achieved. In other words, someone has not relapsed unless they have been in recovery *first*. So, the individual who goes through the motions of entering rehab or attending a few meetings but does not internalize the solution, and then uses after a period of abstinence, is really not relapsing. For such a person, the brief pause in his or her regular pattern of using (with or without exposure to treatment) is simply part of the same diseased state of active addiction. There are many addicts who do not use daily. It is common for addicts to go through small periods of time without using—being abstinent without recovery. Taking a break from more frequent usage does not constitute recovery, and therefore resumption of use would not represent a relapse. Recovery is necessary before relapse can occur. Relapse is not the same as using. Relapse is resumption of use after a period of recovery.

Hence, an addict can be said to have relapsed only if he or she has achieved a state of recovery by exhibiting evidence of a voluntarily maintained lifestyle that includes abstinence, healthy behaviors, and enhanced social functioning. This is a critical distinction. There is a grave misunderstanding about the effectiveness of treatment that stems from

- mistakenly equating detox with treatment; and
- characterizing any resumption of mood- and mind-altering substances subsequent to any treatment episode as a relapse.

I believe that when such better, clearer definitions of recovery and relapse are widely accepted and utilized in outcome evaluation for addiction treatment, success rates will increase. If we use standard definitions to measure recovery or relapse, treatment's effectiveness would be more accurately applied to what we are actually aiming to establish. A return to use without an established period of abstinence would not be considered a relapse. Relapse requires a period of abstinence; otherwise, it's simply continuing to use. Experience has taught me that although there are no guarantees, far less relapsing occurs after recovery has been established. The vast majority of people who I have witnessed return to using substances have not achieved any degree of recovery first. Also, there is a correlation between length of time in recovery and likelihood of relapse: the longer the time spent in recovery, the less likely relapse becomes.

Like the development of addiction, recovery is a process. Moreover, the process of recovery and preventing relapse entails different stages of healing, growth, and challenge. Initially in recovery, addicts learn how to stop using mind-altering substances and then begin to learn and practice how to stay stopped. Next, addicts learn how to manage emotions, stress, and success. Using the knowledge and skills gained in these earlier stages, addicts then learn how to live without using, one day at a time.

I have found that avoiding a relapse is not a sustainable lifestyle. Removing the drug doesn't lead to a fulfilled life any more than removing depression guarantees one's happiness. My theory is that addiction develops when people pursue happiness ineffectively. With relapse rates so high both during and soon after treatment, I developed an approach to treating addiction that aims to make life so fulfilling and rewarding that the risk of relapse is small. I named it Positive Recovery, and it combines effective modalities with the science of well-being—positive psychology.

Early recovery, including detoxification, is extremely challenging and intense. Physical, spiritual, and psychological pains are powerful. Addicts also have to navigate through the phase of postacute withdrawal in early recovery. More frequent cravings, difficulty concentrating, trouble with short-term memory, mood swings, sleep disturbances, and physical problems are typical and can make staying in recovery during the first few months especially difficult.

Middle recovery is where addicts begin to "get their brain back." It is generally agreed that it takes about five years of uninterrupted recovery for the brain to resume normal and age-appropriate functioning. During this time there is more reconditioning of the neuroplastic brain as recovering addicts achieve a higher degree of stability in their recovery and learn how to cope better with life on life's terms.

Late recovery is a maintenance-oriented phase in which addicts consistently apply the things they have learned, one day at a time. The challenges in late recovery are not as great as in the other phases, unless, of course, addicts become complacent and stop doing the things that helped them to achieve and maintain their recovery. When recovering addicts in any phase discontinue doing the things necessary to maintain their recovery, the relapse process begins. Contrary to what many people assume, relapse does not begin with the resumption of drug use itself; it actually begins with the discontinuation of recovery-supportive practices and activities.

Addiction is a chronic, relapsing, potentially fatal disease characterized by physical dependence, obsession and compulsion, loss of control, unmanageability, insanity, catastrophic negative consequences, and ultimately, institutionalization and death. Sound like fun? Of course not. Active addiction is a living hell. Addicts who can remember that their addiction is a deadly and insane illness greatly enhance their chances of staying in recovery. On the other hand, for those who forget or otherwise lose their appreciation of the true nature of addiction, the likelihood of relapse increases dramatically. Relapse is a process whereby the more subtle, indirect signs and symptoms of addiction— the maladaptive mental, emotional, and spiritual aspects—return after a period of recovery. There is deterioration in recovery beliefs, recovery behaviors, and recovery attitudes over time that culminates in resumption of use of mind-altering substances.

Relapse occurs for many reasons. Let us explore a few. There is a nonscientific notion pervasive in recovery that is worth reviewing here, and that is that *addiction is the only disease that tells you that you don't have a disease.* This aphorism contains wisdom and merit, though it cannot be explained scientifically. Obviously, a disease cannot actually talk, but the saying has a powerful message: denial is very pervasive and strong in addiction, and it can reemerge at any stage in recovery. In recovery, denial is what essentially facilitates the loss of the appreciation of addiction as a chronic, deadly, insanity-causing disease.

While human beings across the board have minds that can fabricate all kinds of nonsensical notions, rationalizations, and denial, addicts can be especially clever in this regard. For example, an addict I know claims that one side of his brain manufactures bullshit while the other side of his brain purchases it in large quantities. He happens to be in recovery and has a colorful way of explaining that he has a twisted internal dialogue essentially telling him that he can drink and use other drugs again—despite the fact that every time he has done so in the past, his life has unfailingly imploded into catastrophe.

I have witnessed human beings with other diseases who are very capable of denial and rationalization, are noncompliant with courses of treatment designed to improve their lives, and continue to act in self-destructive ways. Like denial, relapse as a phenomenon is not unique to addicts. Just look at how many "normal" people do not take their medications or otherwise follow doctors' advice. In fact, engaging in some degree of denial and rationalizing is simply part of being human. Addicts are, however, extraordinary in that they can colorfully make an art form of the process.

Addiction is no less chronic, less relapsing, or less fatal than cancer. Most cancer patients would not dispute the claim that they have cancer and require intensive treatment. Cancer has no usefulness whatsoever to a person. On the other hand, alcohol and other mind-altering drugs were at one time an important and useful part of the coping skill set for the addict—there was a benefit to using them at some point. Over time, though, that benefit is replaced with a "need." The subconscious has assigned an enormous value to mind-altering substances, and the state of being without the substance is painful and empty. The need, though, remains subconscious while the delusional thought that mind-altering drugs are beneficial lingers in the cortex.

Postacute withdrawal syndrome (PAWS) is the name given to the time period that ensues once the addict passes through the acute withdrawal or detoxification period. PAWS can last from several weeks to several months to a year or more, depending on how much and for how long an addict has used. Many relapses occur during PAWS. It is particularly challenging to stay sober in this time period because the drive to avoid suffering from the discomfort of the anxiety, irritability, depression, and sleep problems that are characteristic of PAWS is tremendous.

Addiction is a brain disease that causes dysfunction in memory, reward, motivation, attention, emotional regulation, social interactions, spiritual connection, and cravings. So, when the brain is subject to dysfunction, the ability to do the right thing is compromised. Even for those who are very eager, vulnerability to relapse is high during the period of brain repair. Treatment and relapse-prevention planning ought to recognize that addicts early in recovery have dysfunctional brains. Treatment cannot be of too short a duration because the healing process takes time, and lots of it. The good news is that healing happens and cognitive function returns. The bad news is that it can be challenging to teach fish to ride a bicycle.

A fish cannot ride a bike for several reasons, not the least of which is the absence of legs. What an addict in early recovery lacks are healthy coping skills. During active addiction, addicts perfect the art of escape and numbing themselves out. Asking someone to cope entirely on his or her own after his or her primary coping mechanism is no longer available is an incredibly daunting request. It is comparable to getting pushed out of an airplane without a parachute. Without a good set of alternative coping skills (that can only be learned over time), people will revert back to what is known and comfortable, even if it is self-defeating and self-destructive.

The unknown is frightening for everyone. The biblical story of Moses and the Jews escaping from the tyranny of enslavement in Egypt illustrates the point well. During the Exodus, it is said that many of the Jewish people asked to return to Egypt because the journey through the desert to the Promised Land was harrowing, painful, mysterious, and frightening. Even though as slaves the Jewish people were beaten, were robbed of their rights, and had their male offspring killed, some of them still wanted to return. The point is that even though conditions were obviously worse in Egypt, it was at least what they were accustomed to. Even though a life with active addiction is traumatic, a new life in a wilderness of the unknown of early recovery with a dysregulated brain can be extremely frightening.

Getting out of the desert is one thing. Entering and remaining in the Promised Land, and living life on life's terms, is an entirely a different matter. Becoming abstinent is tough; staying abstinent and maintaining recovery is tougher, by virtue of the fact that it is a lifelong task. In essence, a good relapse-prevention plan accounts for PAWS and the brain's need to heal, as well as for as many other potential relapse triggers and triggering events as possible. Addicts are encouraged to change their playmates, playthings, playpens—the people, places, and things in their life that are associated with their active addiction or are otherwise unhealthy. For instance, anyone in early recovery is well advised to avoid going to bars. Why go to a bar to order a Diet Coke? That would be like going to a brothel for a kiss. You can see it makes no sense. As addicts in recovery quip when discussing such risky scenarios, "If you go to a barbershop often enough, you are going to get a haircut."

The process of recovery involves developing and practicing new coping skills to be able to handle life on its own terms. Learning new and healthy coping skills is also part of a comprehensive relapse-prevention plan that can enable addicts to withstand the entire spectrum of emotional and stressful situations without using. While these new coping skills are being mastered, it is invaluable to have safe, supportive stopgaps in place. Such resources help bridge the transition from the past coping strategy of mood-altering substances to the adoption of healthy, recovery-oriented skills.

Holidays, anniversaries, and other life milestones can be particularly difficult for people new to recovery. Knowing that such times are challenging, having a solid support system, and being prepared with a strategy when stress or emotions begin to feel overwhelming can make the difference between another day in recovery and a relapse. It is important to have a twelve-step meeting or other supportive resource available when needed. Being aware of meetings one can attend around Thanksgiving or July Fourth, or on anniversaries and other significant occasions, is a great strategy.

Vacations are another prime opportunity to engage in a tailored relapse-prevention plan. There are twelve-step meetings all over the world, and even if the Twelve Steps are not part of your primary recovery plan, they can still provide a safe, recovery-oriented haven for anyone struggling with thoughts of using. There are many other strategies that can be employed in a good recovery plan. For example, I recommend outlining a list of ten things to do as an alternative to using mind-altering substances or acting out in other self-destructive ways, especially when faced with boredom, loneliness, or other potential triggers.

Emphasizing relapse prevention does not imply that relapse is inevitable. Even though, in my experience, the majority of people in recovery do not get and stay abstinent after their first attempt, relapse is not mandatory. It is entirely possible for any addict to successfully achieve and maintain recovery the first time around—and many do. Again, it is important to understand that relapse does not mean failure, either! Remember, someone with high blood pressure is not considered a failure if they have a relapse and their blood pressure does not remain at 120/80 from the minute they are diagnosed.

Relapse is an opportunity to look at the recovery plan and review what is working well in addition to what is not. It can provide a powerful learning experience that presents unique opportunities for the professional to work with the addict to identify and set aside residual or reemerging denial, and adjust and strengthen the plan. It is also a time to build on whatever successes the addict may have achieved instead of merely reinforcing the sense of failure or causing unhelpful shame and guilt.

When relapse does occur, it does not have to last a long time or be excruciatingly painful. When a relapse-prevention plan is comprehensive and includes agreements to participate in aftercare treatment and twelve-step or other support programs, and when the family is committed to participating in appropriate interventions where necessary, relapse can be prevented or terminated rapidly. When an addict gives his or her support system open permission to honestly express their concern over warning signs and behaviors, the higher degree of accountability that creates can, in turn, prevent or terminate a relapse much earlier in the process and minimize the consequent suffering.

Red Flags

"Mark" is a forty-four-year-old history teacher at a prestigious, local private college. He has been widely published and has won several awards. His students frequently give him positive feedback, and his peers and administrators also respect him. One day he awoke to find his friends and family standing at his hospital bed. He had drunk too much one night and was suffering from a delusional blackout when he walked into the middle of a busy street and was hit by a car. Thankfully, he recovered from that and no one else was hurt . . . sort of. His friends and family were deeply troubled by his recent behavior, and the accident was the final straw. During an emergency intervention at his bedside, they expressed their love and told him of the pain he was causing them by his drinking. They cried, he cried, and he agreed to enter treatment.

He was hardly a model guest at his residential treatment facility, but slowly and surely he began to internalize that the solution to his plight was to engage in a recovery program. After some resistance, he accepted the fact that he had a chronic and potentially fatal disease that was full of insanity, obsession, and compulsion. He also put a lot of his old ways behind him. He swore off the English pub and jazz clubs he had frequented. He erased the numbers of his drinking buddies from his cell phone. His treatment team helped him identify some untreated anxiety and family-of-origin issues, and he made a plan to treat his whole person. He got a sponsor, a doctor, and a therapist. He went to ninety twelve-step meetings in ninety days.

His semester ended and he had some time off. Everyone in his support system was amazed at how well he was doing, and they would frequently comment about it and encourage him to continue. He often would share with me that among the blessings in his recovery were the salvaged relationships that he held dear. He was a loving man and, in many ways, I learned much from his good heart. However, as the summer wore on, he began to skip some of our sessions, until finally he stopped coming altogether. I later heard that he had ceased attending his regular twelve-step meetings, and his therapist shared with me that he had not been attending sessions with her, either. I began to fear that I was going to see his name in the obituaries.

What I would later learn is that he let his recovery plan fall by the wayside after four months. He decided that since he had stayed abstinent for that long, he had it licked on his own. He went back to his favorite nightspots "for entertainment" because he was feeling overconfident and cavalier, until one night he took a drink. His active addiction resumed with a fury, but no one knew about his relapse until he failed to show up for his first day of class. He had retreated from his recovery plan and his support system, and was left to his own devices—resulting in relapse.

Mark's story demonstrates a few key elements of the relapse process. His initial abstinence and time in recovery were authentic. He was wholeheartedly in recovery, working a good program, attending meetings, compliant with his medications, and beginning to work the steps. Over time, as he began to rebuild his life, his behavior began to change. What went wrong in his case is typical of a relapse process. After some time in recovery, addicts may grow complacent and start to rest on their laurels. Some forget that the disease of addiction is chronic, progressive, and fatal, and decide they do not have it any longer.

Mark's *actions* changed. Recovery is about *doing*. His *doing* while in recovery included twelve-step meetings, regular therapy sessions, and consistent communication with his sponsor. His relapse began a few weeks prior to that first drink. His isolation and complacency sparked the process of the relapse. As he began to withdraw from the recovery community and other successful elements of a recovery plan, his relapse started ever so slowly. He stopped calling his sponsor and attending regularly scheduled appointments; he discarded the support and accountability that contributed directly to his recovery as well. His mood changed. I later learned that he would become angry at the smallest provocation and let the resentments fester internally without processing his emotions. He fell into a state of self-pity and began to frequent his old haunts until the relapse process ended in a drink.

Contrary to what many people assume, relapse does not occur on the spur of the moment. Relapse is always a process, and there are warning signs evident throughout that process. As in Mark's case, there are many red flags that may indicate a relapse process is starting. These can include, but are not limited to:

- Increasing isolation, denial, defensiveness, boredom
- Feeling like a victim, self-pity, diminished sense of meaning in life
- Complacency, minimizing need for further treatment, casting aside elements of the recovery program—starting with decreasing, then discontinuing, meeting attendance
- Seeking conflict with others, crisis building, option reduction, emergence of other forms of addiction like gambling, overeating, sexually acting out, or shopping/shoplifting
- Disregard for rules, deterioration in appearance, mood changes

Of course, many more red flags exist. A useful strategy to identify red flags and stop a potential relapse from taking root is to include some of the addict's support system. This strategy works best if guided by a trained professional, because many family systems slip into old behaviors and mistake involvement for opportunities to control. However, if the family and other support systems are given permission by the addict to gently intervene (not be in charge) with observations and concerns, then it is more likely that the addict will be able to receive feedback in the proper context. In the case of someone who is in a twelve-step program, a sponsor is often the unofficial point person to gently or not-so-gently encourage modification or intensification of the recovery plan. Otherwise, a therapist, physician, clergy member, or some other capable, respected adult can play that role.

When the addict in early recovery is left to his or her own devices, the likelihood of slipping into old behaviors and heading blindly into a relapse cycle is high. Recall that brain dysfunction and postacute withdrawal syndrome pose a challenging set of circumstances to navigate. The brain is not operating on all cylinders, and help from other functional and recovering brains can bridge the gap during this early taxing time. In short, when there is a trusted and reliable set of supports that can gently yet assertively assist addicts in maintaining recovery-oriented actions, they are much less susceptible to relapse. The addict must also remain in a state of openness, because when red-flag behaviors are identified and intervened on early enough, the addict has to be willing to take the feedback to heart and adjust course.

Relapses can be anticipated in order to be prevented. Competitive athletes will tell you that often the best defense is a good offense. A good relapse-prevention plan requires honesty, accountability, willingness, action, and anticipation. Addicts must adapt their entire lifestyle consistent with the plan and the process of recovery. Changing people, places, and things and learning how to modify thoughts and tolerate uncomfortable emotions are extremely difficult but fundamentally vital to success in recovery.

Adopting old habits and associating with old friends and places activates mental, emotional, and physiological triggers to use that can be overwhelming early in recovery. Remember that addiction lives in the part of the brain that reacts independently of one's will and, when triggered, operates at a subconscious level. Even with the best of intentions, an addict who is exposed to certain people, places, emotions, and things can inadvertently be triggered to relapse. Many patients who return after a relapse confirm that they were "caught off guard." But upon dissecting the anatomy of each relapse, we learn the particulars of how it happened gradually and progressively. Each opportunity to learn from mistakes grants wisdom. We can also apply knowledge of others' mistakes in order to better anticipate and prepare for the kinds of high-risk situations mentioned throughout this chapter.

There are emotional, physical, subconscious, and spiritual ties in the control center of addicts' brains that connect cues like people, places, emotions, and things to using. In essence, a crucial first step is to identify these ties and cues, which are known as triggers. Triggers can be of any type, and a helpful practice is to assist each addict to identify their strongest ones. I find the best strategy to identify and label triggers includes focusing on four areas in the addict's life: stress and emotions, cues, substance avoidance, and appropriate medical care.

Stress

Emotional maturity, generally absent during active addiction, is not achieved the minute abstinence starts. Instead, it is developed slowly over time while in recovery, as experience and wisdom build. Because the brain gets emotionally arrested at the stage of development at which the addict begins using, there is not an abundance of emotional maturity present in early recovery. Stress and emotions are often the bane of an addict's existence. Many people, addicts included, find stress and emotions challenging. Financial insecurity, attachment, yearning, and fear can plague us all. The coping skill set of an addict in the active disease state and in early recovery is immature and inadequate. Many addicts cope with stress and uncomfortable emotions in ways that may help them feel better in the very short term but are ultimately self-defeating and destructive.

Coping effectively with stress and emotions requires a degree of acceptance, delayed gratification, and resiliency that is not common in early recovery. Using alcohol or other drugs, overworking, emotional eating, and so forth may initially work to lower anxiety, yet over time these activities create additional stress and harmful negative consequences.

Imagine a type-A-personality businessman who comes home at the end of a stressful workday and has one drink in order to relax. Then, he plays with his kids and attends to his wife's needs. No problems. He repeats this stress-reducing drink after work on most days because it does help him chill out; then it turns into an everyday routine. Over time, as tolerance and dependence ensue, that one drink turns into two, then three, or even four. Time spent with family and social obligations takes away time from the drinking, and so nonessential socialization decreases as he focuses more and more on what has now become a need. Progressive drinking, changes in behavior, activation of his MDS, isolation, marital and family discord, and other manifestations of addiction create a self-perpetuating set of stressors. What started out as an effective tool to relax ends up stressing out him and his whole family. His drinking manages his life while he continues to drink in order to try to manage his life.

It is easy to see that, as this man's wife, children, employer, and social network begin to complain, he will rationalize the "necessity" to drink more in order to quiet his mind and his emotions. He will then isolate more, drink more—thereby inflicting more pain on his loved ones—and experience even more stress. And the cycle continues.

During sober moments when his brain's cortex can process his situation, he can appreciate the extent of his drinking-related consequences, and experience what are called "moments of clarity." Many addicts resolve never to use or act out again during these moments. But when the activated MDS overwhelms his cortex, he continues to drink even when he does not want to. Using a drink to manage stress creates more stress in the long run. This is just one example of how some short-term-focused coping skills can create more stress than those they were initially intended to relieve.

A Chinese proverb best sums up this dynamic: "First the man takes a drink, then the drink takes a drink, then the drink takes the man." What was at first a harmless, stress-reducing habitual drink after work turned into a stress-provoking need. The servant becomes the master.

Until the addict in early recovery develops healthy alternative coping skills, he or she is vulnerable to the MDS's drive to soothe itself with drugs and/or addictive behaviors. The effects of stress on the body and mind of an addict can trigger particularly undesirable physical consequences and emotional states. I used to contend that stress avoidance is key to well-being and relapse prevention. However, it is not stress, but the way in which an individual views and handles stress that determines whether stress is harmful or helpful.

In a blog last year, I wrote on how stress is inaccurately considered by many to be inherently "bad." As it turns out, while stress is very real, it does not have to be bad. Stress has an upside—it all depends on how you explain the stress. Studies teach us that when you use stress to your advantage, you can experience more "good stuff." This all starts with how you understand stress, or, in other words, what meaning you assign to the stress you experience.

Some of us seem to shine under stress. For example, some people do their best when facing a deadline. They seem to almost *need* the stress of a deadline in order to perform. For them, stress is an important and positive motivator. Meanwhile, other people do their best work without the weight of time limits and other such external pressures. In either case, delegate tasks and plan ahead to increase your chances of goal attainment, but not necessarily to reduce stress. Stress is normal; stress happens.

People who don't view stress as the enemy—the potentially fatal boogeyman that many well-meaning health advocates claim we should avoid like the plague—are much less susceptible to the ravaging effects it can have on people who do.

Stress is actually a physiological response, and, like the myriad events that happen in life, you choose how to perceive it. You give stress meaning, and the way you explain it to yourself is not a trivial matter. While a more in-depth exploration of stress is beyond the scope of this book, the bottom line is this: embrace stress and you may actually improve your overall health.[172]

An important relapse-prevention consideration concerning emotions that often goes unaddressed is that intense positive emotions can be just as risky as intense negative emotions. Emotions and stress do not necessarily need to be negative in order to trigger strong cravings. Sure, fear, stress, anger, and resentment are atop the list of negative offenders for most people, but good feelings such as joy or the satisfaction that accompanies experiences of success can also trigger urges to drink or use drugs, and lead to relapse. As strange as it may sound to some, there are many addicts who have an extremely difficult time coping with emotions on the positive side of the spectrum.

Too much self-satisfaction, confidence, or praise can be unsettling enough to trigger a relapse for some, especially early in recovery. Even money can be a powerful trigger—"burning a hole" in an addict's pocket and taking him or her to the dealer's doorstep. Sometimes addicts believe that they deserve the reward of using for having been abstinent for a time or for doing well in their recovery process, or for some other success. It is important for each individual to identify his or her own set of stressors and challenging emotions. Awareness of the potential for both positive and negative emotional stress to trigger a relapse helps those in recovery to better anticipate and avoid potholes.

Emotional development for recovering addicts takes time, action, patience, hope, and guidance. Stressful events challenge the addict's immature coping skills. There are three main types of stressful events. One includes emergencies, where the body is in actual physical danger—real life-and-death circumstances. A Bengal tiger trying to eat you is a good example. The next type of stressful event is a long-term stressor where the stress is not acute but chronic—for instance, the stress inherent in wartime or famine. The third type of stressful event, which is most applicable to the disease of addiction, includes psychological stress, such as stress related to the serious negative consequences of using—damage to marriage/primary relationship, career/job, health, finances, self-esteem, and so on.

Stress contributes directly to the addiction cycle through the ways it affects us psychologically and physically. Addicts often have one foot in the past and one foot in the future. Checking out of one's reality through escapism is reinforced and thoroughly honed in the cycle of addiction. In habituating self-destructive coping mechanisms like escaping one's reality, addicts become masters at not being present. For many addicts, stressors and fears are born from sheer inexperience in remaining mindful and present. There is a great quote from Mark Twain that sums up this type of situation best: "I have been through some terrible things in my life, some of which actually happened."

Any of the three types of stress outlined on the previous page stimulate the body's stress response system. Even stress that is created by fear of the future or guilt about the past can have as powerful an effect on the mind and body as the stress of wartime. Stress, regardless of the specific cause, activates a common physiologic set of reactions that disrupt the body's natural balance and homeostasis. In fact, worrying about the future and regretting the past are enormous human stressors, and in addiction these stressors perpetuate the cycle of addiction by creating enough discomfort to result in substance use.

What is the stress response? It is the brain's response to threatening situations, real or imagined. In the stress response, the brain orchestrates a reactive set of chemical and behavioral changes that include the starting and stopping of different parts of the nervous system, as well as activation and deactivation of specific hormone chemicals. Stress is a force that places strain on our minds and bodies and disrupts our balance and homeostasis. The stress response is the body's way of counteracting the force of stress in an attempt to restore balance. One thing the stress response does is turn off nonessential activities like digestion, sexual reproduction, and the immune system. While the body is in a crisis state, these activities are not essential. For example, in a truly stressful event, like when somebody is chasing you with a knife, it would be a waste of energy and downright dangerous if the body was interested in copulating or stopping off for a bite to eat. In a crisis, those drives would get you killed.

A very important aspect of the stress response is that the brain does not distinguish between true emergencies and psychological stress. When there is stress, the response is the same regardless of the type of stressor. So, the chronic stress of addiction activates the same physiologic response pathways in the body as an acute life-threatening event or the chronic stress of war or famine.

There are consequences of a chronically activated stress response. One such consequence is a weakened immune system. This helps explain, in part, why addicts are more vulnerable to getting sick. Research also demonstrates that there are higher-than-normal circulating levels of the stress hormone cortisol in those with active addiction. Addiction is traumatic in and of itself, and with higher circulating levels of stress hormones there is an elevated level of anxiety as well, which leads to more habitual self-soothing through the use of substances. This is another way that the addictive cycle is perpetuated and exacerbated. In effect, the stress of addiction causes the addict to use more, but in turn, this use causes even more long-term stress.

Psychological stress and physiological stress perpetuate the cycle in the same manner. Addiction causes addicts to behave in disturbing ways. While the disease is active, the brain is hijacked so that addicts will do anything, even it means crawling through hazardous waste, in order to get more of what they "need." Addicts will lie, cheat, steal, fail to meet obligations, and behave in many ways that range from generally unattractive to abhorrent. This "bad" behavior creates an enormous amount of shame and guilt in addicts.

Speaking from personal experience, I can confirm this paradox. If we care at all about others, we are in pain as a result of our destructive actions. When we are out of integrity and fail to fulfill our potential, we can be in pain. Looking in the mirror, or seeing the disappointment or anger in the faces of our loved ones, is painful. So, what can we do to quickly, easily, and powerfully change the way we feel? What do we know best? Naturally, we use more. Using numbs the psychological pain. Guilt and pain caused by addiction can be dulled by continued use of mind-altering substances so that the psychological stress itself also drives continued use, perpetuating the cycle.

The activation of the body's stress response over extended periods of time generates considerable costs for the long-term health of the individual. The stress response is a type of physiological crisis intervention and, although it is helpful for immediate danger evasion, it causes damage when chronically activated. Over time, the individual's entire homeostatic balance is distorted. So much of our health depends on allocating attention and effort to preventing disease and maintaining the health we have. When a large amount of energy is applied to crisis intervention, less attention is available for prevention and maintenance, and so health suffers.

What exactly happens in our brains and bodies during the stress response? When there is an actual or imagined stressor, the hypothalamus in the brain releases corticotrophin-releasing hormone, or CRH, which in turn activates the anterior pituitary gland to secrete corticotrophin, or ACTH, which then causes the adrenal gland to release glucocorticoids. Then, the sympathetic nervous system releases epinephrine and norepinephrine. Epinephrine and norepinephrine act very quickly, within seconds. Glucocorticoids, on the other hand, act over minutes or hours. Epinephrine and norepinephrine are the hormones primarily responsible for preparing the body for fight or flight.

The fight-or-flight automatic response is a survival tool that prepares our body to survive through the activation of our heart and muscles, and it turns off nonessential activities like digestion and reproduction. Research has demonstrated this by showing that the stress hormone cortisol is as elevated in addicts as it is in those suffering from post-traumatic stress disorder.

A brief overview of how coping skills progress is warranted here. By trying to manage the stressors of life through numbing themselves, addicts are masters at not being present and not feeling emotions. Active addiction is a state in which the lack of presence and feeling are obvious. Even before addiction is present, however, repetitive behaviors that may be used as coping strategies are often effective enough to use as a way to "check out." For instance, drinking at the end of a hard day's work can help relieve stress. Shopping when depressed can elevate mood. Eating a pint of ice cream while watching TV is a way to distract from boredom. Working long hours can provide a needed escape from demands at home. Gambling can cause some excitement in a life that may seem tedious. Sexual activity provides an effective distraction from whatever.

Of course, hard work or making love or placing an occasional wager are not self-destructive in and of themselves. These and other activities are used moderately and successfully by millions of people every day. But over time, in the right host-environment-agent combination and through repetition, these coping strategies turn into habits and a lifestyle that cause self-destruction and fuel the cycle of addiction.

Developing healthy alternative coping skills requires awareness where there was none. When addicts enter recovery and break out of the cycle of addiction, they are able to feel their emotions and begin to glimpse a new way of living. The influence of the thinking cortex, with its ability to weigh and measure decisions, is reintroduced over the slow process of healing in early recovery. Instead of reacting impulsively with old behaviors, addicts in recovery can begin to choose a healthier way to respond to difficult or stressful situations. While the brain and body are healing and an addict is learning how to cope with life without the use of mood-altering substances, it is critical that he or she use the support and safe havens of twelve-step and/or other self-help recovery groups. Recall that to expect an addict to become abstinent and intuitively know how to navigate life on life's terms is like pushing someone out of an airplane without a parachute and expecting him or her to be okay.

Cues

Cues are a significant source of potential relapse triggers. Cues come in many forms: visual, auditory, tactile, temporal, and olfactory. As discussed earlier, an addict new to recovery should stay away from *people* who are associated with their active addiction, *places* that were part of their addiction, and addiction-related *things* lest the temptation to use stirs strongly within. In fact, such people, places, and things offer ample examples of all five of the above forms of sensory cues.

Visual cues are things we see that set off internal switches and stimulate brain changes that can cause us to act. The convenience store or a pill bottle, when gazed upon, can seriously stir the desire to use. Running into your drinking buddy, bartender, or drug dealer can have the same effect.

Auditory cues are triggering sounds that have an established association with rewarding the MDS. For example, if you are a cold-beer-loving alcoholic and you decide to torture yourself by pouring a nonalcoholic beverage into a frosted beer-style mug, there are several auditory cues that may stir you to drink. The clang of a cold mug or the *glug glug glug* sound of a drink filling a glass may stimulate and motivate you to repeat the behavior with an alcoholic beverage next time.

Tactile cues are things we touch that may trigger a relapse. Examples of tactile cues include the feel of a bar stool or the bar itself, the feel of a chair that an addict routinely sat in when he or she used, or touching or holding alcohol bottles or other drugs. Other examples include drug paraphernalia such as glass tubes, scales, cigars, rolling papers, and glasses.

Temporal cues are cues that occur at specific times. These can be particular times of the day—for instance, 5:00 p.m. or the conclusion of the workday; times of the week—Friday or the weekend; or times of the year—holidays, anniversaries, or birthdays. Temporal cues are especially important for the addict who has developed patterns of using at specific times. For those who are triggered intensely by temporal cues, managing time becomes especially important in their relapse-prevention plan. One way to do this is to schedule therapy sessions or, whenever possible, plan to attend self-help meetings at the riskiest times.

Finally, olfactory cues are those things we smell that trigger the desire to use. The smells of a bar or of a basement where substances were used, as well as the sweet aroma of marijuana, the earthy smell of ale, or the pungent and acrid smell of crack burning, are just a few examples of olfactory cues that can be dangerous for the addict seeking recovery.

Cues also include any mind-altering, abusable substance other than the "drug of choice." In my experience, this is the cue that is the most dangerous and insidious. Too many prescriptions are written for addicts by physicians who are unaware of the risks or choose to ignore them. I have witnessed far too many addicts relapse through the use of a prescribed medication or a little alcohol (in cases where alcohol was not the abused substance). Introducing mind-altering substances into an addict's body is a form of playing with fire. Very often, when put into the body of an addict, any abusable substance—alcohol, marijuana, opioids, cocaine, sedatives, and so forth—carries an extremely high risk of becoming a "priming dose" that activates the phenomenon of craving and leads to reinitiating the addiction cycle. Any mind-altering substance, by virtue of its site of action, has the potential to overwhelmingly and subconsciously motivate addictive behavior.

It is essential to emphasize that recovery is an inside job. That means that recovery is a way of life independent of external circumstances, and when in stable and solid recovery an addict can go anywhere with anyone at any time. Healthy recovery goes with the addict everywhere he or she goes. The difference is that when they are in recovery, addicts will not want to go to a bar to order a Diet Coke, they will not fabricate a reason to get controlled substances from their physicians, and they will not find it necessary to drive by their old dealer's house.

Let us next explore how cues trigger cravings. As an example, we'll use environment as the cue. Cues can trigger cravings and become part of a relapse process because they activate automatic stimulus-responses in the subconscious. For example, if an addict who is early in recovery visits the pub he or she usually drank in, that addict's neural pathways that connect being in that pub with drinking alcohol will become activated, trigger craving, and a create a high risk of relapse. For this reason, I instruct my patients that it is better to avoid bars and other high-risk environments if at all possible, especially early in recovery.

An experiment with rats reflects the power of the environment in triggering drug seeking and relapse. The subject rats were given cocaine in a room illuminated by red lights. Every time they received cocaine it was only when they were in the all-red room. So, close associations developed between that environment and drug use. The rats were then removed from this environment, and their habit of drug use was extinguished.

After an extended period of time, the rats were put back into the all-red room, and they exhibited behaviors consistent with strong cravings. Their actions upon returning to this room involved the same drug-seeking behaviors that were evident while they were actively addicted to the cocaine.[173] They would search the room madly for cocaine and scratch the walls. They groomed themselves less often. Some even tried calling their drug dealers, but they didn't have opposable thumbs and so couldn't hold the phone to dial (another attempt at research humor).

Another obvious cue to be avoided whenever possible, and especially early in recovery, includes exposure to people who use mind-altering substances. This is especially important if such people were the addict's using buddies.

The association between that group of people and using is most often too great to overcome. Many addicts who are new to recovery want to try to hold onto friends, even when those friends continue to use. Maintaining these relationships places an addict squarely in harm's way, and has contributed directly to many relapses.

If you can imagine the difficulty encountered by an addict in recovery who attends a function at his or her formerly favorite bar surrounded by his or her best friends who are getting completely wasted, you may have a slight idea of what that person would be up against. I am not suggesting and do not recommend that addicts isolate themselves socially and avoid weddings, birthdays, and holidays. However, self-awareness is essential, and precautions may be necessary to create a safety net. After time in recovery, the exposure to drug use loses its strength and often becomes less of an issue.

All mood-altering drugs work in the brain's pleasure center and are enormous potential activators of addictive thinking and actual substance use. The only gray area in this framework for a relapse-prevention plan is in the use of prescriptive medications. Suffice it to say that this aspect of a relapse-prevention plan has inherent risks. Many people continue to hold the misconception that prescription medications are safe because they are doctor-recommended "medicines." Moreover, many physicians who have not been trained in addiction medicine may unknowingly prescribe medications that work in the pleasure center and increase the risk of setting off addictive thinking, craving, and relapse. Any prescribed mood-altering medications must be dealt with very carefully for anyone in recovery, even those with stable long-term abstinence.

Most patients I treat today actually have a prescription drug problem, either alone or in combination with alcohol and/or illicit drugs. At one time, prescription drugs were considered safer than illicit drugs because they were tightly controlled and, for the most part, were not overprescribed. Today, however, prescription drugs are extremely easy to obtain and can be even more dangerous than alcohol. "But wait a minute," you say. "My doctor prescribes Valium or Xanax or Adderal, and I take it as prescribed." Or "I need the Vicodin or Ambien or Dilaudid in order to function." True, there are some individuals who require certain medications in order to maximize their life functioning. However, when tools that came into use to improve the quality of life begin to have the opposite effect, those tools are no longer helpful. In addition, there is a time and place for everything. I firmly believe that the disease of addiction should not mean a life sentence of inappropriate medical care, either. Everyone should be treated with dignity, respect, and proper medical care. However, whenever feasible and as much as possible, addicts can remain out of harm's way by refraining from mind-altering addictive substances. The wonderful thing about medical care today is that there are viable options for treating anxiety, depression, bipolar disorder, insomnia, and pain with minimal risk of stimulating the reactivation of active addiction.

In cases where addictive substances are prescribed to those in recovery for legitimate underlying conditions, they must be used with special care and according to strict guidelines. When the use of addictive medicines begins to create its own set of harmful negative consequences in addicts and nonaddicts alike, it becomes necessary to utilize other options to manage one's medical status and overall life effectively.

Let us look at "Janie," a thirty-five-year-old divorced mother of two boys. She suffers from fibromyalgia, a painful musculoskeletal disorder that is also associated with psychiatric symptoms including depression and fatigue. After seeking help from the traditional medical community, she found herself taking escalating amounts of painkillers, muscle relaxants, and sedatives. She was prescribed these medications in larger and larger quantities because they stopped working at lower doses. She was compelled to take more than what was prescribed for her because they stopped working even at higher doses.

Her use escalated until she began to feel increasingly worse without them in her system. When she would run out of the medication early, various doctors would eventually tire of her and discharge her from their care, and she would end up in my office, completely devastated and ashamed. I learned that her boys were caring for her as you would care for a disabled elder with Alzheimer's dementia. But she was only thirty-five years old.

She was mostly bedridden, far from the vibrant woman she had been previously. It was a sad life, but she could not stop on her own and could not understand why she had started taking the pills so much in the first place. She wanted to hate these drugs, but she couldn't—she needed them, she would tell me. Without the strong narcotics that her body had become accustomed to, she suffered agonizing pain. As a result, she still enjoyed how they made her feel despite the fact that her life had become a mess.

Janie was reluctant to stop taking these drugs because she was concerned about her fibromyalgia pain, depression, and withdrawals. She tried many times on her own to quit using her pills, but found the withdrawals to be more wretched than she could bear. So, she resigned herself to the sad lifestyle she was living at the time I met her. It took some finessing on my part, but she was able to hear that other options did exist for her condition and that she could be treated in a way that could enrich her life instead of disabling her. Finally, she agreed to inpatient treatment. After some cajoling, Janie grew open to alternative and safer ways to treat her maladies. Today, Janie has over two years in recovery, is a healthy adult role model for her children, has finished school, and works a full-time job.

Most people I treat with prescription pill addiction are not as dramatically disabled as Janie was. Soccer moms, executives, teachers, laborers, and others like them make up the bulk of people asking for help for addiction to prescription drugs. Our insured working, middle, and upper classes are the ones most affected today, like those who were affected when cocaine and opium tonics were rampant in the United States before the Harrison Narcotics Tax Act of 1914. The United States is in the midst of an enormous prescription pill epidemic, the likes of which has not been seen before. The overprescribing and abundant availability of pills can cause people to become addicted just as easily as they can enable identified addicts to maintain or resume their active addiction. Addicts need to be up-front and honest with their physicians about their addiction in order to facilitate communication and reduce the potential for relapse via prescription medications.

The One Thing

I discovered one final piece on relapse prevention worth mentioning. In preparing this book and in order to be more effective in my job, I decided to interview numerous people in long-term recovery. Over the years, I have asked many addicts who had at least ten years of recovery one question: What is the *one* most important piece of advice you can give to someone new in recovery? These veterans were from different walks of life, of different ages, and from different socioeconomic levels. Some were famous and some infamous. My experience was quite interesting, because instead of answering my question directly with that *one* most important piece of advice, most began to say fifty things. "Your joy and enthusiasm are admirable," I would say, "but please tell me just one thing." I was expecting to hear as many different answers as there were people.

To my surprise, the answers were consistent with a single message: *it can't be done alone.* The folks in long-term recovery have much wisdom. Indeed, research confirms that the best prognostic indicator when recovering from any serious illness is one's support system.[174,175] Not surprisingly, the biggest contributor to one's well-being is also the depth and breadth of one's relationships.[176] I know recovery from addiction is not easy, but part of the solution may be that simple.

The disease of addiction isolates people. In isolation, the addict keeps company only with a disease that enslaves.

The sense of connection, community, and support provided both in treatment settings and in twelve-step and other self-help programs is invaluable to the recovery process and to one's general state of happiness. My hope is that everyone suffering directly or indirectly with addiction in any way, shape, or form can find a way out. Treatment is effective. Recovery is possible. Like any chronic condition, optimal management may require several attempts. The work is worth it, because the potential for an amazing life awaits. As Jim Valvano, the inspiring college basketball coach, stated emphatically during his battle with cancer: "Don't give up. Don't ever give up."

Chapter 12:

Gambling, Food, and Sex: A Word on Process Addictions

*W*hen *the Servant Becomes the Master* has thus far been primarily concerned with addiction as it applies to substances. I have purposefully concentrated on substances because the vast majority of what we know today about addiction medicine pertains to studies on the effects of drugs. However, there are forms of addiction that exist that do not involve substances and deserve some attention. The research on these other forms of addiction that include behavioral disorders, also known as process addictions, consistently demonstrates brain changes and processes that are strikingly similar to those of substance addiction. Process addictions used to be understood as obsessive-compulsive behavior, but there are growing numbers of professionals who believe they are actually different forms of addiction because they are closely related to substance addiction in so many ways. Process addictions are behavioral disorders whose object of addiction, instead of an external substance, is an actual behavioral process.

In many people's minds, it is easier to acknowledge that drugs are addictive. Drug addiction has a clear biologic component and tends to run in families. Drugs are also outside the body, cause physical dependency, can be measured, have predictable withdrawal symptoms, can cause overdoses, and are more commonly discussed in the media and in society. Process addictions, instead of involving drug use, can include gambling, eating, sex, exercise, shopping, work, Internet, or gaming. Two forms of process addiction include behaviors that are absolutely necessary and must happen, because without food or procreation the human race would cease to exist. Some argue, then, that addiction to food or sex cannot be real addiction because we must eat to live and have sex to reproduce.

When describing process addiction, we are not referring to someone who has an extra piece of chocolate cake, places an occasional wager, occasionally views pornography, may have an extramarital affair, or shops when depressed. A process addiction describes an excessive drive to repetitively engage in behaviors aimed at producing pleasure, relief, and/or escape despite increasing negative and harmful consequences and the desire to stop. Even when taken to the extreme—with the obsessive-compulsive dynamics that characterize addiction—some professionals continue to view these as disorders of compulsion rather than forms of addiction. Even though the jury is still out, so to speak, I will present the three most common categories of process addiction in order to shed some light on their nature, problems, and treatment because they are very prevalent, serious issues today no matter how they are classified.

Process addiction is like substance addiction in many ways. Addiction related to gambling, eating, and sexual activity costs society hundreds of billions dollars a year; frequently co-occurs with alcohol and other drug use; causes horrible psychological, physical, spiritual, and emotional pain; and leads to higher rates of suicide. In addition, research demonstrates that repetitive behaviors seen in process addiction can cause tolerance and withdrawal. Over time, process addicts escalate in the amount and type of their behavior and exhibit withdrawal symptoms upon discontinuation of that behavior that mimic those seen in drug withdrawal states.

Both substance and process addiction involve the same natural chemicals. Gambling, overeating, and sexually acting out can also be enormously stimulating and rewarding in the same neural pathways and locations as drug addiction. Dopamine, endorphins, and serotonin are released in the limbic system and other addiction pathways when addicts are engaged in process addiction behaviors. Recall that alcohol and other drugs of abuse also have the capacity to alter brain chemistry and influence the expression of genes. Process addiction is similar here as well, because addictive behavior stimulates the addiction center in the brain via a change in brain chemistry.

Another similarity is observed: process addiction and drug addiction share the same fundamental patterns of behavior. Process addiction behaviors are known as "acting out." The addiction cycle described in Chapter Five is present for addicts regardless of whether the form their addiction takes is based on substances or behaviors. In fact, it was Patrick Carnes, a sex addiction therapist and executive director of the Gentle Path program at Pine Grove Behavioral Center in Hattiesburg, Mississippi, who originally devised the addiction cycle model for sex addiction in order to explain the acting-out behavior of an addict while his or her disease is active. Drugs as well as processes (behaviors) are used to escape and change feelings. When an addict is triggered, obsession leads to compulsive use or acting out, which is followed by shame, guilt, and despair. Negative consequences escalate along with the progression of the disease. The addiction cycle is universally applicable; addicts share the same cycle and consequences no matter whether the manifestations of addiction involve substances, behaviors, or both.

Process and substance addictions are also alike in how they develop. Recall that a certain combination of agent + host + environment can result in no use, some use, abuse, or addiction. Biologic predispositions to addiction, coupled with a high degree of availability of sugary and high-fat foods without the availability of drugs in the environment, will cause more of those who are at risk to use food as a way to create chemical changes in their MDS. Regardless of whether the object of addiction is a substance or a behavior, the host's biology is not the only crucial element in the development of addiction; environment, society, development, relationships, exposure to coping strategies, and other cultural variables are extremely important contributors as well. Across the entire spectrum of substances and processes, addicts share many social, environmental, and developmental risk factors.

Even though we are not currently aware of as many genetic markers in process addiction as are known to exist in substance addiction, there are some genetic markers common to both groups. For example, people with eating disorders who binge on sugars have as high a probability of having dopamine receptor abnormalities as do some groups of drug addicts.

Process addiction tends to be more prevalent among certain groups of individuals. Many people struggling with addiction to sex and food have a history of sexual abuse or other trauma as children. Many of those addicted to gambling, food, and sex have a coexisting addiction to alcohol and/or other drugs. In fact, a family history of alcohol addiction can predispose someone to developing a process addiction.[177,178]

The commonalities between process and substance addictions are significant enough to broadly assign them to the same disordered brain process. Whether process addiction is exactly the same as drug addiction makes little difference, ultimately, because they are so similar. More important is the fact that treatment for both is also generally the same and would not change based upon reclassification of the disorders. The repetitive behaviors of process addiction can easily be as debilitating as those of drug addiction, and it is equally imperative that process addicts receive comprehensive biopsychosocial treatment.

Rarely do we find an addict with an isolated drug or process addiction. Many addicts have more than one drug of choice, and many times they will switch their drug of choice. Quite often, addiction to processes coexists with addiction to substances. Food addicts who have weight-reducing surgery frequently develop an addiction to alcohol or other drugs soon after surgery because their drug of choice, food, has been physically and mechanically made less available. However, the broader disease of addiction is not addressed by withdrawing the ability to use food as a drug. When addiction is not treated comprehensively, it will seek a way to manifest itself. In this way, the disease can "come out sideways." Because addiction is the larger issue, the substance or process is merely a symptom. Addicts' brains are motivated to ring the bell of the pleasure center and will cause the host to engage in those addictive behaviors and consume those substances that work in the same limbic system pathways. Active addicts adapt to whatever object is available. If addicts cannot find dope or booze, they may find a pill-happy doctor, go to a casino, or gorge themselves on ice cream. Addiction is not the specific substance or process; it is a deeper brain disease that can make use of a variety of objects.

Gambling

It is estimated that approximately 80 percent of adult Americans will gamble at least once in their lifetime.[179] In the same way that most people who drink do not become addicted to alcohol, the majority of those who gamble do not develop a gambling problem. Less than 5 percent of Americans have gambling disorders, but this percentage has increased with the widespread legalization of casinos, racetracks, lotteries, and other forms of gambling.[180] Some problem gamblers play the stock market. Twice as many men as women develop a significant gambling problem. *DSM-IV*'s label of *pathological gambling* evolved to *gambling disorder* in *DSM-5,* a further step in the direction of *gambling addiction.*

A diagnosis of *gambling disorder* is rendered when someone's gambling involves a progression of negative consequences, loss of control, and other significant impairment and distress. Specific diagnostic criteria include, but are not limited to, a preoccupation with gambling; tolerance as evidenced by the need to gamble with escalating amounts of money in order to get the same desired effect/level of excitement; using gambling as an escape from problems or uncomfortable feelings; lying to others about the extent of one's gambling; and breaking the law to support gambling through theft, fraud, forgery, and so on.

Much like addiction to alcohol and other drugs, gambling addiction has historically been viewed as a moral failing. However, behavioral patterns coupled with brain imaging studies demonstrate that, as with substance addiction, many more factors are involved than weakness of will or poor character. Gambling addicts cannot fix their problem with a desire, a decision, or willpower. Moreover, attempts to self-regulate their gambling are as futile as any other addict's attempts to manage his or her drug use. Gambling addiction essentially describes what happens when the focus (manifestation) of addiction is gambling—it is not curable, but treatment is available, and the condition can be managed.

While financial problems are usually the first issues to surface, gambling addiction affects every area of the gambler's life. Gambling addicts experience changes in personality, irritability, and legal problems; fail to meet social obligations; and have unfinished projects, conflicts at work, health problems, trouble concentrating, and sleep disorders. Family members and significant others become as affected as their counterparts in any other form of addiction— gambling addiction is a family disease too, affecting the health, as well as the emotional and psychological well-being, of everyone. As a matter of fact, spouses in equal-property states can be even more affected because they assume 100 percent liability for any debt, and often for any criminal activity as well.

As is the case with any manifestation of addiction, a family history of addiction is a risk factor for gambling addiction. Family systems also adapt to gambling addiction just as they do when drug addiction is present. There are attempts to control the gambler, enabling occurs as the gambler is bailed out with money, conflicts and fights arise, and family members feel angry, hopeless, and helpless. Long-term effects are predictable as well. Children of addicted gamblers are more likely to experience depression, have poor school performance, and develop addictions themselves.

Like other forms of addiction, gambling addiction is progressive. The disorder typically progresses through three stages and gets worse unless it is treated and the addict becomes abstinent and begins a process of recovery. The first stage is the fun, **winning** stage. Excitement, winning, and adventure typify this stage. Self-esteem is closely linked to how much money is won—gamblers interpret their wins as reflections of their personal merit. Losses that occur in this stage are rationalized as "bad luck."

In the second, **losing** stage, preoccupation grows as the gambler chases his or her losses with more money and personally feels insulted at the losses. It is said that Las Vegas wasn't built on winners. Continued gambling inevitably leads to losses, which the gambler experiences as a personal attack. In an attempt to rescue his or her self-worth, the gambler will borrow money, extend credit lines, spend more time gambling, and hide losses. Relationships, work, health, social obligations, and other areas of the gambler's life begin to deteriorate as more and more time is spent gambling.

Next, in the **desperation** stage, gamblers' resources are depleted, psychological consequences arise, health further declines, and crimes may be committed. Pathological gamblers at this stage maintain the twisted belief that the next gambling event will cure their problems, so they keep gambling—taking the very "medicine" that is poisoning them. This is known as "chasing," where panic at the depth of losses causes irrational behavior and, often, criminal activity. The progression of gambling addiction ends in financial and family ruin, prison, suicide, running away (to Las Vegas or another gambling hot spot), or treatment.

Gambling may start as a thrill-seeking activity or as an occasional escape, or it may be used as a coping device to provide relief from anxiety and other unwanted emotions or as an escape from a tumultuous relationship or other problems. It is not necessary for gambling addicts to pass through every stage, and the order of the stages may vary. Until a gambling addiction progresses to the point where it creates noticeable problems, it is difficult to identify. Like addicts of any kind, gamblers often go to amazing lengths to deny, minimize, and conceal their behavior and its consequences.

It is not uncommon for pathological gamblers to enter into a dissociative state while gambling. The addiction can progress to a point where they gamble without care for their basic needs. In many casinos there exists a specific job to change the seats on chairs when gamblers have urinated or defecated on themselves, unable to give up their seat at a poker table or slot machine. The disease can clearly be as overwhelming as any chemical dependency. Pathological gambling has all of the hallmarks of addiction. Addicted gamblers cannot stop despite the desire to do so and despite the mounting harmful and often disastrous emotional, physical, psychological, and spiritual consequences. Neuroimaging studies demonstrate that gambling activates the same dopamine pathways in the MDS that are activated in drug addiction. Consistent with this neurochemical connection, many addicted gamblers are also addicted to substances.

Cravings can be as intense in gambling addiction as they are in drug addiction. Gambling addicts show tolerance through their need to increase the frequency and amounts of their betting, and they experience highs comparable to those of many substances. Moreover, many pathological gamblers show withdrawal symptoms that appear like a mild form of substance withdrawal—including anxiety, sleep disturbance, sweating, irritability, and intense craving. Like those addicted to drugs, they are also at risk of relapse even after years of abstinence.

Treatment for pathological gambling is available and strikingly similar to that for other addictions. The opiate blocker naloxone has been shown to diminish the excitement and the highs people experience while gambling. The fact that naloxone also diminishes the euphoria of alcohol and other drug use (as described in Chapter Nine) underscores the common neurochemical disease process at work. Pathological gamblers benefit from intensive residential treatment, individual psychotherapy, family therapy, twelve-step fellowships, and management of co-occurring disorders. Gamblers Anonymous is the twelve-step program for those addicted to gambling. Gam-Anon is the twelve-step program for their family members and significant others.

Food

The United States is facing a major health crisis. Every year more than 300,000 people die from illnesses related to weight and obesity. Some estimates indicate that 40 to 60 percent of Americans are either overweight or obese.[181] At any given time, over forty-five million adults in the United States are dieting.[182] According to US Centers for Disease Control and Prevention statistics, one-third of adults and 17 percent of children are now considered overweight, and we are witnessing an epidemic of childhood type 2 diabetes as a result.[183]

Obesity is far from the only manifestation of an addictive relationship with food. Its opposite, excessive starvation, is another. There are three major eating disorders: compulsive overeating, bulimia nervosa, and anorexia nervosa. All three of these disorders are based on unhealthy, dysfunctional relationships with food. Compulsive overeating is usually considered synonymous with food addiction, where the object of the addiction is food and food is used excessively despite significant negative consequences.

Anorexia nervosa is the name given to deliberate weight loss to more than 15 percent below a person's normal weight based on height. It is an extremely serious eating disorder that is incredibly difficult to treat. Some people view anorexia, as it is generally referred to, as an addiction to a pathologically distorted body image. Anorexia can be considered a "negative" addiction insofar as it is based on *withholding* or *depriving* rather than *consuming* behaviors. Those who suffer from it starve themselves in an obsessive-compulsive manner. Instead of taking drugs or taking up more gambling, sex, or shopping, it's a state of going without (food). Alarmingly, upwards of 15 percent of people with anorexia die from it. It is estimated that anorexia affects 1 percent of the population, with women having ten times more risk for it than men.[184] Eighty-five percent of cases of anorexia begin in childhood or early adolescence.[185]

Anorexia is unique among psychiatric disorders because relatively greater wealth is a risk factor for developing it. Other psychiatric disorders typically do not have a higher incidence in families with many resources and healthcare treatment options. Quite the contrary; excluding anorexia, there is a strong correlation between lower socioeconomic status and mental illness in general. Although the association is not clearly understood, many experts believe the stress of poverty is a major causative agent.[186] Anorexia also has unique endocrine (stress, sex, growth, and thyroid hormone) abnormalities and dysfunctions, as well as high psychiatric comorbidities (depression, obsessive-compulsive disorder, anxiety, addiction, attention-deficit disorder, and borderline narcissistic, histrionic, and avoidant personality disorders). Some argue that self-starvation, which can produce a state of serenity, is a self-medicating behavior for anxiety or other emotions. Sufferers go to great lengths to conceal their problem, and continue with their excessive and unhealthy behaviors despite life-threatening consequences.

Bulimia nervosa is an eating disorder based on a repetitive cycle of bingeing and purging. It consists of the binge eating of large quantities of food followed by a compensatory behavior meant to offset the effects of the binge. Such compensatory behaviors include self-induced vomiting, excessive exercise, fasting, enemas, and use of diuretics or laxatives. Bulimia affects more women than men and affects 2 to 3 percent of the US population.[187] Depression, anxiety, substance abuse, and a family history of addiction are risk factors for bulimia. There is also a higher incidence of bulimia among actors, dancers, models, gymnasts, figure skaters, and other groups involved in activities with rigorous weight requirements or expectations of *thin beauty*. As with addiction to drugs, bulimic behavior is initially voluntary but seems to progress to the point where it is beyond conscious choice. Bulimia and binge eating both have an impulsive component where pleasure and arousal are closely followed by guilt and remorse.

A substantial subset of bulimics selectively binge on carbohydrate-dense foods. Both compulsive overeating and bulimia involve bingeing, where massive amounts of food are consumed in one sitting. When carbohydrates are consumed, more serotonin is formed. Dopamine is also increased in the limbic system after meals. As Dr. Mark Gold told me, "The limbic system is interested in survival and is hardwired to respond favorably to fatty, sugary foods." Since serotonin and dopamine are mood-enhancing neurotransmitters, an argument can be made that sugar is the equivalent of a drug. We know that food and drugs compete for the same reward system in the brain. Dr. Gold later reviewed brain-imaging studies showing that food creates the same types of brain changes seen in drug addiction. There is an intriguing parallel found in "comfort food's" richness in carbohydrates and fats. Food, especially when highly caloric and dense, is reinforcing in the same ways that drugs are. Further, drug addicts in early recovery frequently turn to sugary foods as a way to feel better.

There may be a group of people who are highly sensitive to the effects of sugar. Dopamine gene markers found in many alcoholics and other drug addicts are also often found in obese individuals who binge on sugar. Many self-proclaimed food addicts in recovery maintain that abstinence from sugar is the only means of effectively managing their addiction. Like the first drink to the alcoholic, the first sugar to this type of food addict will trigger a binge. On the other hand, compulsive overeating without regard for the types of foods consumed reflects a more global dysfunction in satiety and self-regulation. Consuming vast amounts of fats and sugars triggers the brain to produce endorphins, the natural rewarding and pleasurable neurotransmitters.

The only eating disorder that appears in *DSM-5* is *binge eating disorder* (BED). In *DSM-IV, binge eating* appeared only in an appendix, not as an official diagnosis. Hundreds of research studies published over the last two decades support the legitimacy of BED. BED is actually the most common eating disorder in America, afflicting over 3 percent of women, 2 percent of men, and 1.5 percent of teens. BED is defined by recurring and chronic binge eating episodes (eating more food than one's hunger would normally prompt one to eat, eating more rapidly than one would normally eat, eating until painfully full, and so forth) that are associated with feelings of shame and distress, without compensatory behaviors like purging, as seen in bulimia. BED is not simply a fancy term for morbid obesity. Indeed, most people who are obese do not have BED. However, nearly two-thirds of people with BED are obese. Like other forms of addiction, BED is associated with co-occurring illnesses such as alcohol abuse, anxiety, and depression.[188]

When food is used as a coping mechanism and when it is used excessively, compulsive overeating in any form creates similar brain changes to those seen in other forms of addiction. Brain imaging shows that the parts of the brain that process pleasure associated with food grow larger in compulsive overeaters. Tolerance develops because more food is needed to produce the same degree of mood-changing experience. Withdrawal symptoms can also occur, and have been confirmed in animal research—rats that were given a sugar solution and then given an opiate blocker demonstrated physical signs of withdrawal.[189] In addition, images of foods can trigger cravings, and this poses a problem if you watch any television at all. A colleague enlightened me on this by cleverly remarking, "America is great. We are the only country where every other commercial is for food, and then you see commercials following those for carving abs in bed or for pills that make you lose weight when you are sleeping."

Compulsive overeating affects men and women fairly equally. Compulsive overeaters have a higher incidence of depression, personality disorders, trauma, family dysfunction, alcohol and other drug addiction, and family histories of addiction. Although socially stigmatizing, discomforting, and extremely unhealthy, obesity is only a symptom of the disease. Losing weight does not cure the problem. This form of addiction is more complicated than just using food as a drug. Studies on select groups demonstrate that some people may have more hormones driving hunger or fewer hormones signaling fullness. In other words, the drive to eat may be physiologically stronger in people who are overweight. Even if they are successful at dieting, eventually the body's drive to keep eating will overwhelm their willpower. At its core, compulsive overeating is a chronic disorder that does not disappear when sugar is removed or weight is lost, any more than the disease of addiction disappears when an addict becomes abstinent from substances.

Unlike with substance use or gambling, we have an actual, literal need to eat. Food, some argue, is completely different from alcohol and other drugs because it is necessary for survival. According to this view, eating is natural, so obsessive-compulsive behaviors related to food cannot be considered addiction. Others make the familiar argument that the idea of an addiction to food is merely an excuse for lack of willpower. Yet the relationship that compulsive overeaters have with food mirrors the relationship that drug addicts have with substances. Food takes precedence over other parts of their lives; they use food for nurturing and to feel good, better, or just normal. Food, like drugs, supplies a mood-enhancing high, provides a temporary escape from life, and creates the same progression of harmful negative consequences experienced with other manifestations of addiction.

Those with addiction centered around food don't have the option to "just say no" or use their willpower to stop any more than those addicted to alcohol or other drugs or gambling can. Like addicts with other forms of addiction, compulsive overeaters and people with other eating disorders, such as bulimia, typically make repeated efforts to control their eating behaviors, and feel despair over their consistent failure to do so. As with addiction based on substances, relapse is common. A friend of mine who has struggled with this addiction for years often quips, "I have lost 5,000 pounds in my life!" Like Mark

Twain's comment on quitting cigarettes hundreds of times, his point reflects the reality that recovery is not maintained simply through desire and willpower, and addiction does not disappear.

Diets rarely work, and multiple attempts to limit or eliminate certain foods more often than not have the paradoxical effects of rebound bingeing and weight gain. While obesity has other causes, it is a common sign of food addiction. Compulsive overeaters' inability to control their eating and weight engenders stigma and prejudicial treatment from others. This contributes to increased feelings of shame and despair, further eroding self-esteem and creating even more reasons to numb or escape through addictive behaviors. Like any addict in the cycle of addiction, food addicts become trapped in self-perpetuating behaviors.

Structured treatments are available for addiction to food, including intensive inpatient, outpatient, and aftercare programs. Mutual-aid support groups like Overeaters Anonymous, individual psychotherapy, and other modalities are also options to help achieve and maintain a state of recovery. Self-proclaimed food addicts who participate in twelve-step programs reinforce the similarities between compulsive overeating and other forms of addiction. The process of admitting powerlessness over food and its creation of unmanageability in one's life is identical to the recovery process in other twelve-step programs.

As with other forms of addiction, success in recovery should be clearly defined and treatment must be individualized. Compulsive overeaters are encouraged to design food plans, the main vehicle of a food addict's recovery plan, with the help of a professional dietician. Treatment for anorexia nervosa and bulimia nervosa requires medical supervision. However, unlike with substance addiction, recovery from eating disorders is complicated by the human need to eat in order to live—complete abstinence is not an option. Those who struggle with a dysfunctional relationship with food must regularly and unavoidably come in direct contact with the object of their addiction.

As challenging as it can be, every day with the help of twelve-step programs such as Overeaters Anonymous, Anorexics and Bulimics Anonymous, other self-help resources, and professional treatment providers, thousands of people overcome the daily struggle with compulsive overeating, self-starvation, and bingeing-purging behaviors, and find recovery one day at a time.

Sex

In the same way that our brains are hardwired to respond to drugs and high-fat and sugary foods, we are designed to enjoy sex. As with drugs, repeated exposure to sexually charged events in the right personal and environmental conditions can cause someone to develop sex addiction. Sex addicts experience the cycle of addiction exactly like drug addicts do. When, in any phase of the cycle, a chemical reaction is triggered in the MDS of the brains of sex addicts, that serves to keep the pleasure center singularly interested in maintaining arousal. Chemicals activated during planning or engaging in sexual activities release endorphins and dopamine that capture the attention of the MDS in the same way drugs do. Sex addiction is progressive. Tolerance develops as well; over time, sex addicts increase the frequency of their behaviors and often have to find novel, alternative, dangerous, deviant, or other out-of-the-norm behaviors in order to get the same amount of chemical arousal and satisfaction they experienced previously.

Sex sells. Prostitution may be the world's oldest profession, but the mainstreaming of pornography is a recent phenomenon. In the last few decades, sexual content has become increasingly available. As a result, millions of Americans have been exposed to and have become involved with a new agent with which to escape or change the way they feel. Internet sites, cable networks, and hotel chains make enormous amounts of profit every year from pornography. The pornography industry is a multibillion-dollar business, and the Internet makes pornography accessible through any computer. Before videos, CDs, and the Internet gave the protection of anonymity, sexual activity usually mandated face-to-face contact that required a greater degree of motivation and effort. Many activities, from the passive to the more interactive, that are now easily available via the Internet have external stigma and internal shame linked to them, especially for women. Instead of going to an adult theatre, a porn shop, or a house of ill repute where someone could be seen and forever "marked," now folks can partake in many behaviors from behind the shroud of secrecy that cyberspace provides.

Sex addiction is not defined by any one behavior. It includes a number of sexually related obsessive-compulsive behaviors. These behaviors may include any of the following, alone or in combination: pornography, cybersex, compulsive masturbation, anonymous sex, compulsive heterosexual and/ or homosexual relationships, chronic affairs, voyeurism, indecent phone calls, fetishism, and exhibitionism. These behaviors are not unhealthy or dysfunctional in and of themselves. Obviously, viewing pornography does not by itself constitute an addiction. When the sexual behavior reaches a critical stage in a person's life where it has obsessive-compulsive qualities and begins to interfere with his or her functioning, a downward progression ensues, with the same set of harmful consequences that are found with other forms of addiction. Like drug addicts, sex addicts are capable of breaking the law and engaging in behaviors that society finds abhorrent. While sex addiction is not necessarily synonymous with deviancy, some addicts become involved in prostitution, rape, dangerous sex, incest, or violent sexual activity.

Though not formally recognized in *DSM-5*, sex addiction continues to wreak havoc in the lives of many people and their families. In recent years, this form of addiction has garnered mainstream attention due to the well-publicized tribulations of Tiger Woods and certain other celebrities. Nonetheless, the existence and label of sex addiction remains a highly controversial issue among many in the general public. In short, sex addiction is a disorder with close similarities to substance addiction. A leader and pioneer in the field of sex addiction, Patrick Carnes, PhD, has written many articles and books on the subject. His breakthrough book, *Out of the Shadows,* formally crystallized a common and widespread problem that healthcare professionals have been aware of for a long time. It is estimated that 5 percent of the US population has a sexually related behavioral dysfunction. More people seek treatment every year, and experts report that the number of reported sex addicts is only increasing. Again, the explosion of the online availability of pornography and cybersex is a contributing factor to the increasing number of sex addicts.

Some argue that unlike alcohol and other drugs, sex is necessary for survival, and that because relationships and love are natural, sex "addiction" is merely a compulsive behavior. Others make the case that sex addiction is simply an excuse for loose morals. Sex addiction is not just about the sex. As Dr. Carnes has described it, addictive sexual behavior is more about pain—about numbing, or escaping, or decreasing anxiety and other uncomfortable emotions—than it is about sex. It functions as a temporary solution. For addicts, sex serves the same purpose that drugs serve. Addiction to substances and addiction to sex share several fundamental common elements. The same excessive and unhealthy relationship with the object of the addiction exists—regardless of whether it is sex or substances.

Sex, like drugs, supplies a mood-enhancing high, provides an escape from life, and is used to feel better or just to feel normal. Brain chemistry changes are similar to those with drugs as well. When someone addicted to sex views pornographic images or when someone addicted to alcohol sees an image of alcohol, the exact same brain regions activate. Both drug addiction and sex addiction afflict more people with family histories of addiction, histories of trauma, lack of emotional support by caregivers, and other forms of addiction.

Cocaine and methamphetamine addiction, in particular, have a close relationship with sex addiction.

Sex addicts experience the same range of emotional states as addicts with other forms of addiction, from stress and fear of getting caught to shame and guilt for engaging in behaviors that are inconsistent with their core values. As the disease of addiction evolves, sex progressively takes precedence over other parts of the addict's life. Emotional, physical, social, legal, spiritual, and financial problems arise and, over time, increase in severity. Sex addicts will replace healthy relationships with unhealthy ones, isolate from their support systems, put themselves at high risk to sustain bodily injury, or contract dangerous infectious diseases like HIV or hepatitis, as well as less lethal sexually transmitted diseases. Several behaviors associated with sex addiction are illegal, and it is not uncommon for sex addicts to face legal consequences for their actions. Subsequently, they often also incur occupational consequences such as termination and/or loss of licensure. Financial troubles frequently follow loss of employment or spending of vast amounts of money on pornography or prostitution.

As the disease progresses, addicts often try harder and harder to control their sexual behaviors. Many go through periods of no sexual activity at all, known as *sexual anorexia,* but this attempt usually results in a rebound period of acting-out behavior. Like other forms of addiction, sex addiction causes enormous pain. Those who dismiss it as an excuse for poor choices do not appreciate that the behavior of those addicted to sex is driven by changes in a brain that has been hijacked and programmed to continue despite negative consequences. However, having a disease does not absolve the addict from personal responsibility and accountability for his or her behavior. Sex addiction is a valid condition, but there should be appropriate consequences for unethical and illegal behavior, no matter the cause.

Often sex addicts enter treatment only after leverage is applied. When sex addicts stop their acting-out behavior, we observe another similarity to those with other forms of addiction: painful emotional withdrawal symptoms.

Recovery is challenging, but entirely possible. Healthy sexual behaviors and intimate relationships must be learned and practiced. Recovery from sex addiction is not as simple as abstaining from all things sexual—as is the case with addiction to food, complete abstinence is not realistic. Sex addiction and drug addiction are similarly treated. First, acceptance of the disease is essential as a starting point for recovery. Next, an admission of the addict's lack of control, followed by a commitment to change, is necessary. Finally, open-mindedness to participation in twelve-step groups such as Sex Addicts Anonymous and Sex and Love Addicts Anonymous, treatment with trained professionals, and support from others in recovery provide the greatest chance of success. Available structured treatment programs include intensive inpatient, outpatient, and aftercare groups for both the sex addict and his or her family and significant others.

Summary

Throughout time and across different cultures, mind- and mood-altering substances have often been considered to be "gifts of the gods." Drugs are used in healing, religious, and other culturally significant ceremonies. People have used, do use, and will continue to use these substances because they provide meaning, and since they exert potent effects in the pleasure and survival pathways of the brain, these substances capture our attention like nothing else. They provide a powerful, effective, and easy way to change how we feel. Drugs are thus used not only to augment the sacred or simply to make us feel better; they are also used as tools, as coping devices, and as an escape. Buyer beware. In the right alignment of drug, person, and environment, these substances enslave the user as he or she becomes caught up in forces beyond his or her control. This, in turn, causes great pain and destruction.

Addiction is a chronic, relapsing, and potentially fatal disease that imposes vast social as well as individual and family costs. As many as 15 percent of those who use alcohol and other drugs develop the disease of addiction. In the United States, it is estimated that more than twenty-three million people fulfill the diagnostic criteria for substance addiction, but most do not receive treatment.[190] Many end up dead or incarcerated.

Continued use of mind- and mood-altering substances is necessary, but not sufficient by itself, to explain the disease of addiction. Addiction is a multifaceted illness with contributing factors that extend beyond merely using too much for too long. In the right person and under the right circumstances, however, drugs powerfully and, in some ways, permanently change the chemistry in the brain. Recall the analogy of cucumbers and pickles: cucumbers can always become pickles, but pickles can never return to being cucumbers. In my humble opinion, addiction develops when people pursue happiness ineffectively. It's a simple and easy-to-remember definition that fits.

Studies of the brain and its structures involved in drug use, tolerance, pleasure, withdrawal, and relapse provide clear evidence that the relationship between the addict and the object of his or her addiction involves neural pathways that permeate the whole person—body, mind, and soul. At the neurochemical level, the disease primarily affects the mesolimbic dopamine system (MDS), but this in turn affects every aspect of the person, including his or her environments and relationships. Addiction comes about with a genetic predisposition, a psychological predisposition, and an environmental predisposition, after repeated exposure resulting in a neurochemically changed brain. Addiction is possible in anyone; it does not target the poor, the dumb, or the "bad." If you are human, you are potentially susceptible. However, as with other chronic diseases like diabetes or high blood pressure, the chances of developing addiction increase if you have low socioeconomic status, co-occurring mental health issues, or inadequate social and family support systems.

The choice-versus-disease debate should be over. Reliable scientific research has provided the data to move us past archaic explanations about addiction and addicts. Reactions that view addiction and its sequelae as "bad behavior" perpetrated by "bad people" are rife with inaccurate judgments that run contrary to science. Imaging studies and microscopic molecular research have identified dysfunctional reward, motivation, and impulse-control mechanisms, along with other factors that explain the behaviors that are symptomatic of the disease.

Addiction is no longer a mystery—it is a disease-causing dysfunction in the mesolimbic dopamine system, a part of the brain that functions below the level of conscious choice. Addiction resides in the primitive recesses of our brains that focus on survival, operating independently of our will. Chemical reactions in the MDS excite and captivate the bundle of cells that evolved to motivate us to repeat behaviors such as eating and sex that help us survive and pass on our genes. Once addiction commandeers this part of the brain, it robs the person of his or her free will, specifically because the MDS operates subconsciously through a stimulus-response mechanism. When this happens, our frontal lobes, the most highly evolved parts of our brain that give us the awareness to makes choices, are not as in charge as we would like to believe.

There may have been elements of choice during the development of addiction, but there are also substantial elements of choice in other chronic diseases. What separates addiction from other chronic diseases is that volition is lost at some point along the continuum of use, abuse, and dependence. The initial choice to use or experiment with drugs or processes is voluntary (although the drive to self-medicate increases the propensity to make that choice), but the effects of drugs and processes in the brain are profoundly influenced by genetic, environmental, and other factors beyond the addict's control. Once addiction is activated, avoiding the wretched state of being without the object(s) of one's addiction becomes the main driver. However, it is important to stress again that classifying addiction as a disease that robs the host of volition does NOT relieve the addict of personal responsibility and accountability for his or her behavior and its effects on others.

Addiction is complex; it is not solely a behavioral problem, a biological problem, a psychological problem, or a spiritual problem. Addiction is a dysfunction in all these systems. At first, drugs and processes may serve the person well. Alcohol and other drugs, sex, gambling, and food can be effective and powerful coping tools that relieve stress, provide pleasure, or otherwise offer an escape. These choices are fraught with danger, however. After a variable period of time, those coping tools commandeer and change the brain, and activate addiction. When that line has been crossed, it is too late to ever go back; once someone develops the disease of addiction, he or she will always have it. There is no cure, and it never goes away. However, an addict, any addict, does not have to continue to suffer in active addiction—recovery is possible.

Treating addiction is effective. More than thirty years of research demonstrates that addiction responds to treatment. It should also be clear that punishing addiction does not work. In order to truly measure treatment's effectiveness, it's necessary to view success rates related to the management of other chronic diseases. Comparing addiction treatment to the treatment of other chronic diseases reveals that management of addiction is as effective as management of other chronic diseases such as high blood pressure and diabetes. Due to the limitations set by managed care or one's own resources, many patients receive less than the recommended level of care. Treatment that is inadequate is usually ineffective, and failure is likely. When patients are able to receive appropriate treatment and follow the recommended care, they have positive outcomes.[191,192,193,194]

Addiction is a relapsing disease, but so are most other chronic diseases. Approximately 60 percent of patients with high blood pressure or asthma and 40 percent of patients with diabetes experience recurrence or relapse of their symptoms, and require more intensive medical care to gain better management. This information makes clear the fallacy that if an addict relapses following treatment, treatment for addiction does not work. Nobody expects a single episode of care to cure diabetes or high blood pressure, yet unreasonable expectations persist that one treatment encounter for addiction, whether inpatient or outpatient, will be curative. Recovery is management, not absolution. In the treatment community, we know that each therapeutic intervention adds to an evolving process of learning and growing. We see treatment work, and we know not to give up before the miracle of healing happens.

Since addiction is a complicated disease, its treatment must be multifaceted. Behavioral treatment (talk therapy) engages addicts in the process of recovery, enhances their coping skills, changes their attitudes and behaviors, and increases the chances of long-term abstinence. Medication management is increasingly becoming more sophisticated and specific, and can be an effective adjunct to increase the effectiveness of behavioral therapies. Medication strategies can also target brain pathways responsible for reward, motivation, and relapse. Together, behavioral and medical treatment strategies can be synergistic.

However, the medical community has yet to reach a consensus on the use of medications in addiction treatment, especially for addiction to opioids, which remains controversial among doctors. Practicing medicine is still an art form of sorts, and we are continuously "practicing."

Addiction is one disease that takes a variety of forms. Process addiction and substance addiction have enough in common to be broadly assigned to the same disordered brain process. The question of whether process addiction is exactly the same as substance addiction is stimulating but fundamentally immaterial, because they are much more similar than different. In addition, they respond to roughly identical treatment. Even the medications discussed in Chapter Nine that are indicated for substance addiction can be effective with process forms of addiction—though they are used creatively, or "off-label." Even limited success is success and reinforces the similarities between addictions of all forms.

Moreover, the repetitive behaviors of process addiction and the harmful consequences they create can be equally debilitating as they are in addiction to alcohol and other drugs. It is especially imperative that, like those addicted to substances, those addicted to processes receive comprehensive biopsychosocial treatment and participate in programs and activities that provide meaning and balance if they are to find recovery and discover a new way of life.

We have and will continue to have our challenges in the field of addiction treatment. That being said, the future looks brighter than ever. "Big Pharma" is taking a more concerted interest in the field than ever before. As more medications show promise, more are entering the research pipeline and are being developed. Since the publication of the first edition of *When the Servant Becomes the Master,* there have been several new medications introduced into the market. While these new medications are generally variations on existing ones, academics are working arduously on enhancing our understanding of the genome in addicts and on developing medications targeted at very specific brain receptors.

The availability of different treatment modalities that can effectively address individual needs and goals continues to expand, and further research will demonstrate which of these have the greatest merit. Although on the whole, twelve-step programs are accepted as being the most available and successful option, they are not necessarily the best fit for everyone. Fortunately, other effective modalities are available today, and as the fruit of more research becomes ready to pick, newer and perhaps even more effective treatments will be used in the future. No matter the route that people take, recovery from addiction is the path to an amazing life worth living, one day at a time.

No one is immune to relapse. The disease of addiction does not care how many therapy sessions, vitamins, exercises, or twelve-step meetings an addict has had in the last week, month, or year. The potential for a relapse process to germinate is ever present. It exists in the environment outside the addict as well as in his or her internal patterns of thinking and emotional responding. Preventing a relapse is a comprehensive task that involves many acts of doing. There is a saying in recovery that sums it up best: all an addict has to change is *one* thing: *everything*. With proper support and guidance, recovery is possible, but it is never easy. If treatment in the form of a recovery-supportive lifestyle and activities is maintained, recovery can last a lifetime. The choice for recovering addicts is evident: prevent relapse or surrender your recovery and risk returning to full-blown active addiction.

Avoiding a relapse alone will not suffice. One must add goals, the ones that enrich one's life, such as positivity, engagement, relationships, meaning, and achievement. Only then will life be so rewarding that relapse will be less likely. The payoff for actively working a balanced recovery program is beyond words and is certainly not bland. As a recovering addict once said, "Addicts demand to feel good. If staying sober were not ultimately good and often better, none of us would do it."

Resources

Professional Resources

American Society of Addiction Medicine

(301) 656-3920

email@asam.org

www.asam.org

National Institute on Drug Abuse (NIDA) of the National Institutes
of Health (NIH)

www.drugabuse.gov

Substance Abuse and Mental Health Services Association (SAMHSA),
Department of Health and Human Services (DHHS)

(877) SAMHSA-7 ((877) 726-4727)

www.samhsa.gov

The National Council on Problem Gambling

(202) 547-9204

www.ncpgambling.org

National Association of Anorexia Nervosa and Associated Disorders

(630) 577-1333

ww.anad.org

Mutual-Aid/Self-Help Resources

Alcoholics Anonymous

(212) 870-3400

www.aa.org

Al-Anon and Alateen
(757) 563-1600

www.al-anon.alateen.org

Narcotics Anonymous
(818) 773-9999

www.na.org

Gamblers Anonymous
(213) 386-8789

www.gamblersanonymous.org

Gam-Anon
(718) 352-1671

www.gam-anon.org

Anorexics and Bulimics Anonymous
(780) 318-6355

aba12steps.org

Food Addicts Anonymous
(561) 967-3871

www.foodaddictsanonymous.org

Overeaters Anonymous
(505) 891-2664

www.oa.org

Sex Addicts Anonymous (SAA)

(713) 869-4902

www.sexaa.org

Sex and Love Addicts Anonymous (SLAA)

(210) 828-7900

www.slaafws.org

Sexual Compulsives Anonymous (SCA)

(310) 859-5585

www.sca-recovery.org

Sexual Recovery Anonymous (SRA)

www.sexualrecovery.org

Sexaholics Anonymous (SA)

(866) 424-8777

www.sa.org

Notes

Foreword to the First Edition

1 Daniel M. Blumenthal and Mark S. Gold, "Neurobiology of food addiction." *Current Opinion in Clinical Nutrition and Metabolic Care,* volume 13, issue 4 (July 2010): pp. 359–365.

2 Yijun Liu, Karen M. Von Deneen, Firas H. Kobeissy, and Mark S. Gold, "Food addiction and obesity: Evidence from bench to bedside." *Journal of Psychoactive Drugs,* volume 4, issue 2 (July 2010): pp. 133–151.

3 Mark S. Gold, D. Eugene Redmond, Jr., and Herbert D. Kleber, "Clonidine blocks acute opiate-withdrawal symptoms." *The Lancet,* volume 312, issue 8090 (September 1978): pp. 599–602.

4 Charles A. Dackis and Mark S. Gold, "New concepts in cocaine addiction: The dopamine depletion hypothesis." *Neuroscience and Biobehavorial Reviews,* volume 9 (October 1984): pp. 469–477.

5 Kenneth Blum, Thomas J. H. Chen, B. William Downs, et al., "Neurogenetics of dopaminergic receptor supersensitivity in activation of brain reward circuitry and relapse: Proposing 'deprivation-amplification relapse therapy' (DART)." *Postgraduate Medicine,* volume 121, issue 6 (November 2009): pp. 176–196.

6 Lisa J. Merlo and Mark S. Gold, "Prescription opioid abuse and dependence among physicians: Hypotheses and treatment." *Harvard Review of Psychiatry,* volume 16, issue 3 (2008): pp.181–194.

7 Robert L. DuPont, A. Thomas McLellan, William L. White, Lisa J. Merlo, and Mark S. Gold, "Setting the standard for recovery: Physicians' health programs." *Journal of Substance Abuse Treatment,* volume 36, issue 2 (March 2009): pp. 159–171.

8 Betty Ford Institute Consensus Panel, "What is recovery? A working definition from the Betty Ford Institute." *Journal of Substance Abuse Treatment,* volume 33, issue 3 (2007): pp. 221–228.

Preface to the Second Edition

9 R. Saitz, "Things that work, things that don't work, and things that matter—including words." *Journal of Addiction Medicine,* volume 9, issue 6 (2015): pp. 429–430.

10 Michael H. Baumann et al., "Bath salts, spice, and related designer drugs: The science behind the headlines." *Journal of Neuroscience,* volume 34, issue 46 (2014): pp. 15150–15158.

Chapter One

11 Lisa Girion, Scott Glover, and Doug Smith, "Drugs now deadlier than autos." *The Los Angeles Times,* September 18, 2011, http://www.latimes.com/health/la-me-drugs-epidemic-20110918,0,3886090.story (accessed September 19, 2011).

12 https://www.cdc.gov/drugoverdose/data/statedeaths.html (accessed March 22, 2017).

13 https://www.samhsa.gov/data/sites/default/files/NSDUH-FRR1-2014/NSDUH-FRR1-2014.pdf (accessed March 22, 2017).

14 National Institute on Drug Abuse, InfoFacts, "Treatment approaches for drug addiction." National Institutes of Health, US Department of Health and Human Services (September 2009).

15 National Institute on Drug Abuse, InfoFacts, "Understanding drug abuse and addiction." National Institutes of Health, US Department of Health and Human Services (March 2011).

16 Justice Policy Institute, "Substance abuse treatment and public safety" (January 2008), http://www.justicepolicy.org/images/upload/08_01_REP_DrugTx_AC-PS.pdf (accessed August 4, 2011).

17 National Institute on Drug Abuse, InfoFacts, "Treatment for drug abusers in the criminal justice system." National Institutes of Health, US Department of Health and Human Services (July 2006).

18 http://www.asam.org/quality-practice/definition-of-addiction (accessed March 23, 2017).

19 https://www.samhsa.gov/disorders/substance-use (accessed March 23, 2017).

20 Jerome C. Wakefield, DSW, PhD, Neuroethics, "Addiction and the concept of disorder, Part I: Why addiction is a medical disorder," DOI 10.1007/s12152-016-9399-9.

21 "American Medical Association Timeline, 1941–1960," http://www.ama-assn.ort/ama/pub/about-ama/our-history/timeline (accessed September 9, 2011).

22 US Department of Health and Human Services (HHS), Office of the Surgeon General, Facing Addiction in America: The Surgeon General's Report on Alcohol, Drugs, and Health. Washington, DC: HHS, November 2016.

23 US Supreme Court, Traynor v. Turnage, volume 485 (1988): p. 535.

24 Horace Day, The Opium Habit. New York: Harper Brothers, 1868, p. 152.

25 Ernest Able, "Was the fetal alcohol syndrome recognized by the Greeks and Romans?" Alcohol & Alcoholism, volume 34, issue 6 (1999): pp. 868–872.

26 Carlton K. Erickson, PhD, The Science of Addiction: From Neurobiology to Treatment. New York: W. W. Norton & Company, 2007, p. 83.

27 Bernice Porjesz and Henri Begleiter, "Visual evoked potential and brain dysfunction in chronic alcoholics." in Henri Begleiter (Ed.), Evoked Brain Potentials and Behavior. New York: Plenum, 1979, pp. 277–301.

28 William F. Gabrielli, Jr., Sarnoff A. Mednick, Jan Volavka, Vicki E. Pollock, Fini Schulsinger, and Turan M. Itil, "Electroencephalograms in children of alcoholic fathers." Psychophysiology, volume 19, issue 4 (July 1982): pp. 404–407

29 Email coresspondence with Howard Wetsman, MD, DFASAM, 2017.

30 Ting-Kai Li, Lawrence Lumeng, William J. McBride, and James M. Murphy, "Rodent lines selected for factors affecting alcohol consumption." Alcohol and Alcoholism Supplement, volume 1 (1987): pp. 91–96.

31 Marc A. Schuckit, "Self-rating of alcohol intoxication by young men with and without family histories of alcoholism." Journal of Studies on Alcohol and Drugs, volume 41, issue 3 (March 1980): pp. 242–249.

32 Christina Gianoulakis, Brinda Krishnan, and Joseph Thavundayil, "Enhanced sensitivity of pituitary beta-endorphin to ethanol in subjects at high risk of alcoholism." Archives of General Psychiatry, volume 53, issue 3 (March 1996): pp. 250–257.

33 Marc A. Schuckit, "Biological vulnerability to alcoholism." *Journal of Consulting and Clinical Psychology,* volume 55, issue 3 (June 1987): pp. 301–309.

34 Peter R. Finn, Nathalie C. Zeitouni, and Robert O. Pihl, "Effects of alcohol on psychophysiological hyperactivity to nonaversive and aversive stimuli in men at high risk for alcoholism." *Journal of Abnormal Psychology,* volume 99, issue 1 (February 1990): pp. 79–85.

35 Christina Gianoulakis, "Endogenous opioids and excessive alcohol consumption." *Journal of Psychiatry and Neuroscience,* volume 18, issue 4 (1993): pp. 148–156.

36 Christine Gianoulakis, Brinda Krishnan, and Joseph Thavundayl, "Enhanced sensitivity of pituitary β-endorphin to ethanol in subjects at high risk of alcoholism." *Archives of General Psychiatry,* volume 53 (1996): pp. 250–257.

37 Joseph R. Volpicelli, "Uncontrollable events and alcohol drinking." *British Journal of Addiction,* volume 82, issue 4 (April 1987): pp. 381–392.

38 Marc A. Schuckit, "Low level of response to alcohol as a predictor of future alcoholism." *American Journal of Psychiatry,* volume 151 (1994): pp. 184–189.

39 https://www.prisonpolicy.org/reports/pie2016.html (accessed March 29, 2017).

40 https://www.cancer.gov/about-cancer/understanding/statistics (accessed March 29, 2017).

41 US Department of Health and Human Services (HHS), Office of the Surgeon General, *Facing Addiction in America: The Surgeon General's Report on Alcohol, Drugs, and Health.* Washington, DC: HHS, November 2016.

42 National Institute on Drug Abuse, "Measuring and improving costs, cost-effectiveness, and cost-benefit for substance abuse treatment programs." National Institutes of Health, US Department of Health and Human Services (1999).

43 NIDA (2012). Principles of Drug Addiction Treatment: A Research-Based Guide (Third Edition). Retrieved March 29, 2017, from https://www.drugabuse.gov/publications/principles-drug-addiction-treatment-research-based-guide-third-edition.

Chapter Two

44 Carlton K. Erickson, *The Science of Addiction: From Neurobiology to Treatment.* New York: W. W. Norton and Company, 2007, p. 25.

45 A. Thomas McLellan, Davis C. Lewis, Charles P. O'Brien, and Herbert D. Kleber, "Drug dependence, a chronic mental illness: Implications for treatment, insurance, and outcomes evaluation." *Journal of the American Medical Association,* volume 284, issue 13 (October 4, 2000): pp. 1689–1695.

46 George E. Valliant, "A long term follow-up of male alcohol abuse." *Archives of General Psychiatry,* volume 53, issue 3 (March 1996): pp. 243–249.

47 National Institute on Drug Abuse Research Report Series, "Therapeutic community" (August 2002), US Department of Health and Human Services, National Institutes of Health.

48 Substance Abuse and Mental Health Services Administration, "Briefing on substance use treatment and recovery in the United States," Partners for Recovery, Executive Summary, page 3 (undated), US Department of Health and Human Services, http://pfr.samhsa.gov/docs/Briefing_Substance_Use_Treatment.pdf (accessed September 12, 2011).

49 Yih-Ing Hser, Elizabeth Evans, David Huang, and Douglas M. Anglin, "Relationship between drug treatment services, retention, and outcomes." *Psychiatric Services*, American Psychiatric Association, volume 55, issue 7 (July 2004): pp. 767–774.

50 Satoshi Kanazawa, "More intelligent people are more likely to binge drink and get drunk." Blog: The Scientific Fundamentalist, A Look at the Hard Truths About Human Nature, *Psychology Today*, published February 13, 2011 (accessed September 7, 2011).

51 H. P. Monsour, et al. "Liver Transplantation in Patients Actively Drinking Less Than 6 Months Before Transplant Presenting with Acute Decompensation: A Single Center Experience." *Transplantation*, Vol. 100.

Chapter Three

52 Nora Volkow, "The addicted brain: Why such poor decisions?" *Director's Column, NIDA Notes,* volume 18, issue 4 (November 2003), National Institute on Drug Abuse, National Institutes of Health, US Department of Health and Human Services.

53 Fulton T. Crews, "Alcohol-related neurodegeneration and recovery, mechanisms and animal models." National Institute on Alcohol Abuse and Alcoholism Publications, http://pubs.niaaa.nih.gov/publications/arh314/377-388.htm (accessed August 1, 2011).

54 Paula K. Shear, Terry L. Jernigan, and Nelson Butters, "Volumetric magnetic resonance imaging quantification of longitudinal brain changes in abstinent alcoholics." *Alcoholism: Clinical and Experimental Research,* volume 18, issue 1 (February 1994): pp. 172–176.

55 Ann Julian, "Meditation can slow down Alzheimer's." *Alzheimer's Weekly,* Therapy Article Week, July 22–28, 2007, http://alzheimersweekly.com/content/meditation-can-slow-down-alzheimer-s (accessed September 7, 2011).

56 J. M. Lewohl, L. Wang, M. F. Miles, L. Zhang, P. R. Dodd, and R. A. Harris, "Gene expression in human alcoholism: Microarray analysis of frontal cortex." *Alcohol: Clinical and Experimental Research,* volume 24 (May 2000): pp. 1873–1882.

57 William M. Freeman, Michael A. Nader, Susan H. Nader, Daniel J. Robertson, Lynda Giola, Samara M. Mitchell, James B. Daunais, Linda J. Porrino, David P. Friedman, and Kent E. Vrana, "Chronic cocaine-mediated changes in non-human primate nucleus accumbens gene expression." *Journal of Neurochemistry,* volume 77, issue 2 (April 2001): pp. 542–549.

58 Marlene Oscar-Berman, Barbara Shagrin, Denise L. Evert, and Charles Epstein, "Impairment of brain and behavior: The neurological effects of alcohol." *Alcohol Health & Research World,* National Institute on Alcohol Abuse and Alcoholism, volume 21, issue 1 (1997): pp. 65–75.

59 David A. Gansler, Gordon J. Harris, Marlene Oscar-Berman, Chris Streeter, Robert F. Lewis, Iqbal Ahmed, and Dwight Achong, "Hypoperfusion of inferior frontal brain regions in abstinent alcoholics: A pilot SPECT study." *Journal of Studies on Alcohol,* volume 61, issue 1 (January 2000): pp. 32–37.

60 Joanne M. Lewohl, Long Wang, Michael F. Miles, Li Zhang, Peter R. Dodd, and R. Adron Harris, "Gene expression in human alcoholism: Microanalysis of frontal cortex." *Alcoholism: Clinical and Experimental Research,* volume 24, issue 12 (2000): pp. 1873–1882.

61 John C. Crabbe, Tamara J. Phillips, Kari J. Buck, Christopher L. Cunningham, and John K. Belknup, "Identifying genes for alcohol and drug sensitivity: Recent progress and future directions." *Trends in Neurosciences,* volume 22, issue 4 (1999): pp. 173–179.

62 Assunta Imperato and Gaetano Di Chiara, "Preferential stimulation of dopamine release in the nucleus accumbens of freely moving rats by ethanol." *Journal of Pharmacological Experimental Therapy,* volume 239, issue 1 (1986): pp. 219–228.

63 Assunta Imperato, Angelina Mulas, and Gaetano Di Chiara, "Nicotine preferentially stimulates dopamine release in the limbic system of freely moving rats." *European Journal of Pharmacology,* volume 132, issues 2–3 (December 1986): pp. 337–338.

64 Assunta Imperato and Gaetano Di Chiara, "Drugs abused by humans preferentially increase synaptic dopamine concentrations in the mesolimbic system of freely moving rats." *Proceedings of the National Academy of Sciences,* volume 85 (July 1988): pp. 5274–5278.

65 Nora D. Volkow, Gene-Jack Wang, Frank Telang, Joanna S. Fowler, Jean Logan, Anna-Rose Childress, Millard Jayne, Yeming Ma, and Christopher Wong, "Cocaine cues and dopamine in dorsal striatum: Mechanism of craving in cocaine addiction." *The Journal of Neuroscience,* volume 26, issue 24 (June 14, 2006): pp. 6583–6588.

66 Jaak Panksepp, Brian Knutson, and Jeff Burgdorf, "The role of brain emotional systems in addictions: A neuro-evolutionary perspective and new 'self-report' animal model." *Addiction,* volume 97 (August 2001): pp. 459–469.

67 Roy A. Wise, "Brain reward circuitry: Insights from unsensed incentives." *Neuron,* volume 36 (October 2002): pp. 229–340.

68 Nora D. Volkow and Ting-Kai Li, "Drug addiction: The neurobiology of behavior gone awry." *Nature Reviews Neuroscience,* volume 5 (December 2004): pp. 963–970.

69 Eliot Gardner and David James, "The neurobiology of chemical addiction." In Jon Elster and Ole-Jorgen Skog (eds.), *Getting Hooked: Rationality and the Addictions.* Cambridge: Cambridge University Press, 1999, pp. 93–136.

70 James Olds, "Satiation effects in self-stimulation of the brain." *Journal of Comparative and Physiological Psychology,* volume 51, issue 6 (December 1958): pp. 675–678.

71 Aryeah Routenberg and Janet Lindy, "Effects of the availability of rewarding septal and hypothalamic stimulation on bar pressing for food under conditions of deprivation." *Journal of Comparative and Physiological Psychology,* volume 60, issue 2 (October 1965): pp. 158–161.

72 Michael A. Bozarth and Roy A. Wise, "Toxicity associated with long-term intravenous heroin and cocaine self-administration in the rat." *Journal of the American Medical Association*, volume 254 (1985): pp. 81–83.

73 Chris E. Johanson, Robert L. Baister, and Kathryn Bonese, "Self-administration of psychomotor stimulant drugs: The effects of unlimited access." *Pharmacology Biochemistry and Behavior*, volume 4 (1976): pp. 45–51.

74 Lin Lu, Jeff W. Grimm, Yavin Shaham, and Bruce T. Hope, "Molecular neuroadaptations in the accumbens and ventral tegmental area during the first 90 days of forced abstinence from cocaine self-administration in rats." *Journal of Neurochemistry*, volume 85 (2003): pp. 1604–1613.

75 Nora D. Volkow, "Addiction science: From molecules to managed care." The Science of Drug Abuse & Addiction: Drug Use Changes the Brain. PowerPoint presentation, National Institute on Drug Abuse, http://www.drugabuse.gov/pubs/teaching/Teaching6/Teaching4.html (accessed August 1, 2011).

76 Mark S. Gold, Firas H. Kobeissy, Kevin K. W. Wang, Lisa J. Merlo, Adriann W. Bruijnzeel, Irina N. Krasnova, and Jean Lud Cadet, "Methamphetamine- and trauma-induced brain injuries: Comparative cellular and molecular neurobiological substrates." *Biological Psychiatry*, volume 66, issue 2 (July 2009): pp. 118–127.

77 Walter Adriani, Sabine Spijker, Veronique Deroche-Gamonet, Giovanni Laviola, Michel Le Moal, August B. Smit, and Pier Vincenzo Piazza, "Evidence for enhanced neurobehavioral vulnerability to nicotine during periadolescence in rats." *The Journal of Neuroscience*, volume 23, issue 11 (June 2003): pp. 4712–4716.

78 Denise B. Kandal and Kevin Chen, "Comparison of the onset of hypoactivity and anxiety-like behavior during alcohol withdrawal in adolescent and adult rats." *Alcoholism: Clinical & Experimental Research*, volume 28, issue 4 (2004): pp. 598–607.

79 Bridget F. Grant, Frederick S. Stinson, and Thomas C. Harford, "Age at onset of alcohol use and DSM-IV alcohol abuse and dependence: A 12-year follow-up." *Journal of Substance Abuse*, volume 13, issue 4 (2001): pp. 493–504.

80 Thomas M. Kelly, Jack R. Cornelius, and Duncan B. Clark, "Psychiatric disorders and attempted suicide among adolescents with substance use disorders." *Drug and Alcohol Dependence*, volume 73, issue 1 (2004): pp. 87–97.

81 Bureau of Justice Statistics, "Comparing federal and state prison inmates" (1991), Office of Justice Programs, US Department of Justice.

82 Bureau of Justice Statistics Special Report, "Substance abuse and treatment, state and federal prisoners" (1997), US Department of Justice, Office of Justice Programs.

83 Frederick P. Rivara, Beth A. Mueller, Grant Somes, Carmen T. Mendoza, Norman B. Rushforth, and Arthur L. Kellermann, "Alcohol and illicit drug abuse and the risk of violent death in the home." *Journal of the American Medical Association*, volume 278, issue 7 (August 1997): pp. 569–575.

Chapter Four

84 https://www.drugabuse.gov/publications/drugfacts/nationwide-trends (accessed April 3, 2017).

85 https://www.cdc.gov/alcohol/fact-sheets/alcohol-use.htm (accessed July 6, 2017).

86 M. Stahre, J. Roeber, D. Kanny, R. D. Brewer, and X. Zhang, "Contribution of excessive alcohol consumption to deaths and years of potential life lost in the United States." *Preventing Chronic Disease*, 2014; 11:130293. DOI: http://dx.doi.org/10.5888/pcd11.130293.

87 Jeffrey J. Sacks et al., "2010 national and state costs of excessive alcohol consumption." *American Journal of Preventive Medicine*, volume 49, issue 5:pp. e73–e79.

88 Ronald J. Peters, Jr., Angela F. Meshack, Steven H. Kelder, Patrick Webb, Dexter Smith, and Kevin Garner, "Alprazolam (Xanax) use among Southern youth: Beliefs and social norms concerning dangerous rides on handlebars." *Journal of Drug Education*, volume 37, issue 4 (2007): pp. 417–428.

89 Albert Hofmann, "The Road to Eleusis: Unveiling the Secret of the Mysteries," http://www.hofmann.org/papers/rak_1.htm (accessed October 14, 2011).

90 Ibid.

91 https://www.drugabuse.gov/publications/drugfacts/nationwide-trends (accessed April 3, 2017).

92 http://www.ncbi.nlm.nih.gov/pubmed/11363932 (accessed October 31, 2011).

93 http://www.csam-asam.org/sites/default/files/pdf/misc/Legalization.pdf (accessed April 3, 2017).

94 W. Hall, N. Solowij, and J. Lemon, *The Health and Psychological Consequences of Cannabis Use*. National Drug Strategy Monograph No. 25. Canberra: Australian Government Publication Services, 1994.

95 National Academies of Sciences, Engineering, and Medicine. 2017. *The health effects of cannabis and cannabinoids: The current state of evidence and recommendations for research*. Washington, DC: The National Academies Press. doi: 10.17226/24625.

96 Ibid.

97 "Tobacco use—Targeting the nation's leading killer at a glance." Centers for Disease Control and Prevention, 2011. http://www.cdc.gov/chronicdisease/resources/publications/aag/osh_htm (accessed December 28, 2011).

98 "The National Survey on Drug Use and Health: 2004 Detailed Tables, Tobacco Brands." Substance Abuse and Mental Health Services Administration, Office of Applied Studies, 2005.

99 "2005 National Survey on Drug use and Health." Substance Abuse and Mental Health Services Administration, Office of Applied Studies. NSDUH series H-27, DHHS Publication no. SMA 05-4061.

100 "Preventing tobacco use among young people: A report of the surgeon general." US Department of Health and Human Services.

101 World Health Organization Report on the Global Tobacco Epidemic, Implementing Smoke-Free Environments, 2009.

102 The health consequences of smoking: A report of the surgeon general." Centers for Disease Control, US Department of Health and Human Services, 2004, http://www.cdc.gov/tobacco/data_statistics/sgr_2004/index.htm (accessed March 16, 2011).

103 M. Ballbé and J. M. Martínez-Sánchez, "Cigarettes vs. e-cigarettes: Passive exposure at home measured by means of airborne marker and biomarkers." *Environmental Research,* volume 135 (November 2014): pp. 76–80.

104 https://www.cdc.gov/tobacco/stateandcommunity/pdfs/cdc-osh-information-on-e-cigarettes-november-2015.pdf (accessed July 12, 2017).

105 https://www.drugabuse.gov/publications/drugfacts/nationwide-trends (accessed July 12, 2017).

Chapter Six

106 George R. Uhl and Robert W. Grow, "The burden of complex genetics in brain disorders." *Archives of General Psychiatry,* volume 61 (2004): pp. 223–229.

107 Michael Bohman, Soren Sigvardsson, and C. Robert Cloninger, "Maternal inheritance of alcohol abuse: Cross-fostering analysis of adopted women." *Archives of General Psychiatry,* volume 38, issue 9 (1981): pp. 965–969.

108 Kenneth S. Kendler, Carol A. Prescott, Michael C. Neale, and Nancy L. Pedersen, "Temperance board registration for alcohol abuse in a national sample of Swedish male twins born 1902–1949." *Archives of General Psychiatry,* volume 54 (1997): pp. 178–184.

109 Terry Reed, William F. Page, Richard J. Viken, and Joe C. Christian, "Genetic predisposition to organ-specific endpoints of alcoholism." *Alcoholism: Clinical and Experimental Research,* volume 20, issue 9 (December 1996): pp. 1528–1533.

110 Yushu Rao, Ewa Hoffmann, Mohammad Zia, Laurent Bodin, Marilyn Zeman, Edward M. Sellers, and Rachel F. Tyndale, "Duplications and defects in the CYP2A6 gene: Identification, genotyping, and in vivo effects on smoking." *Molecular Pharmacology,* volume 58, issue 4 (2000): pp. 747–755.

111 Kalyani Kathiramalainathan, Howard L. Kaplan, Myroslava K. Romach, Usoa E. Busto, Ning-Yuan Li, Juliette Säwe, Rachel F. Tyndale, and Edward M. Sellers, "Inhibition of cytochrome P450 2D6 modifies codeine abuse liability." *Journal of Clinical Psychopharmacology,* volume 20 (2000): pp. 435–444.

112 Danielle M. Dick, Howard J. Edenberg, Xiaoling Xuei, Alison Goate, Sam Kuperman, Marc Schuckit, Raymond Crowe, Tom L. Smith, Bernice Porjesz, Henri Begleiter, and Tatiana Foroud, "Association of GABRG3 with alcohol dependence." *Alcoholism: Clinical and Experimental Research,* volume 28, issue 1 (2004): pp. 4–9.

113 Drake Morgan, Kathleen A. Grant, H. Donald Gage, Robert H. Mach, Jay R. Kaplan, Osric Prioleau, Susan H. Nader, Nancy Buchheimer, Richard L. Ehrenkaufer, and Michael A. Nader, "Social dominance in monkeys: Dopamine D2 receptors and cocaine self-administration." *Nature Neuroscience,* volume 5, issue 2 (2002): pp. 169–174.

114 Matt McGue, Irene Elkins, and William G. Iocono, "Genetic and environmental influences on adolescent substance use and abuse." *American Journal of Medical Genetics (Neuropsychiatric Genetics),* volume 96, issue 5 (2000): pp. 671–677.

115 Richard Rende, Cheryl Slomkowski, Elizabeth Lloyd-Richardson, and Raymond Niaura, "Sibling effects on substance use in adolescence: Social contagion and genetic relatedness." *Journal of Family Psychology,* volume 19, issue 4 (2005): pp. 611–618.

116 Marianne B. M. van den Bree, Eric O. Johnson, Michael C. Neale, and Roy W. Pickens, "Genetic and environmental influences on drug use and abuse/dependence in male and female twins." *Drug and Alcohol Dependence,* volume 52, issue 3 (November 1998): pp. 231–241.

117 Cong Han, Matthew K. McGue, and William G. Iocono, "Lifetime tobacco, alcohol and other substance use in adolescent Minnesota twins: Univariate and multivariate behavioral genetic analysis." *Addiction,* volume 94, issue 7 (July 1999): pp. 981–993.

118 B. Douglas Bernheim and Antonio Rangel, "Addiction and cue-triggered decision processes, addiction." *The American Economic Review,* volume 94, issue 5 (December 2004): pp. 1550–1590; http://www.rnl.caltech.edu/publications/pdf/aer04addiction.pdf (accessed February 17, 2011).

119 Li-Tzy Wu and Dan G. Blazer, "Substance use disorders and psychiatric comorbidity in mid and later life: A review." *International Journal of Epidemiology,* volume 43, issue 2 (2014): pp. 304–317.

120 D. A. Reiger et al., "Comorbidity of mental disorders with alcohol and other drug abuse." *Journal of the American Medical Association,* volume 264, issue 19 (1990): pp. 2511–2518.

121 Lawrence M. Scheier et al., "Social skills, competence, and drug refusal efficacy as predictors of adolescent alcohol use." *Journal of Drug Education,* volume 29, issue 3 (1999): pp. 251–278.

122 S. E. Young et al., "Substance use, abuse and dependence in adolescence: Prevalence, symptom profiles and correlates." *Drug and Alcohol Dependence,* volume 68, issue 3 (2002): pp. 309–322.

123 Susan T. Ennett et al., "Parent-child communication about adolescent tobacco and alcohol use: What do parents say and does it affect youth behavior?" *Journal of Marriage and Family,* volume 63, issue 1 (2001): pp. 48–62.

124 Sharon M. Flicker et al., "Ethnic background, therapeutic alliance, and treatment retention in functional family therapy with adolescents who abuse substances." *Journal of Family Psychology,* volume 22, issue 1 (2008): p. 167.

125 Karol L. Kumpfer, "Prevention interventions: The strengthening families program." *Drug Abuse Prevention Through Family Interventions* (1998): pp. 160–207.

126 Stephen J. Bahr, John P. Hoffmann, and Xiaoyan Yang, "Parental and peer influences on the risk of adolescent drug use." *Journal of Primary Prevention,* volume 26, issue 6 (2005): pp. 529–551.

127 J. David Hawkins et al., "Early effects of Communities That Care on targeted risks and initiation of delinquent behavior and substance use." *Journal of Adolescent Health,* volume 43, issue 1 (2008): pp. 15–22.

128 Kimberly Hoagwood et al., "Evidence-based practice in child and adolescent mental health services." *Psychiatric Services,* volume 52, issue 9 (2001): pp. 1179–1189.

129 Gilbert J. Botvin et al., "Preventing illicit drug use in adolescents: Long-term follow-up data from a randomized control trial of a school population." *Addictive Behaviors,* volume 25, issue 5 (2000): pp. 769–774.

130 J. David Hawkins, Richard F. Catalano, and Michael W. Arthur, "Promoting science-based prevention in communities." *Addictive Behaviors,* volume 27, issue 6 (2002): pp. 951–976.

Chapter Seven

131 Eric J. Nestler, "Molecular basis of long-term plasticity underlying addiction." *Nature Reviews Neuroscience,* volume 2 (February 2001): pp. 119–128.

132 A. Thomas McLellan, David C. Lewis, Charles P. O'Brien, and Herbert D. Kleber, "Drug dependence, a chronic medical illness: Implications for treatment, insurance, and outcomes evaluation." *Journal of the American Medical Association,* volume 284, issue 13 (October 2000): pp. 1693–1695.

133 A. Thomas McLellan, David C. Lewis, Charles P. O'Brien, and Herbert D. Kleber, "Implications for treatment, insurance, and outcomes." *Journal of the American Medical Association,* volume 284, issue 13 (October 2000): pp. 1719–1720.

134 Noah E. Adrans, "Current practices and optimal futures for the treatment of substance use disorders through client-treatment matching: A Delphi Study." (2011). Paper 115, http://epublications.marquette.edu/dissertations_mu/115 (accessed August 2011).

135 Thomas F. Babor, Bonnie G. McRee, Patricia A. Kassebaum, Paul L. Grimaldi, Kazi Ahmed, and Jeremy Bray, "Screening, brief intervention, and referral to treatment (SBIRT): Toward a public health approach to the management of substance abuse." (2007). http://suba.haworthpress.com (accessed February 14, 2011).

136 "Taking burden off physicians key to SBI growth, new report says." The Partnership at drugfree.org (March 2009), http://drugfree.org/join-together/alcohol/taking-burden-off-physicians (accessed October 20, 2011).

137 Betty Ford Institute Consensus Panel, "What is recovery? A working definition from the Betty Ford Institute." *Journal of Substance Abuse Treatment,* volume 33, issue 3 (2007): pp. 221–228.

138 "Recovery defined—Give us your feedback." Substance Abuse and Mental Health Services Administration, US Department of Health and Human Services, http://blog.samhsa.gov/2011/08/12/recovery-defined-%E2%80%93-give-us-your-feedback/ (accessed September 6, 2011).

139 Ibid.

Chapter Eight

140 https://www.drugabuse.gov/publications/drugfacts/nationwide-trends (accessed April 5, 2017).

141 "Principles of drug addiction treatment: A research-based guide." NIH Publication No. 09-4180, printed October 1999; reprinted July 2000, February 2008; revised April 2009. National Institute on Drug Abuse (NIDA), National Institutes of Health, US Department of Health and Human Services.

142 National Institute on Drug Abuse, InfoFacts, "Understanding drug abuse and addiction." National Institutes of Health, US Department of Health and Human Services (March 2011).

143 "Principles of drug addiction treatment: A research-based guide." NIH Publication No. 09-4180, printed October 1999; reprinted July 2000, February 2008; revised April 2009. National Institute on Drug Abuse, National Institutes of Health, US Department of Health and Human Services.

144 Bankole A. Johnson, "Update on neuropharmacological treatments for alcoholism: Scientific basis and clinical findings." *Biochemical Pharmacology,* volume 75, issue 1 (January 2008): pp. 34–56; published online August 9, 2007, 10.1016/i/bcp.2007.08.

145 National Institute on Drug Abuse, InfoFacts, "Treatment approaches for drug addiction." National Institute on Drug Abuse, National Institutes of Health, US Department of Health and Human Services (September 2009).

146 "Minnesota Model: Description of counseling approach." National Institute on Drug Abuse Approaches to Drug Abuse Counseling, National Institute on Drug Abuse, National Institutes of Health, US Department of Health and Human Services, undated (accessed October 13, 2011).

147 "*Time* 100 persons of the century: Heroes and icons." *Time,* June 14, 1999.

148 "Self-Management and Recovery Training (SMART)." Pamphlet, http://www.smartrecovery.org/resources/pdfs/bod2011.pdf (accessed August 3, 2011).

Chapter Nine

149 "The Clinician's Ultimate Reference, Addiction Aids: Acamprosate (Campral)," http://www.globalrph.com/addiction.htm (accessed July 19, 2011).

150 Barbara J. Mason, Anita M. Goodman, Sylvie Chabac, and Phillipe Lehert, "Effects of oral acamprosate on abstinence in patients with alcohol dependence in a double-blind, placebo-controlled trial: The role of patient motivation." *Journal of Psychiatric Research,* volume 40, issue 5 (2006): pp. 383–393.

151 Henning Sass, Michael Soyka, Karl Mann, and Walter Zieglgänsberger, "Relapse prevention by acomprosate." *Archives of General Psychiatry,* volume 53, issue 8 (August 1996): pp. 673–680.

152 Francois M. Paille, Mulien D. Guelfi, Alan C. Perkins, Rene J. Royer, Lucien Steru, and Phillippe Parot, "Double-blind randomized multicentre trial of acamprosate in maintaining abstinence from alcohol." *Alcohol & Alcoholism,* volume 30, issue 2 (1995): pp. 239–247.

153 I. Pelc, P. Verbanck, O. Le Bon, M. Gavrilovic, K. Lion, and P. Lehert, "Efficacy and safety of acamprosate in the treatment of detoxified alcohol-dependent patients: A 90-day placebo-controlled dose-finding study." *The British Journal of Psychiatry*, volume 171 (1997): pp. 73–77.

154 Bankole A. Johnson, Nassima Ait-Daoud, Charles L. Bowden, Carlo C. DiClemente, John D. Roache, Kevin Lawson, Martin A. Javors, and Jennie Z. Ma, "Oral topirate for treatment of alcohol dependence: A randomized controlled trial." *The Lancet*, volume 361, issue 9370 (May 2003): pp. 1677–1685.

155 Bankole A. Johnson, Norman Rosenthal, Julie A. Capece, Frank Wiegand, Lian Mao, Karen Beyers, Amy McKay, Nassima Ait-Daoud, Giovanni Addolorato, Raymond F. Anton, Domenic A. Ciraulo, and Henry R. Kranzler, "Improvement of physical health and quality of life of alcohol-dependent individuals with topiramate treatment: US multisite randomized controlled trial." *Archives of Internal Medicine*, volume 168, issue 11 (2008): pp. 1188–1199.

156 Giovanni Addolorato, Fabio Caputo, Esmeralda Capristo, Marco Domenicali, Mauro Bernardi, Luigi Janiri, Roberta Agabio, Giancarlo Colombo, Gian Luigi Gessa, and Giovanni Gasbarrini, "Baclofen efficacy in reducing alcohol craving and intake: A preliminary double-blind randomized controlled study." *Alcohol and Alcoholism*, volume 37, issue 5 (2002): pp. 504–508.

157 David Yamini et al., "Utilization of baclofen in maintenance of alcohol abstinence in patients with alcohol dependence and alcoholic hepatitis with or without cirrhosis." *Alcohol and Alcoholism*, volume 49, issue 4 (2014): pp. 453–456.

158 Olivier Ameisen, *The End of My Addiction*. New York: Farrar, Straus & Giroux, 2008.

159 Lorenzo Leggio et al., "A preliminary double-blind, placebo-controlled randomized study of baclofen effects in alcoholic smokers." *Psychopharmacology*, volume 232, issue 1 (2015): pp. 233–243.

160 Bankole A. Johnson, John D. Roache, Martin A. Javors, Carlo C. DiClemente, Claude Robert Cloninger, Thomas J. Prihoda, Patrick S. Bordnick, Nassima Ait-Daoud, and Julie Hensler, "Ondansetron for reduction of drinking among biologically predisposed alcoholic patients: A randomized controlled trial." *Journal of the American Medical Association*, volume 284, issue 8 (2000): pp. 963–971.

161 Henning Krampe, Sabina Stawicki, Thilo Wagner, Claudia Bartels, Carlotta Aust, Eckart Rüther, Wolfgang Poser, and Hennelore Ehrenreich, "Follow-up of 180 alcoholic patients for up to 7 years after outpatient treatment: Impact of alcohol deterrents on outcome." *Alcoholism: Clinical and Experimental Research*, volume 30, issue 1 (January 2006): pp. 86–95.

162 Henry R. Kranzler, "Evidence-based treatments for alcohol dependence: New results and new questions." *Journal of the American Medical Association*, volume 295, issue 17 (2006): pp. 2075–2076.

163 Raymond F. Anton, et al, "Combined pharmacotherapies and behavioral interventions for alcohol dependence, the COMBINE Study: A randomized controlled trial." *Journal of the American Medical Association*, volume 295, issue 17 (2006): pp. 2003–2017.

164 R. A. Rudd, P. Seth, F. David, and L. Scholl, Increases in Drug and Opioid-Involved Overdose Deaths— United States, 2010–2015. MMWR Morbidity and Mortality Weekly Report 2016; 65: pp. 1445–1452. DOI: http://dx.doi.org/10.15585/mmwr.mm655051e1.

165 Krupitsky & Blokhina, "Long acting depot formulations of naltrexone for heroin dependence: A review." 2010.

166 http://www.philly.com/philly/health/addiction/Scientists-say-they-can-make-a-vaccine-against-heroin-whats-the-holdup.html (accessed July 14, 2017).

167 National Institute on Drug Abuse, InfoFacts, "Cigarettes and other tobacco products." National Institute on Drug Abuse, National Institutes of Health, US Department of Health and Human Services (updated August 2010).

168 National Center for Biotechnology Information, US National Library of Medicine, PubMed Health, Lung Cancer, at http://www.ncbi.nlm.nih.gov/pubmedhealth/PMH0004529 (last reviewed September 26, 2010).

169 Centers for Disease Control and Prevention, "Tobacco related mortality." March 2011; Centers for Disease Control and Prevention, "Fast facts: Morbidity and mortality," March 2011.

170 David Gonzalez, Stephen I. Rennard, Mitchell Nides, Cheryl Oncken, Salomom Azoulay, Clare B. Billing, Erik Watsky, Jason Gong, Kathryn E. Williams, and Karen R. Reeves, "Varenicline, an a4ß2 nicotinic acetylcholine receptor partial agonist vs. sustained-release bupropion and placebo for smoking cessation: A randomized controlled trial." *Journal of the American Medical Association–JAMA Express*, volume 296, issue 1 (2006): pp. 47–55, 10.1001/jama.296.1.47. For the Varenicline Phase 3 Study Group: *JAMA*, volume 296, issue 1 (2006): pp. 47–55, 10.1001/jama.296.1.47.

Chapter Eleven

171 Peter M. Milner, "Brain stimulation reward: A review." *Canadian Journal of Psychology Outstanding Contributions Series*, volume 45, issue 1 (1991): pp. 1–36.

172 Alia J. Crum, Peter Salovey, and Shawn Achor, "Rethinking stress: The role of mindsets in determining the stress response." *Journal of Personality and Social Psychology*, volume 104, issue 4 (April 2013): pp. 716–733.

173 Robert J. Carey, Ernest N. Damianopoulos, and Arielle B. Shanahan, "Cocaine conditioned behavior: A cocaine memory trace or an anti-habituation effect." *Pharmacology Biochemistry and Behavior*, volume 90, issue 4 (October 2008): pp. 625–631.

174 W. Eugene Broadhead et al., "The epidemiologic evidence for a relationship between social support and health." *American Journal of Epidemiology*, volume 117, issue 5 (1983): pp. 521–537.

175 Gregory D. Zimet et al., "The multidimensional scale of perceived social support." *Journal of Personality Assessment*, volume 52, issue 1 (1988): pp. 30–41.

176 Sonja Lyubomirsky, *The How of Happiness: A Scientific Approach to Getting the Life You Want*. New York: Penguin, 2008.

Chapter Twelve

177 Richard A. Grucza, Robert F. Krueger, Susan B. Racette, Karne E. Norberg, Pamela R. Hipp, and Laura J. Bierut, "The emerging link between alcoholism risk and obesity in the United States." *Archives of General Psychiatry,* volume 67, issue 12 (December 2010): pp. 1201–1308.

178 John W. Welte, Grace M. Barnes, William F. Wieczorek, Marie-Cecile O. Tidwell, and John C. Parker, "Risk factors for pathological gambling." *Addictive Behaviors,* volume 29, issue 2 (February 2004): pp. 323–335.

179 National Opinion Research Center, "Gambling impact and behavior study." *Report to the National Gambling Impact Study Commission* (April 1999): p. 6.

180 National Council on Problem Gambling FAQs, Problem Gamblers, http://www.ncpgambling.org/i4a/pages/index.cf?pageid=3390 (accessed December 28, 2011).

181 US Department of Health and Human Services, "Overweight and obesity: A major public health issue." *Prevention Report,* volume 16, issue 1 (2001).

182 "Diet plan success tough to weigh," CBS News, February 11, 2009.

183 Centers for Disease Control and Prevention, "US obesity trends," July 2011, http://www.cdc.gov/obesity/data/trends.html (accessed December 28, 2011).

184 James Hudson, Eva Hiripi, Harrison G. Pope, Jr., and Ronald C. Kessler, "The prevalence and correlates of eating disorders in the national comorbidity survey replication." *Biological Psychiatry,* volume 61, issue 3 (2007): pp. 348–358.

185 "Emergent management of anorexia nervosa." *Medscape,* Drugs, Diseases & Procedures, July 17, 2011, http://emedicine.medscapt.com/article/805125-ove rview (accessed July 27, 2011).

186 Christopher G. Hudson, "Socioeconomic status and mental illness: Tests of the social causation and selection hypothesis." *American Journal of Orthopsychiatry,* volume 75, issue 1 (January 2005): pp. 3–18.

187 "National survey finds eating disorders on the rise." Health & Science, *International Herald Tribune, The New York Times,* February 6, 2007, http://www.nytimes.com/2007/02/06/health/06iht-sneating.4491388.html (accessed December 28, 2011).

188 S. A. Swanson, S. J. Crow, D. Le Grange, J. Swendsen, and K. R. Merikangas, "Prevalence and correlates of eating disorders in adolescents. Results from the national comorbidity survey replication adolescent supplement." *Archives of General Psychiatry,* volume 68, issue 7 (2011): pp. 714–723.

189 Carlo Colantuoni, Pedro Roda, Joseph McCarthy, Caroline Patten, Nicole M. Avena, Andrew Chadeayne, and Bartley G. Hoebel, "Evidence that intermittent excessive sugar intake causes endogenous opioid dependence." *Obesity Research,* volume 10, issue 6 (June 2002): pp. 478–488.

190 Results from the "2008 National Survey on Drug Use and Health: National Findings." US Department of Health and Human Services, Substance Abuse and Mental Health Services Administration, Office of Applied Studies.

191 National Institute on Drug Abuse, "Principles of drug addiction treatment: A research based guide." National Institutes of Health, US Department of Health and Human Services, NIH pub. 99-4180 (1999).

192 Rudolf H. Moos, John W. Finney, and Ruth C. Cronkite, *Alcoholism Treatment: Context, Process and Outcome*. New York: Oxford University Press, 1990.

193 A. Thomas McLellan, D. C. Metzger, A. I. Alterman, et al., "Is addiction treatment 'worth it'? Public health expectations, policy-based comparisons." In *Proceedings of Josiah Macy Conference on Medical Education*. New York: The Josiah Macy Jr. Foundation, 1995, pp. 165–212.

194 Dean R. Gerstein and Henrick J. Harwood, *Treating Drug Problems: Volume 1, A Study of the Evolution, Effectiveness, and Financing of Public and Private Drug Treatment Systems*. Washington, DC: National Academy Press, 1990.